# PLEASE
# YELL AT
# MY KIDS

What Cultures Around the World Can
Teach You About Parenting in Community,
Raising Independent Kids, and
Not Losing Your Mind

# PLEASE YELL AT MY KIDS

Marina Lopes

**balance**

New York   Boston

Balance

Hachette Book Group

1290 Avenue of the Americas

New York, NY 10104

GCP-Balance.com

@GCPBalance

First Edition: April 2025

Balance is an imprint of Grand Central Publishing. The Balance name and logo are registered trademarks of Hachette Book Group, Inc.

The publisher is not responsible for websites (or their content) that are not owned by the publisher.

The Hachette Speakers Bureau provides a wide range of authors for speaking events. To find out more, go to hachettespeakersbureau.com or email HachetteSpeakers@hbgusa.com.

Balance books may be purchased in bulk for business, educational, or promotional use. For information, please contact your local bookseller or the Hachette Book Group Special Markets Department at special.markets@hbgusa.com.

Print book interior design by Amy Quinn.

Library of Congress Control Number: 2024951415

ISBNs: 978-0-306-83441-7 (hardcover); 978-0-306-83443-1 (ebook)

Printed in the United States of America

LSC-C

Printing 1, 2025

*For Oliver and Dahlia, citizens of the world*

# Contents

# Introduction

MY FRIEND MELISSA HAS THE VOICE OF A PRINCIPAL YOU DON'T want to cross. It's calm but firm, steady, and—when the occasion calls for it—dripping with disapproval. When Melissa means business, she pairs the voice with her signature look. Lips pressed, eyes fixed, it's a face that welcomes any toddler's challenge. I've seen the combination make both children and adults stop dead in their tracks. Last Wednesday night, I watched as she aimed the combo at my five-year-old son.

"Ollie. Down!"

He was scaling her midcentury modern table, seconds away from toppling a plant onto a Persian rug. Ollie had crossed a line, and he knew it. But he did not move. Instead, he stared at Melissa, who met his gaze straight on. The two squared off in a silent duel, each waiting for the other to break.

But I knew it was no match. Eventually, Ollie inched his body down, each limb accepting defeat individually. Head hung, he braced for his scolding. "The table is not for climbing. If you do it again, I'll send you home."

As mothers, Melissa and I are very different. Even if I wanted to, I'd never be able to pull off "the look." The one time I tried, my two-year-old giggled, assuming I was playing pretend. At

Melissa's, there is no gentle parenting. Rules are set, expectations are high, and compliments are sparse. She is much more likely to say "Do better" than "Great job!" It's a parenting philosophy that might horrify my American friends. Still, several times a week, I send my children over to eat, play, and, occasionally, earn the look.

This was not a babysitting arrangement I settled for. In fact, my husband and I uprooted our family and moved across the world so that our best friends, Melissa and her husband, Jeremy, could help us share the joys and burdens of parenthood—and, in the process, yell at our children.

We are not hippies, polyamorous, or cult followers. But, having lived abroad for much of our adult lives, both my husband and I were wary of raising our kids in a nuclear American family. Parenthood in America was isolating. We wanted to raise our children in a proverbial village with the strong community network and multigenerational ties we had seen sustain families abroad. So, we packed our lives and moved across the world to live next to our best friends, who happened to be in Singapore. We created an informal commune sharing childcare, playdates, and parenting each other's kids.

I knew if my American friends had seen Melissa scolding Ollie, they would be uneasy. Discipline, they would assume, is a job best left to parents. To let someone else do it for you risks confusing or even damaging your child. But if those friends looked long enough, here's what else they would have seen: my shy, introverted son giggling through the night at weekly sleepovers with his best friend, Melissa's son Jay. Jeremy cooking dinner for us all at the end of a long week. All of the kids squeezed into the back of my car, singing the *Frozen* soundtrack at the top of their lungs on the way to class. They would see homemade soup delivered to our door when we are sick, and bottles of champagne popped in our living rooms to celebrate promotions.

When, after nearly ten years of living abroad, we moved our family back to the States, I saw a very different dynamic play out. American parents draw boundaries, protect their personal space, and value their independence. But they are also harried, tired, and, most of all, lonely. Many live across the country from both their families and their closest friends. Even if they know their neighbors, they can't count on them. American individualism, especially when it comes to parenthood, is failing them.

*Please Yell at My Kids* is not a book about discipline or the merits of different parenting philosophies. It isn't about how to start a commune. (But you'll see some ways we make it work!) And it isn't about the myriad ways that American structures are failing families, especially mothers, because we all know that already. Somehow, despite the number of books written about the exhaustion of American parenting, we still don't have reliable childcare or meaningful paid family leave—and let's be real, it's going to take a while. Though much has been written about the unsustainable workload American parents shoulder, we've left out a crucial part of the discussion: culture.

*Please Yell at My Kids* is about taking apart the cultural rules and norms we follow almost instinctively in order to examine whether they actually help us. Is it really wrong for another mother to discipline my kids, or does it open them to other parenting styles in important ways? Should childbirth be an intensely private experience or one where the mess and the bliss are laid bare for your friends and family to see? Should grandparents be left to enjoy their retirement or asked to stand in line at school pickup? These aren't just hypothetical questions. Each chapter includes practical steps for parents who want to adapt these traditions for themselves.

The book calls on Americans to recognize what parents around the world already know: that raising children should not be a private project, but a shared one. Each chapter examines a parenting rule that bucks American traditions and offers an alternative vision of what's possible when we bring others into the fold of parenting. These traditions challenge us to invite aging grandparents and meddling neighbors to our breakfast table, carpool lanes, and delivery rooms. Instead of defending what we stand for, they urge us to make room for who we stand with. The book follows the parenting journey chronologically, from pregnancy to childcare, tapping into wisdom from parents in ten countries along the way. In addition to our own experience in Singapore and Brazil, I profile parents in China, Denmark, Sweden, Malaysia, France, Mozambique, the Netherlands, and Finland.

These countries were not chosen at random, but rather because parents there have hacked an aspect of parenting Americans struggle with. Much has been written about the benefits of raising children in Europe. But we can learn just as much from the Scandinavian welfare system as from Mozambique's sense of solidarity.

NONE OF THE COUNTRIES ANALYZED IN THIS BOOK OFFER PERFECT solutions. The parents profiled here are just as bleary-eyed and turned around as the rest of us. They have morning sickness and back pain. They have had postpartum depression and, in some cases, even psychosis. The difference is that they are not doing it alone.

You may find some of these approaches ridiculous. That's okay! They aren't prescriptions meant to be followed to the letter. Rather, I try to whittle down each of the eleven traditions in the book to their central message, and extract a lesson about parental support that Americans can apply to their everyday lives. You may not want to invite guests to your C-section the way mothers in Brazil do or skip showers for forty days after you give birth as prescribed by Chinese confinement practices, but how can opening up to your friends help you find support in the chaos of the postpartum period? Perhaps you don't want to let your baby sleep outdoors like the Danish, but what can the practice teach us about preserving our pre-baby identities? Can the Dutch tradition of dropping children off blindfolded in the woods help us find an antidote to helicopter parenting?

Some rules may seem irrelevant to American families, at least until the United States adopts legislation to better support parents. But they, too, hold wisdom for US families. Even if your office lacks a paternity leave policy, Swedish fathers can teach us how to split household chores more equitably. French daycare activists can tell us how to fight for better childcare in our own communities.

Parenthood is hard everywhere. But in America, it is broken. Traditional ties that shore up young families in countries like Brazil have fallen away, but unlike in Europe, government support has not stepped in to fill the gap. A historical reverence for individualism puts help—communal, family, or government-sponsored—at arm's length. The thin webs of support that do exist, like community networks and religious ties, are quickly fraying.

At the same time, parenthood is intensifying. You know this already, but it bears repeating: American moms today spend four more hours a week doing active childcare than mothers in 1965. Dads spend triple the amount of time caring for their kids than their fathers' generation did. With income inequality in America reaching a fifty-year high, everyday parenting decisions, like what school to send your children to, or what activities to sign them up for, weigh on parents. As wealthy families shower their children with extracurricular classes, tutors, and standardized test prep, the race to the top is steeper than ever before. For the first time, Americans have a 50 percent chance of being less well off than their parents. With their children's future on the line, American parents are trying to do it all by themselves, all the time. It isn't working.

Of course, every country has its problems. In pointing out what each is doing right, especially in supporting parents, I'm not issuing a blanket endorsement of any culture or absolving it of faults.

Yet the conversations I've had with American parents from Oakland to North Carolina are infused with a hopelessness I have not encountered elsewhere. Battered by the pandemic, rising childcare costs, and mounting anxiety about their children's future, parents across the United States are echoing the same refrain: this is not sustainable.

Americans have a long tradition of blending the ideas and values of other cultures into our own ways of life—that's how we ended up with TexMex burritos and oat milk chai lattes. I'm suggesting you do the same when it comes to parenthood—learn from other cultures and create a blend that works for you.

Throughout the book, I look to American policymakers, activists, and families around the country who are already experimenting with imported solutions. I examine which elements have translated well and which haven't.

Because so much of the historical burden of parenthood has been placed on women, many of my conversations are with mothers. Throughout the book, I use both gendered and gender-neutral language to acknowledge the breadth of experiences encountered by parents. But, as you will see in the chapters that follow, the ideas and tips discussed here can benefit people of all genders and families of all shapes and sizes. In fact, one of the primary challenges I pose to readers, namely to cultivate a chosen family, was an idea practiced and popularized by the LGBTQ+ community long before it became a common mainstream practice.

Parenting in America is hard. Our cultural assumptions about childbirth, family, and community only make it that much harder. Join me as we rethink the practices handed down to us as parents. Let's trade the overwhelm, relentlessness, and stress that has become synonymous with American parenting and replace it with community, balance, and, most of all, fun.

## RULE 1

# Invite Guests to Your C-Section

## Uncovering the American Dream

A few years ago, I found myself in a Brazilian hospital watching a stranger's C-section surgery, along with forty of her coworkers, friends, and relatives. I was reporting on my favorite kind of story: both quotidian—hers was one of many C-section parties the hospital was hosting that day—yet completely alien to my readers at the *Washington Post*, where I had been writing about Brazil for years. Stories like this were the reason I became a foreign correspondent and why I moved back to Brazil after spending much of my childhood in the United States.

I come from a long line of immigrants seeking better lives abroad. My great-grandfather first came to Brazil in the early twentieth century, trading an impoverished life as a fisherman in Italy for a fresh start in a new continent. He found what he was

1

looking for and convinced the rest of his family to join him before long. My family grew roots in Brazil, a country they loved and never planned on leaving. But in the 1970s, my father spent a year in the United States as an exchange student and knew right away he had uncovered an even better place to live.

My dad loved the efficiency of America, the way it rewarded hard work and innovation. Exhausted by Brazil's pervasive corruption, he spent the next fifteen years saving for his own American dream. He wanted it all: the white picket fence, the Thanksgiving turkey, and bicycles for his children.

When I was nine, my parents announced we were moving to the United States. At first, it seemed like a sweet deal. I was eager to leave polluted, crime-ridden São Paulo, where riding a bike around the block was out of the question. I was in awe of the American suburbia that colored the Mary-Kate and Ashley movies I watched on repeat. My parents, it turns out, were also enamored.

So, we moved to Miami and my dad embraced American culture with the fervor of the converted. He erected an American flag on our front door and blasted Billy Joel and Shania Twain from the car radio. He signed me up for the quintessential American sport: cheerleading. And, taking a page out of a movie he must have watched, bought a beagle named Billy to wait for us after school.

I blossomed in American schools. Unlike in Brazil, where intelligence seemed like a fixed trait, in the United States, it was something teachers invested in. We exchanged the pervasive fear of crime in Brazil for a freedom we had never known before. My brother and I spent hours shooting hoops in our driveway and looping the block on our bikes.

But I soon saw there were downsides to our American dream. The United States shrank my family to the people inside my house. I missed the three-hour Sunday lunches at my grandmother's house, where my extended family would gather to argue about politics and gossip about the neighbors. Every weekend, I would play hide-and-seek with my band of cousins until it was too dark to see.

The move split my identity down the middle. I spent summers in Brazil attempting to piece together a Brazilian self. I'd try to pick up new slang from my cousins, mimic the style of Brazilian actresses I saw on TV, and listen to sad bossa nova songs on repeat, hoping the lyrics would seep into me. I constantly compared the two cultures, evaluating and reevaluating their strengths and weaknesses, and thinking of what my life would have been like had we stayed.

After university, I became a foreign correspondent and found it was, in many ways, a continuation of the way I had grown up: straddling countries with one foot permanently outside the United States. My first international assignment straight out of journalism school took me to Mozambique, a sleepy nation off the coast of Southern Africa.

I was there to report on coal and gas discoveries that investors hoped would put the country on the map. But the assignment impacted my life in a way I never expected. It was in Mozambique that I met my husband, Rudy.

Rudy worked as a diplomat at the US embassy and like me, he built a life in the gaps between cultures. His parents moved to the United States from Taiwan before he was born. But after a decade of living around the world, he felt more at home dancing the bachata in Guatemalan clubs and surfing off the coast of

Angola. Rudy loved curating bits of cultures and value systems from his different postings and absorbing them into his everyday life. He fought Brazilian jiu-jitsu, ate popcorn with chopsticks, and danced to Bollywood music.

When Rudy and I decided to get married, we chose to move back to the United States. We settled in Washington, DC, and dreamed of the kind of home we wanted to create. I wanted to ensure my kids grew up surrounded by the love I experienced in my extended family. Even as an adult, wherever I was, whatever I faced, I knew fifty of my relatives in Brazil had my back. Rudy also craved the warmth of Latin American families but wanted to interweave it with the respect for elders and the Asian work ethic he grew up with. He looked back fondly on memories of his mother helping him with calculus homework late into the night, a plate of cut strawberries turning up on his desk when he needed a boost.

But as our friends and families started their journeys into parenthood in the United States, we began to rethink our plan. The chaos of parenting engulfed them, receding now and then to reveal shells of their personalities. They were just trying to survive another day. Parenthood in the United States seemed to be all sacrifice. My friends couldn't finish their sentences, let alone their lunches. They didn't seem able to enjoy their partners or kids very much.

The contrast between the Brazilian parents and American parents I knew was stark. Parenthood in Brazil did not require a psychotic break the way it seemed to in the United States. My aunts and cousins in Brazil had maintained their own lives and interests years into parenthood. They went out dancing, traveled, and went to dinner with friends. In big families, childcare was plentiful, and family and friends were constantly around, ready to help.

So, as we prepared to start our own family, Rudy and I reversed the journey my parents had made twenty years earlier, searching for a better place to parent.

## Preferential Treatment

Though Brazil had changed, Rio de Janeiro, where Rudy and I had moved in 2016, looked as dazzling as ever. Lush green mountains braided in and out of the city, crashing into the ocean in spectacular cliffs. Brazil had undergone tremendous progress in the two decades I had been gone. The country had ridden a commodities boom to prosperity, pulling forty million people out of poverty, thanks partly to a cash transfer program targeted at mothers.

Fond childhood memories drew me back to the tight-knit network of family and friends who were still there. Brazilians are never alone, I learned. Even though Rio de Janeiro wasn't close to many members of my Brazilian family, they took it upon themselves to connect me to distant friends and relatives who toured me around the city on the weekends and constantly invited me over for dinner.

About a year after we moved, the Zika epidemic that had prevented us from trying for a baby receded, and Rudy and I received a long-awaited green light from our doctor. In February, a wave of nausea overtook me while dancing in Rio de Janeiro's carnival parade. I shrugged it off, blaming the heat, the crowd, and my heavy costume. But two weeks later, my hands shook as I spotted a thin line on a cheap pregnancy test.

Little did I know those faint pink stripes would become my ticket to Brazil's most exclusive club: I was officially a card-carrying member of the preferential line.

Many countries give pregnant women privileged status. But Brazil takes it to another level. While regular Brazilians toil away hours in line at famously inefficient banks, supermarkets, and post offices, pregnant women saunter in and are ushered to counters designed for them, with shorter lines and faster service. And the privileges don't just apply to running errands. Pregnant women in Brazil get to skip the line at museums, theaters, and—to my family's delight—even restaurant waitlists.

By my second trimester, my phone was ringing off the hook. "What are you doing Thursday night?" my Aunt Cris wanted to know. She was in town, and the hottest Italian restaurant didn't take reservations. Would seven work for me?

Clearly, the system was being abused, I mused as I dug into my overpriced gnocchi with Aunt Cris. But Brazil's preferential lines got me thinking. Where else did pregnant women feel their support network amplify, not diminish, with their growing belly?

Sure, there were downsides to pregnancy in Brazil. Strangers everywhere would casually reach over and touch my stomach, seemingly forgetting that I—not the baby—was the one feeling their caresses.

Their questions shocked me. "How much weight have you gained?" one taxi driver asked, looking me up and down. "You're lucky it's a boy," said another dude at the checkout line. "Labor with a girl is much more painful."

These comments mostly creeped me out, and sometimes—to my cousins' delight—I'd snap back at the people who delivered them to mind their own business. But the pregnancy experience felt unexpectedly shared. Every time the baker would ask me how many weeks I had to go, or neighbors would help me bring my groceries up to my apartment, I was reminded that I was bringing this baby into an existing community. He was a new addition to this bustling city that everyone was ready to welcome.

In America, pregnancy is a personal project, one that polite society avoids remarking on and meddling with. While pregnant women in America are unlikely to have a cab driver question them about their weight gain, I wondered how many go through the nine months of pregnancy without anyone in the community asking them how they are doing or offering substantial support.

At my baby shower, my family took photos of my pregnant belly and chanted "Come, Oliver," a tradition meant to tell the baby that it is safe for them to come into the world, that there are people on the other side of the birth, waiting to catch him.

As THE BABY GREW, SO DID HIS PILE OF GIFTS. MY GODMOTHER quilted diaper bags and bibs, and my grandmother knit blankets.

At the end of June, Rudy was transferred to São Paulo, the country's financial capital, and we moved just a few blocks from where I grew up. I spent the last months of pregnancy spinning around our new apartment in frantic bursts of energy. After years of moving from place to place, I was nesting—hard. A week before I was due, I installed the batteries in the baby swing and taped a hopeful sleep schedule to the wall. But there was one task I hadn't given a thought to.

My mom was helping me fold onesies into symmetrical Marie-Kondo–sized rolls when her hands suddenly stopped.

"Marina, what about the gift bags?"

I looked at her, puzzled.

"For the guests, sweetie."

What guests? I was going into labor, not throwing a sweet sixteen. And anyway, shouldn't any visitors who came to the hospital be bringing *us* gifts?

"Marina, you can't expect people to come all the way to the hospital to see the baby and leave empty-handed. You have to think about these things beforehand."

Birth in Brazil, she explained, was a celebration. The mother's closest family and friends and even coworkers show up at the hospital to celebrate the birth, watching scheduled C-sections from a window into the operating room. It was a tradition that crossed class lines. Lower-income families save money for birth parties and adorn their hospital room doors with handmade signs announcing their child's birth to visitors. But Brazil's upper classes take it to another level. Wealthy families routinely spend over $10,000 for services that include floral arrangements, guest books, monogrammed sheets for the hospital bed, personalized water bottles, and silver-plated favors for dozens of guests. There were even party planners standing on call, ready to jump into action when the mother went into labor or booked months in advance for scheduled C-sections. At the São Luiz private hospital in São Paulo, a mother-to-be can rent out the $500-a-night presidential suite, which includes a living room and bathroom for guests, a balcony, and a minibar. Parents can request their favorite flowers and magazines and even change the furniture if it clashes with their planned decorations. Even if Rudy and I had the money to put on such a lavish party (we didn't!), it wouldn't be for me, I explained to my mom. I was still getting to know my extended family again. Of course, I wanted my immediate relatives to meet the baby, but everyone else could wait.

The baby books I had read were clear on the matter. Mothers-to-be were to cocoon at home alone with their partners after birth. Relatives were to be managed, dismissed, and put in their place when necessary. Like most American women, I'd been told to guard myself and my baby against the meddling of extended family members. *What to Expect When You're Expecting*, a canon of pre- and postpartum advice, urges: "Everybody else will get their chance for the first moments with your baby, but for now, they need to take a number..."

I told my mom that on my massive list of things to do, making gift bags for the guests didn't make the cut. My new family should be my priority, not random relatives. "Okay, okay," she said, smiling, as she pulled a stack of baby blue, stroller-shaped gift bags out of her purse. "I'll just leave these here then."

## When the Party Doesn't Go as Planned

My son's birth, it turned out, was anything but festive. The night before he was born, I spiked a fever and started throwing up. My doctor ordered me to the hospital for an emergency C-section, where he discovered an infection brewing in my uterus.

Thankfully, Oliver's wails echoed through the surgery room and confirmed what the doctors told us: he was a strong and healthy baby.

I, however, was not doing as well. I hemorrhaged throughout the surgery, and the doctors struggled to control my bleeding. Awake through it all, though heavily anesthetized, I remember registering the look of panic in my obstetrician's eyes as they pumped me with injections and discussed whether I would need a transfusion. Eventually, the bleeding stopped, and I was able to hold our son for the first time. In the photos of those initial moments with him, my face is ghostly, pale from both the blood loss and the fear.

I had always wanted a hospital birth. I couldn't understand friends who swore by home births, their newborns emerging from inflatable kiddie pools in their living rooms. There was a comforting order to the sterile halls of the hospital, the rhythmic hums and beeps of the machines, I thought. I busied myself throughout my pregnancy, going on hospital tours asking about infection rates and dining options—questions the Internet advised me to pose.

But most of all, I longed for a team of experts in white coats to usher me into this new phase of life. Secretly, I hoped that their board-certified knowledge would mask the gaps in mine. After all, what did I know about caring for, let alone delivering a baby?

I will forever be grateful for my hospital birth and those doctors who, it turned out, saved my life from an infection that could have killed me. But in all my research to find an expert medical team, I never once considered a world where our prerogatives would diverge, in which I would want a louder say in our care. When Oliver's temperature dipped, the nurses placed him in an incubator and wheeled him away to the NICU.

Our new little family was forced apart. Rudy went with Oliver to the NICU while I tried my best to heal my body back in my hospital room.

Meanwhile, the infection coursed through me, delivering bouts of vomiting and diarrhea. Racing to the bathroom, I felt sharp pains in my abdomen as my stitches pulled. I was too dehydrated for an IV, so the doctors ordered the antibiotics to be injected directly into my body. Looking at the empty bassinet next to me, I felt like a failure as a mother before I had even begun. I replayed the events of his birth over and over again, reliving the physical and emotional agony. I have always been told that meeting your baby for the first time is one of the most magical experiences of life. But these were, without a doubt, the most challenging moments of mine.

I was at my worst, emotionally and physically beaten, when the guests arrived.

Dozens of them showed up unannounced at the hospital to greet a baby that was nowhere to be seen. It wasn't just my close family. Great uncles, cousins I hadn't seen in decades, and childhood friends showed up, smiling wide.

At first, the visits irritated me. I wanted privacy to nurse my physical and emotional wounds alone. But the guests kept coming, and I was too emotionally drained to stop them. Watching them arrive, my dad quickly dug through his backpack and pulled out the stack of stroller-shaped gift boxes that my mom had packed, just in case. The sight of my Sunday-football-watching dad trying to fold fifty miniature cardboard boxes with his large hands faster than the guests could take them made me laugh for the first time since I arrived at the hospital.

Eventually, I decided to cut the charade. No, I was not happy, I admitted to my visitors. I was terrified, in pain, and unsure of myself. Most of all, I worried I wasn't bonding with Oliver. Our interactions were laced with pain and exhaustion.

My whole life, I felt like I had been prepared for the beauty of motherhood. The apple-pie-baking mother was practically a cultural institution in the United States. She beamed in ads and movies all around me. She was a natural, at home in her role, never flustered, always prepared. Most of the women in my life had spoken about motherhood as important, fulfilling work that they cherished. Now, I was getting a crash course on the difficult, the ugly, the traumatic, but equally real parts of motherhood. I wore my despair openly, too tired to be embarrassed or try to hold it together in front of the guests. But they did not recoil or make excuses to leave. Instead, one by one, they sat with me. I realized that beyond the silver platter and the tiny sandwiches, this was the point of birth parties—to hold the new mother through the transition. My guests held my hand as nurses administered injections and exams; they wiped my tears when I talked about the gulf between my expectations and reality. Most importantly, they shared their own wisdom.

My cousin, who had a baby a year before, reassured me that I had eighteen years to bond with Oliver. The hospital separation would be a blip in our relationship, she said. She listened to the doctor's evaluations and pushed the hospital to reunite me with Oliver faster.

A family friend talked about her own traumatic birth and difficulties breastfeeding when her baby wouldn't latch on. It was all so much harder than she had anticipated.

My aunt, whose daughter had to undergo several surgeries in her first year of life, commiserated about the mental weight of pulling the trigger on critical medical decisions for your child, especially when you disagreed with their doctors.

The visits didn't stop at the hospital. People who had not been a part of my life for decades before I gave birth integrated themselves into my postpartum recovery. There was no fear of invading privacy or personal space. My great-uncle's girlfriend (talk about a distant relative), was an esthetician well into her sixties whom I had only met once before the birth. Still, she showed up at my door unannounced the week after I came home from the hospital, armed with a laser gun. She instructed me to strip down to my underwear and lie on the couch while she zapped my body with red beams she insisted would help reduce my C-section scarring. (They did.) She continued coming by twice a week. Sporting cow-print bell bottoms and winged eyeliner, she told me stories about her postpartum recovery, the best way to swaddle a fussy baby, and how to get rid of colic. By the end of the sessions, I felt physically and emotionally lighter.

My cousin came over to cut up papaya peels she said would heal my broken nipples (they didn't) and keep me company through the never-ending cycles of breastfeeding. Visiting with her eighteen-month-old, she was living proof that there was life after the newborn stage when the baby no longer dictated your wardrobe or schedule. These visitors served as cheerleaders and sages, encouraging me where the experts failed and helping me to find answers to motherhood within myself in those uncertain days after birth.

As the months passed, I couldn't stop thinking about my visitors and how wrong I had been about their presence. When I told my friends about my experience, it was clear that something wasn't translating. "That sounds exhausting," my American friends said. "All that entertaining."

But it felt less like hosting and more like being rescued. Once I quit acting like I had it all together, my community became a source of comfort and knowledge. In Brazil, I was surrounded by women who had been through this and come out the other side. They had so much to teach me. Who was I protecting by keeping them at arm's length? I wondered why I had ever thought to.

The American baby books I'd read talked about the importance of hunkering down with your newborn and shooing guests away.

But none spoke about how difficult it is to unpack the psychological stressors of the birth experience, and how isolating it was to have to do it alone.

I found I was wondering about this omission more than ever as I spoke with girlfriends in the United States who whispered traumatic details of their birth stories like closely guarded secrets.

It turns out that my situation was not unique. Millions of women around the world experience birth trauma every year. Up to 45 percent of women in the United Kingdom say their childbirth was traumatic, and 4 percent of them develop post traumatic stress disorder as a result. In the United States, one in three women report experiencing traumatic births.

Like me, my friends were trying to process the trials of their births and delivery, but they were doing it alone, without the support I'd unexpectedly found in Brazil.

I decided to look deeper into this cultural difference in an article for the *Washington Post*, where I was working as a correspondent.

I soon learned that the surge of guests I received was, if anything, a low turnout. In fact, for many Brazilian women, birth was a chance to throw a full-blown party. Brazilian hospitals, eager to accommodate waves of postpartum visitors, now offered access to wine sellers and on-site hairdressers. Guests were not relegated to waiting rooms. They were invited to experience the delivery itself. I had to see it for myself.

## The C-Section Watched Around the World

On the eve of her C-section, Mariana Casmalla, a twenty-eight-year-old dental surgeon, dazzled her guests from her hospital bed. Her eyes were professionally made up with shimmery eyeshadow and fake lashes. Her hair was perfectly blow dried and curled at the end. In her room, white-gloved caterers set up sandwiches and arranged flowers. The guests arrived, mingling, and chatting. Then it was time.

Nurses wheeled Mariana to the operating room as fifteen of her closest family members and friends trailed behind. They gathered in a special area next to the operating room. Ears pressed to the wall, they listened closely for the baby's first wail. When the doctor pulled baby Lorena from the incision in Mariana's abdomen, the frosted operating room window turned transparent. Laying on the operating table, Mariana gave her audience a thumbs-up. "She's here!" said Mariana's mother-in-law, Marisol, tearing up. Relatives watching on FaceTime asked her to zoom in so they could get a closer look.

Mariana's daughter, Lorena, made it on the front page of the *Washington Post* that week when an article I wrote about birth parties went viral. Readers could not believe what they were seeing. Why would anyone want a room full of people present as you gave birth?

Most readers said they wanted privacy and lots of it. Just like my American friends, they agreed that having to entertain family and friends after undergoing one of life's most demanding physical challenges seemed like an unnecessary burden. The BBC called and asked to speak to me on air. But *why*, my interviewer demanded. Why would those women do that to themselves?

The comment section was a bloodbath. There were xenophobic comments depicting Brazilians as superficial partiers. "Please tell me this is a skillful work of dystopian fiction," one person wrote. "The worst part of this is that the baby is an afterthought, taking a back seat to the mother's ego."

I had accidentally stumbled upon a difference in values so great that my readers simply could not fathom the rationale behind the tradition. But in Brazil, it all made sense.

In speaking to dozens of new Brazilian mothers, I learned that having their family and friends present as they become parents is a rite of passage for many. Like a Jewish Bat Mitzvah, relatives gather to welcome the mother into a new phase of life.

"I love it," said Bruna Viera, a thirty-five-year-old new mother who received eighty guests at the hospital in the days following the birth of her son Arthur. "You feel the tenderness people have for you. Many moms suffer from postpartum depression and feel isolated. Your hormones are raging. But to be surrounded by the people you love, people who saw you grow up, is extraordinary."

As a half-dozen of Bruna's friends cooed at the baby, her husband popped open a bottle of wine. Grandmother Lucimeire Viera swayed baby Arthur in her arms while holding a glass of merlot. "You see, darling," she explained to the baby. "Life's a party."

The message to Brazilian parents is clear: through the good and the bad, you are not alone. In the case of traumatic births or unexpected complications like mine, guests are there to comfort and counsel the mother and even advocate for her desires and preferences. And as over the top as these parties can be, there is no question that society recognizes the transformation that has just transpired. The mother's closest family and friends are there to honor the start of her journey into motherhood. Mothers who have come before her are there to usher her into their world. Matrescence, the process of becoming a mother, is a family activity.

Most importantly, the support Mariana and Bruna received from their families will be there long after the champagne stops bubbling. The Brazilian relatives who gathered to welcome their newborns will be at their fifth birthday parties, communions, graduations, and weddings. These parents have a network to turn to when things get rough, ready to step in and help with childcare, household chores, or advice. Like weddings, birth parties help to solidify these ties among extended families and friends. They celebrate new life but also ensure that new mothers can access aid when they need it.

It's not just parents throwing lavish birth parties who benefit. One 2012 study of Brazilian mothers with babies under six months old showed that 92 percent of them relied on family for help after giving birth, including emotional, financial, and material support. The vast majority of women saw an increase in social support during their pregnancy and the first six months of motherhood. Family members stepped in and did chores, grocery shopping, and provided childcare. One mother in the study said her father-in-law would give up his bed and sleep on the floor when she came to visit.

The impact of this aid is stark. Some studies show that mothers in Brazil who said they felt "well cared for" after birth have reported lower rates of postpartum depression. It makes sense. The wider the network of support available to new mothers, the more alternative caregivers they can turn to when times get tough. Far from a selfish act, the Brazilian tradition of surrounding new mothers with care from the first moments of parenthood is essential for the health of the family.

## Laboring Alone

My American readers might have been appalled at the tradition of birth parties. But it was also clear to me that many felt an absence of community support postpartum, especially those who, like me, had traumatic births. After being wheeled into emergency C-sections or stitched up after unexpected episiotomies, my friends often found themselves nursing their wounds and processing their experiences alone.

It wasn't always this way. The isolated, hospital-centric birth common in the United States today is a relatively new phenomenon. Until the start of the twentieth century, most Americans gave birth at home, surrounded by family and friends. These were female-dominated spaces where, in the absence of formal medical training, older women applied knowledge gained from their own births and experience to guide their neighbors and kin through labor. It was only in the 1760s that women began inviting male doctors into birthing rooms in cases of emergency. Women still decided where and with whom to labor, sometimes traveling back to their childhood home to deliver in a safe place where they felt most comfortable.

Of course, birth at home was often deadly, and even women who survived birthing an average of seven children were often left with debilitating consequences, including cervical prolapses, painful intercourse, and unrepaired lacerations.

In 1762, Dr. William Shippen Jr. founded the first maternity hospital in the United States, and through the nineteenth century, the urban elite began to increasingly rely on doctors for birth. With the introduction of anesthesia and advancements in sterilization, hospital births steadily replaced home births.

By 1950, 88 percent of white and 56 percent of nonwhite patients gave birth in hospitals. Maternal mortality rates declined dramatically, from 670 per 100,000 live births in 1930 to 37 per 100,000 births in 1960.

But, for many women, the rigid protocols, anonymity, and professionalized care of the hospital chafed against the sense of familiarity, communal care, and control they had once experienced at home. Visitors were discouraged, and fathers were segregated to all-male waiting rooms known as "Stork Clubs" through the 1960s.

The experience proved isolating for many women. In her book *Brought to Bed*, Judith Walzer Leavitt profiles several women who spoke out against hospital labors after being disillusioned by their own births.

"I experienced the sensation, which has always seemed to me worse than any pain—of struggling for consciousness, going down into blackness, coming up only to know that something big and dreadful is happening, to feel fear, to hear oneself moaning, to sense strange people with offensive professional voices," Lenore Pelham Friedrich, one woman profiled in the book, said about her three hospital deliveries in the 1930s. "It became obvious to me that... an important thing had happened to me, and I knew nothing about it."

Even today, American hospitals don't have the infrastructure for communal care. Rooms are not designed with guests and visitors in mind, like many Brazilian hospitals. Most American hospitals have a five-person visitor cap, and even then, guests are only admitted at specific hours.

While hospital births dramatically cut the maternal morbidity rate throughout the twentieth century, those gains have stabilized and, in some communities, even reversed. Now, the fight to regain a sense of community during birth has become, for some women, a matter of life or death.

## Communal Birthing as a Safety Net

On a Thursday morning, bellies protruding over their yoga mats, half a dozen Black pregnant women gathered in Oakland, California, to resurrect the communal birth experience. At first glance, the scene could not have been more different from the lavish Brazilian birth parties I had written about in São Paulo. The women gathered in a windowless basement of a former shopping mall in Oakland, California, a city that struggles with some of the nation's highest crime rates. In a community hit hard by racial and economic inequality, the Eastmont Mall was converted into a social service hub that houses the county's Wellness Center clinic. But here, midwives, family support advocates, and doulas were trying to foster a social safety net not so different from the one I had experienced in Brazil.

The Black mothers were part of BE*loved*BIRTH Black Centering, an innovative effort created by Black birth workers in partnership with the county to transform Black birthing experiences and outcomes while restoring community care to pregnancy. Instead of seeing a doctor individually, who may be more likely to dismiss pain and overlook symptoms, the women at BE*loved* are examined together. They meet with other moms at the same stage of pregnancy for 15 group consultations. Midwives lead the visits, which include clinical checkups, review of lab tests, ultrasounds, and educational seminars.

The founders of BE*loved* see safety in numbers. Like the support I found in Brazil, the group care model gives women a safety net and a sounding board that will follow them throughout motherhood. They, too, were sharing stories, exchanging wisdom, processing trauma, and learning from each other. But unlike the silver-plated birth parties, for the women at BE*loved*, communal care was a matter of life or death.

The maternal mortality rate in the United States is among the highest in the developed world, with 32.9 deaths for every 100,000 people giving birth. That's ten times the rate in Spain, Germany, or Japan. While other developed countries have seen their maternal mortality rates decline, in America, they are spiking. The number of women who die within one year of giving birth more than doubled between 1999 and 2019, according to a study published in 2023 by the *Journal of the American Medical Association*. One study found that 13 percent of people giving birth reported experiencing mistreatment or abuse. Rates were higher for LGBTQ+ patients and those who were uninsured, suggesting social stigmas infiltrate birth experiences.

For Black women, the situation is even more dire. They are three to four times more likely to die from pregnancy-related causes than white women in America, according to a 2019 study by the CDC. Black women in America are also twice as likely as their white counterparts to experience life-threatening pregnancy complications and twice as likely to have their child die before their first birthday. Studies attribute the disparity to systemic racism and mistreatment of Black patients that lead to deadly complications, including denial of medication and delayed treatment.

At BE*loved*, it was clear every attempt had been made to transform the sterile retail space, now owned by the county, into a sanctuary. Affirmations were taped to the bulletin boards and Beyoncé cooed from the speakers. On the corner, a flag saluting the Black Panthers, the Black power organization founded in Oakland in the 1960s, was framed on the wall. Maternity shots of the BE*loved*

Birth Alumni hung from the walls. Behind a room divider, women had their bumps massaged by a midwife, after she checked on the baby's growth. Half a dozen baby heartbeats echoed through the room as the women made their rounds through the examinations.

The women also develop birth plans, discuss their symptoms, and undergo tests to catch complications early. Those who lack the support of partners or their families lean on each other as they learn how to advocate for themselves, voice concerns to their doctors, and make decisions about their care.

Many of the women I spoke to at BE*loved* had already experienced medical trauma and neglect. Terilynn Nash, a ballet teacher, said doctors ignored her symptoms and misdiagnosed two ectopic pregnancies as miscarriages. When she told her doctor she had a gut feeling something wasn't right, he told her to go home and rest. Only when Terilynn demanded a pregnancy test did the results confirm her suspicion and secure her a life-saving surgery. Now that she is a patient at BE*loved*, she has the chance to discuss her symptoms every two weeks and talk through any concerns openly. She has also learned from the midwives and the other patients how to create a birth plan, think through questions in her care, and stand up for her own medical choices. "The group helps me advocate for myself and what I want," she said.

Single mom Karinda Williams almost lost her oldest son when an amniotic fluid infection went undetected. Determined that things would be different with this pregnancy, she joined BE*loved*, where she has worked on tapping into her intuition. But she's also learned to rely on others along the way.

"I'm so happy to have that support since I don't have it at home." At BE*loved*, she created a community she turns to when she needs help. At the last visit, she said to the other moms that she wouldn't have a baby shower because "Nobody would show up," she said. Another mother jumped in. "I would." Since then, she and Williams have called each other weekly to discuss their symptoms and worries.

BE*loved*'s group care model has already delivered positive results. Women at BE*loved* are more likely to birth full-term, healthy-weight babies, experience less stress, and report more empowered pregnancy and birth experiences.

Alexis Perryman, one of the doulas at BE*loved*, credits the communal aspect of the group with lowering the stress and anxiety that can lead to complications during birth.

"Imagine going into pregnancy with zero support and love. Programs like this are trying to change that mentality. This is a tribe, a village, and that can counteract these statistics," she said. At BE*loved*, the women become family, she insists. "When your grandma and great grandma are pouring into you their experience and respect for the birthing process, that shows up differently than a doctor who is spitting out what they learned in school. You feel that," she said. "At the end of the day, it's just love."

## BRINGING IT HOME

We spend months planning weddings, hiring experts to guide us through seating arrangements and help us pose for photos. We call on bridesmaids and assign ushers to specific roles for the big day. We should treat birth with the same level of teamwork and preparation.

If the thought of inviting guests to your delivery room makes you queasy, I don't blame you. Privacy is an ingrained birthright in American culture. We have been taught to protect it at all costs, especially during vulnerable times. Of course, every situation is different. Some family dynamics are fraught and inevitably lead to stress. Many of us have spent years creating boundaries to protect ourselves from relatives whose values may not align with ours.

Others don't have a community to rely on—through no fault of their own. We live in a transient society swirling with perpetual change. Career changes and moves can sweep away social networks that take years to rebuild. As anyone who has tried to strike up a conversation with the yogi on the mat next to them knows, few efforts are more humbling than trying to make friends as an adult.

Still, pregnancy is a great time to fortify your network. Sarah Moore, a licensed therapist specializing in postpartum care, tells parents to put their registries aside and focus instead on preparing a social circle to support both you and your baby. "If I had to pick one thing to tell women to prepare before they give birth, it would be community," she said. Many of the families Moore counsels, especially those who have moved far from where they grew up, find that they have little practice when it comes to building a group of friends. She recommends they proactively look for playgroups or parents' meetups specific to their area. She suggests parents investigate everything from local community centers and churches to swimming pools and yoga studios. Neighborhood listservs and social media groups are a great resource to meet other parents. As the women at BE*loved* can attest, group birthing classes and prenatal checkups can be a great way to meet people in similar stages of pregnancy. Best of all, you can continue trading notes as your children grow. If none are available in your area, check social media for pregnancy groups that can play a similar role. But be sure to take the interactions offline as quickly as possible and prioritize real-life coffee dates with members who live locally over online back-and-forths.

Long before your first contraction starts, ask yourself who you want to include in your support team to usher you through the transition ahead.

Consider having advocates at your birth who understand your priorities and can help you find your voice if things take an unexpected turn, whether it is your birth family or your chosen family, a paid doula, or a loving relative. You may still decide to limit your circle of support or favor a secluded experience. But the norm is worth questioning. Here are some tips to get you started:

1. **Expand the Guest List:** In deciding how to approach whom you invite to your birth, consider the following questions:
    - When I go through hardship, do I turn inward or seek help? Which strategy have I found to be most useful? Who has guided me through difficult moments in the past?
    - Who are the friends or family members I can turn to, unpolished and imperfect, when I need advice? If you won't feel comfortable asking them for help, don't invite them over.
2. **Be Raw:** Wherever you find your people, try to be as raw and real as possible from the get-go. Look for nonjudgmental friends who will support you at your worst. "Find the people who you'll walk in with spit-up on your blouse, and they'll give you a knowing smile," says Moore. This idea of presenting myself unfiltered did not come easy to me. I am the type of host who likes to run around the house, nudging the picture frames into place and ensuring my throw pillows are "just so." However, I found the illusion of perfection became much more burdensome to keep up after I became a mom. I felt overwhelmed enough by breastfeeding and sleep schedules in the first few days after Oliver's birth— there was no space for guilt over dirty dishes in the sink. Now, I try to make it a point to invite people over for dinner, knowing the house won't be perfect. I look away from my stained couch and smile through the urge to pick up the toys scattered on the

ground. More often than not, my new friends breathe a sigh of relief and are much more eager to invite me to their homes. These imperfect dinner parties offer a chance to test out the nonjudgmental friends and cement a solid support network before the baby comes, and life inevitably gets messier.

3. **Find Your Vendors:** Research what services your health insurance covers. Many states in the United States now cover doula services and lactation support. Having an advocate at birth can be especially crucial for women of color. Surround yourself with people who understand your birth preferences and can voice your opinions to your care providers or help you think through unexpected decisions.

4. **Call on the Wise:** Professional support is essential, but don't forget to draw strength from the lessons of women who came before you. They will be your guides, helping you make sense of your debut into motherhood. In the weeks leading up to birth, interview the women in your life about their experiences. Ask your mothers, grandmothers, and other parents in your family about the joys of their own experiences, but also their struggles. What surprised or scared them? How do they feel about it now, years or decades later? How did their identities change after becoming parents? What do they wish they knew? If you live far from the people you love, record these conversations and play them back when you feel isolated or depleted. Have faith that just like those who came before you, you too will make it through.

5. **RSVP to Your Friends' Birth Parties:** Live out this philosophy in your own community. Caring for the parents in our lives going through the postpartum period can and should extend beyond flowers or wishes of congratulations. I think back to the days after Oliver's birth, and how my aunts helped me process an experience

that went very differently than I had imagined, one that looked nothing like the manicured photos splashed on the covers of magazines or my social media feed. I try to offer the same sense of support to my friends who have traumatic labors, asking specific questions about their birth stories, avoiding judgment or expectations, and holding space for those taboo but common feelings of disappointment, surprise, or sadness that can accompany birth. "How was it, really?" I ask, no smile stretched across my face. I try not to anticipate a specific response. I find that can open the way for many of my friends to voice the darker side of the experience, the fear or trauma they felt. Airing these grievances freely and openly, I find, is a crucial first step in processing the complex and often life-changing experience that is giving birth. In the United States, it is common to see friends through breakups, unemployment, and even bouts of depression. Why should birth be any different?

# Don't Wash Your Hair for Forty Days

## More Soup for You

My C-section scar was still angry and throbbing when my mother-in-law came to stay in our home in Brazil three weeks after Oliver was born.

My husband's family is Chinese-American, and my in-laws speak limited English and no Portuguese. I had no idea how they would navigate Brazil on their own and worried about how my mercurial mother-in-law would behave. I had been on the fence about the visit for months. My friends called me crazy and urged me to book her a hotel instead. But with my own parents back in America and Rudy returning to the office, I was on my own. "We could use the help," Rudy said, promising to serve as a buffer if things got tense. Cautiously, I agreed.

To my surprise, my mother-in-law was quiet as a mouse when she arrived. She mainly kept to herself and spent hours alone in the kitchen, peeling ginger and crushing garlic while a pot gurgled endlessly on the stove. Her cooking sessions were interrupted by short spurts of activity around the apartment, washing bottles, and cleaning up. Every now and then, she would bolt out of the house for hours at a time with no explanation.

I was surprised but happy to have her out of my hair as I tried to navigate the first few weeks at home. Her long hours in the kitchen meant we were ships in the night. I was free to spend my time figuring out nursing and napping with Oliver, while she cooked away.

That's when the soups started appearing. Chicken soup with goji berries and peanuts placed innocently next to my breakfast oatmeal. Lotus root soup with chunks of papaya floating in a clear broth popped up next to my breast pump. She got confused in the Brazilian market, I thought. Or maybe she just pulled what she could find from our empty cabinets. "Just drink it," Rudy would say. "It's a Chinese thing...it's important to her."

I'd roll my eyes and politely take some sips before making him drink the rest when she wasn't looking. Two weeks in, I noticed my tepid milk supply swelled, and I felt like I had more energy. But the taste lingered, a mix of ingredients I had never tried before. The gamey chicken broth clashed with the tang of the berries and the buttery aftertaste of the peanuts. The soups were clear but rich, making them impossible to chug.

They kept coming faster than I could down them. Soon I was being served several bowls a day. I was swamped with soup morning, afternoon, and night until I couldn't take it anymore. "You have to talk to her; make it stop," I told Rudy. He sighed and, after putting it off for a few days, bit the bullet. As quickly as they appeared, the soups were gone.

Much later, when I dug into research about Chinese birth and postpartum traditions, I pieced together what had happened. My mother-in-law was not trying to drown me in soup for her own amusement. She was silently performing an ancient Chinese ritual of love and devotion for new mothers: confinement.

Confinement is a period of forty days after giving birth, when Chinese women stay home resting and recovering, while a relative, friend, or paid caregiver tends to them and their newborn full time. The caregiver takes over everything from the medical—like basic postpartum checkups—to the mundane, like chores and laundry. The postpartum mother is expected to do no housework, cooking, or cleaning for the full forty days. All her meals are cooked for her, with her recovery in mind.

The earliest records of Chinese confinement, or *zuò yuè zi* in Mandarin, date back to the first century AD, a time when maternal and infant mortality rates were high and "confining" mother and baby at home shielded them from deadly diseases. Known as the sitting month, confinement is still widely practiced across mainland China, Taiwan, Hong Kong, Southeast Asia, and by the Chinese diaspora around the world.

It is a tradition chock full of rules for the new mother. The bans span from the extreme, like not bathing or washing their hair, to the banal, like not drinking cold water. The mother should rest, ideally lying down and be protected from anything that triggers crying.

These rules are not always popular. Some people chafe under them. Many bend their diets and reject restrictions on leaving the house. Most ignore archaic superstitions and jump into the shower. And while the last thing many postpartum people want to deal with is a mother-in-law force-feeding them soup, the confinement tradition also carries an understanding that the care and attention doted on the baby should be extended to the newborn parent.

At first glance, it may seem like confinement is calling for the opposite of Brazilian birth parties—the isolation of the postpartum woman. But in reality, it is a time when her community encircles her. For the postpartum parent, confinement serves as a refuge from societal and career expectations. Throughout the confinement period, there is an unspoken understanding that in this vulnerable time, women need support to keep physical and mental illness at bay.

Like Brazilian birth parties, confinement also marks a reorientation of the woman's place in society as she transitions from woman to mother. She is ushered into this new phase with love and devotion from the women in her life, who feed and nurture her for forty days with traditional soups meant to heal her body and help her breastfeed. Instead of thrusting the mother and baby alone into the world, their village comes to them.

Unbeknownst to me, in those weeks after my son was born, my mother-in-law had been scouring Brazilian markets for hours in search of the specific types of raw peanuts and ginger that would help reduce inflammation and boost my milk supply. She would bring along a notebook to negotiate with Portuguese-speaking vendors, writing down the price she was willing to pay and passing it back and forth to bargain when she found something suitable. In making these soups, my mother-in-law communicated an unspoken understanding: I know what you went through was difficult and traumatic. I'm here to help you heal. It is a beautiful tradition of love and devotion. And I had no idea it happened to me.

## Confinement as a Right

Confinement, I learned, is not a luxury, but rather a child bearer's right. Once a duty relegated to friends and family, confinement is quickly becoming a professionalized service. Throughout China and much of Southeast Asia, paid confinement nannies are a phone call away, available to swoop in and care for the postpartum woman as soon as her contractions end.

In Shanghai, China's financial capital, the popularity of confinement nannies over the last decade has surged. Confinement training schools subsidized by the government have popped up around the city.

Professional confinement nannies are not cheap, and many families save up for months to afford one. Certified professionals in Shanghai charge about $2,500 a month for round-the-clock services, including managing the baby's night feeds and diaper changes, cooking all meals, and even giving postpartum massages. The fee amounts to nearly a full month's salary for the average worker in Shanghai. But even those who cannot afford to hire a nanny have relatives, in-laws, or friends move in to cook, clean, and care for the new mom.

As Xi Weigin, a confinement nanny who has been practicing for eight years in Shanghai, told me, "All women deserve confinement."

"Women are willing to pay this money because it frees them," Shi Yajun, owner of a training center for confinement nannies, told me. "It's not like buying a Louis Vuitton purse. It's an investment." The returns, she said, continue for years, resulting in healthier, more confident mothers eager to have more children. "The body is broken after birth. Confinement is a chance to heal that wound," she said.

While many women in the West would scoff at the notion of birth "breaking" a woman, a little mandated rest doesn't sound so bad when we consider the alternative. I thought about all the mothers who routinely return to work with injured bodies and minds, trying to heal from the visible and invisible wounds of birth. Many of my friends have been forced back to the office weeks after birth, their surgery scars raw under their pencil skirts. They attend meetings while managing incontinence and pump milk in office break rooms between calls.

Culture reflects what a people value. The fact that the confinement tradition survived China's numerous economic and cultural revolutions unscathed says something about its benefit to the wider society. What would it look like, I wondered, to live in a country that shared an understanding of the importance of postpartum recovery?

## Training to Confine

To find out, I went straight to the source. One spring afternoon I followed two dozen women wearing starched pink lab coats into a classroom in an industrial part of Shanghai. The room was lined with empty strollers. Laying by the window, ready for action, were six dolls tightly swaddled in alternating blue and pink blankets.

The nannies-in-training had come to learn how to perform the two-thousand-year-old confinement tradition—professionally. After a month of training, they would be certified and dispatched to live with families around the country, caring for both mother and baby for the first forty days.

Teacher Sunny Xu, wearing a pressed white button-down and a flared black skirt, commanded the students' attention in the center of the room. Sunny lives up to her name. Her round, dimpled face exudes joy and optimism that felt foreign to postpartum life as I've seen it. At forty-one, she has spent half her life helping more than fifty families navigate the postpartum period, and she's a true believer.

Ultimately, the confinement experience helps the women not only recover, but emerge from postpartum stronger than ever, she told the class.

"Confinement allows you to really experience the joy of being a mother." The mothers who undergo confinement, she explained, emerge from postpartum more confident, peaceful, and healthy than the ones who don't.

The session is a masterclass on postpartum care. Sunny teaches the nannies how to comfort both a hungry baby and an insecure mom, how to pat a baby's back to avoid reflux, what to say to a mother in the depths of postpartum depression, how to calm a baby's cries, and how to settle disputes between postpartum mothers and in-laws.

While practices differ throughout Asia, confinement, Sunny explained, boils down to the following nonnegotiable elements:

## Retreat

ISOLATION IS, PERHAPS, THE MOST CONTROVERSIAL ELEMENT OF confinement for Westerners. We associate the word with incarceration and punishment, not the joy of a newborn. But confinement nurses say it is perhaps the most fundamental element in protecting the mother's right to heal. Isolation in confinement does not translate to an alienation but rather a retreat. Confining the mother for forty days forces her to visibly step away from her daily duties, ensuring others respect her recovery period. Being automatically excused from work, social, and family obligations also gives the new mother a say on the pace at which she reenters society. In China, nobody expects the postpartum mom to chair meetings at work in the weeks following her delivery. She won't be at school drop-offs or rushing to meet deadlines. For forty days, she is not responsible for anyone else's well-being. The confined mother is just that—separated from the rest of society, insulated with her newborn, and given the space and time to recover away from the demands of the world outside.

That does not mean she is alone. Rather, she is constantly monitored, checked, and, in many cases, doted on. But instead of having to seek out that support proactively, it is offered to her in the comfort of her house and, many times, from her bed.

## Rest

ALL THE CONFINEMENT NANNIES I SPOKE TO EMPHASIZED REST AS A crucial element in the recovery period. To ensure adequate healing, confined women are urged to avoid exercise, housework, and cleaning.

Unlike in the United States, where rest often comes at the bottom of the postpartum mother's to-do list, in China, it is a family goal. Instead of "sleeping when the baby sleeps," rest is the confined parent's primary responsibility. In some countries confined women are told not only to stay home but to lie in bed for the full forty days. That means everyone else has to be on their feet.

When families know that mom is going to be out of the picture, they are forced to plan. They prepare for confinement ahead of time, calling up in-laws, neighbors, or professionals for help. Partners must step up and fulfill the mother's responsibilities at home. Rest comes even before caring for baby. The postpartum mom will step in to breastfeed, but she returns to rest as soon as possible, while caretakers oversee diaper changes, bathing, and rocking the baby to sleep.

"You must tell the mother 'It's okay. I'll go and see what's going on with the baby,'" Sunny instructs the nannies in training. "Tell her 'You have a good sleep, and I'll take care of it.'"

Sleep is not a last resort. Help is not something exhausted and depleted mothers beg for. It is expected, planned for, and plentiful from the start.

## Nourish

IN CHINESE CULTURE, FOOD OFTEN ACTS THE PART OF MEDICINE. Traditional Chinese medicine employs herbs, mushrooms, spices, and vegetables as tools for specific nutritional outcomes. Ingredients must balance each other out and work together to combat illness.

The postpartum period is no different. During confinement, there are no fast-food meals scarfed down during naps. Food is ingested strategically, with a focus on ensuring the mother's diet is balanced and healing.

Recipes for postpartum confinement diets can even be found in ancient Chinese medical texts as far back as the third century BC. These texts emphasize the importance of restoring a woman's body and replenishing her energy after childbirth. According to traditional Chinese medicine, giving birth depletes a woman's blood and her qi (vital energy), leaving her vulnerable to health issues if not properly cared for during the postpartum period. So, caretakers are laser-focused on ensuring that anything the postpartum woman ingests is serving her recovery and giving her energy.

It is not surprising, therefore, that many parents who undergo confinement strongly associate the tradition with food. Even those who don't abide by some of the tradition's more archaic rules follow confinement diets. Herbal soups cleanse the body of toxins and help heal the perineum. Vinegar and other astringents help to stem blood loss and increase milk supply. Pork strengthens the spleen, while ginger, black pepper, sesame oil, and rice wine help boost energy. Many Chinese mothers swear by these postpartum elixirs.

## Recover

PHYSICAL AND MENTAL RECOVERY IS THE ULTIMATE GOAL OF CONfinement.

While postpartum patients in the United States can go weeks without seeing a doctor after giving birth, confinement caretakers are constantly monitoring their charges for complications. Not only are the nannies trained to tend to the most common physical ailments post-birth, but they are also taught to spot more serious complications that require medical attention.

At the training center, the nannies-to-be fill their notebooks with diagrams showing kegel exercises to strengthen the pelvic floor, instructions on how to care for episiotomies and C-section wounds, and massage techniques to help with uterine contractions and promote lactation.

The psychological healing starts right away too. The nannies are trained on the hormonal cycle of the postpartum woman. They are able to explain to new mothers (and their exasperated partners) the science behind their mood swings and when they can expect them to pass.

They are trained to keep the mother's stress level low at all costs and even dote on her. "When a baby comes, the attention shifts to the newborn, and the mother gets ignored. So, the confinement nanny must focus on the mother. Remind the father and the grandparents to give her care and not transfer all of the love to the child, so she doesn't feel she has lost something," said Sunny.

The nannies also must ensure she does not feel alone as she learns the ropes of parenthood. "The key phrase to comfort the new mother is "Don't worry. I'm here," she says, instructing the nannies to repeat the phrase as often as necessary.

Because nannies often come into multigenerational households at a time of transition, they are trained to deflect conflict and mediate between family members. "We must never add fuel to the fire. Help make the home a place of mutual tolerance," Sunny instructed her class. The nanny, Sunny explains, must protect the energy of the home. "You must learn to digest negative emotions and always look to the positive," she says, reminding the women to always smile big, showing eight teeth if possible. Sunny herself has lectured difficult in-laws on the hormonal fluctuations of a new mother, cradled a crying postpartum woman when her husband had to work late, and reassured countless parents that they too would make it through the transition. "We must be bridge builders."

## Postpartum Doulas in America

Witnessing the twenty-four-hour postpartum care many women in China receive, I was struck by the American alternative. In the

United States it seemed that the moment the baby is safely delivered, the mother's recovery is sidelined as a given. In this context, a forty-day regime for postpartum parents feels like an impractical luxury.

While there are hundreds of books on navigating the postpartum period, the ones I've read seem almost exclusively focused on the newborn's well-being and adjustment. Paragraphs on postpartum maternal care are limited to tips on how to align housework with the baby's feeding schedule. The focus is on regaining a maximum level of productivity as quickly as possible. New mothers are encouraged to pop back into their lives and their work as if nothing has changed.

Asian Americans growing up in immigrant families often have front-row seats to these contrasting attitudes on postpartum care. That was the case for Jin Yoo-Kim, a documentary filmmaker in L.A. For weeks after her brother was born, Korean relatives would pop by her house with iron-rich seaweed soup to help aid her mom's recovery. "My mother's health was so important. It was so different from how Americans were like, "Get back to work," she recalled.

Years later, when she found out she was pregnant, Jin knew she wanted an Asian-style postpartum experience. Still, when her Vietnamese mother-in-law offered to move in for the first month of her postpartum, she hesitated. "I didn't want to have to go into hostess mode, and have to take care of her."

Instead, Jin was the one who was cared for. Her mother-in-law moved in, took care of all the household chores, and told her to focus on rest. Every day, her mother-in-law would cook protein-rich foods and help heal Jin's belly with a warm stone. Meanwhile, her mother would stop by daily with fresh Korean *miyeokguk*, or seaweed soup. The joint effort wove both sides of the family together.

"It was a sweet moment, where both grandparents were really involved in their way. As floundering first-time parents, we felt like we were standing on that."

Compared to the prolonged postpartum recovery in Asia, birth in the United States is practically a drive-through experience, streamlined to get everyone back to work as quickly as possible.

Yet slowly, it seems Americans are rejecting a postpartum attitude that focuses on a return to productivity at all costs. My own friends, especially those who had traumatic births, seem to recognize the need for physical and mental recovery postpartum. In lieu of teddy bears and blankets, they started organizing meal trains for friends and dropping off gift cards for food delivery services.

Some Americans are even adopting Asian confinement practices themselves, regardless of their race and background. Willow Li, the founder of AyiConnect, a service that links Americans with Chinese postpartum nurses, said the interest in confinement care amongst non-Asians has exploded in recent years as more women learn about the tradition.

"Understanding the value behind postpartum care has been eye-opening for Western society. I don't think they were ever exposed to this practice before social media brought attention to the topic," she said.

Li estimates that 10 percent of her postpartum clients today are non-Asian. "Our western patients are looking for rest and recovery. A lot of them come to us and say, 'I may not be inclined to follow postpartum traditions, but I'd like some more help.' They may not have the family support, and they want to be prepared."

For an average of $8,000, customers receive twenty-six days of live-in postpartum services, including meals for the mom, cleaning, and baby care.

Li sees the spike in interest as part of a larger transformation in the way American families view postpartum care. "Independence is one thing, but I think more and more mothers are focusing on their well-being. It helps the mothers shift their mindset from the traditional 'I-can-do-it-all' to 'I need support, and it's okay to ask for help.'"

Shannon Brocks was one of those moms who saw the benefits of confinement all the way from Texas. When she was pregnant with her daughter, Shannon came across a YouTube video of an American expat who underwent postpartum confinement while living in China. The practice seemed like a better alternative to the postpartum experience in America. She was intrigued by the Chinese model and decided to look into it for her own postpartum period. "I feel like American culture intends to prioritize women's health but doesn't create infrastructure to actually assist with a healthy recovery," she said.

A few weeks before her daughter was born, she found herself scouring the aisles of an Asian grocery store with Annie, a Chinese confinement nanny she found online. For thirty days, Annie cooked meals geared toward increasing milk production, took over nighttime feeds while the new parents slept, gave Shannon belly massages, and helped her get the hang of breastfeeding. Meanwhile her husband took over all household chores allowing Shannon to stay in bed for the first two weeks after her daughter was born. When it was time for Annie to leave, Shannon cried. "She was first and foremost a baby-whisperer and taught us so much about caring for a newborn," she said. "She became part of our little family."

While it was hard to see Annie go, the time with her equipped Shannon and her husband with the skills they needed to take on the next few months. "I felt so much better and more confident than I would have been without her."

Confinement nannies aren't the only postpartum support Americans are seeking. Many are now turning to doulas, like LaToshia Rouse, to guide them through the transition. LaToshia grew up in a tightknit community in Grifton, North Carolina, a two-thousand-person town with one stoplight.

"My mother had stories about when she was postpartum, how family would come over and give her breaks, cook for her," she said. As an adult, LaToshia moved away from Grifton and, like so many women today, when it was time to have children of her own she found herself far from her support system.

"I realized that there was a big gap. I remember feeling like, you know, I kind of had to do it. I felt like I had to cover all the bases of the people who usually would be there to help," she said.

The first few years of her son's life were riddled with anxiety as she tried to juggle childcare, housework, and a full-time career with little help from her husband, since his job was less flexible. When she became pregnant with triplets a few years later, LaToshia decided it was time to ask for help, so she turned to a friend from church, who offered to come over for a few hours during the week to take over some housework. The relief was immediate.

"She vacuumed my floors and helped me make baby bottles. But what I treasured the most was that she would talk to me."

After a career working in hospitals, she felt called to give women the support she once craved and became a postpartum

43

doula. While traditional doulas help pregnant women navigate labor, postpartum doulas, much like confinement nannies, guide women through the transition into motherhood.

Like her church friend once did for her, LaToshia shows up at her clients' door ready to assist with calming teas and breastfeeding tips. But mostly, she listens.

The new parents open up, processing trauma from birth, seeking advice on balancing motherhood and marriage, and navigating strained relationships with their families. All of them worry about whether they will be good mothers, she told me. Like Sunny in China, LaToshia is constantly morphing—from a nurse to a housekeeper, a nanny, and a friend. But that, she says, is what her clients need. She understands she is filling in for a village that has evaporated. I was astonished to find that she and Sunny shared a similar motto, which they repeated over and over again to their clients.

"I spend a lot of time during postpartum telling people, 'You're doing it right. It's going to be okay, I'm here.' That's what people are lacking," she said.

## Tackling the Fourth Trimester Together

Asking for help from a relative, neighbors, and even from a healthcare provider can be difficult for postpartum parents anywhere, but in the United States, cultural barriers make it even harder.

"The American streak of independence, this 'pull yourself up by your bootstraps,' really goes counter to what is needed during this period," said Karla Pippa, cofounder of NYC Birth Village, a prenatal and postpartum doula care service in New York City.

Yet anyone who has spent time around a parent during the so-called "fourth trimester," the twelve-week period after birth, can clearly see that better postpartum care options are needed at a societal level.

The postpartum period itself is curtailed in America, the only developed country with no federally guaranteed maternity leave. While paid family leave proposals have advanced in many states, a nationwide policy has yet to be enacted. Postpartum women also receive little in the way of medical support. Most mothers in the United States are sent to a single follow-up appointment at six weeks; even those visits are attended by only 40 percent of moms.

But the first few weeks postpartum are vital in laying the foundation for the mother's and baby's health for years to come. More than half of pregnancy-related deaths occur after the birth of the baby.

Yet, at the University of North Carolina, medical anthropologist Dr. Kristin Tully noticed a cliff in maternal care after labor. "We are hyper visible during pregnancy, and of course, all want what's best for little ones, but it was interesting to think: at what point do we not become valuable in ourselves," she said.

She teamed up with Dr Alison Stuebe, a director of fetal-maternal medicine at UNC, to redefine the fourth trimester.

For two years, Stuebe asked new mothers questions about their unmet health needs. Many of the women felt they were navigating the postpartum transition alone.

Unlike the detailed care they received during pregnancy, their six-week checkup was impersonal and superficial. Less than half of women who attended the postpartum visits felt they received enough information about postpartum depression, healthy eating, exercise, or changes in their sexual response or emotions, according to a 2013 national survey. Women who faced complications felt that their care was fragmented.

Inspired by traditions like confinement, the doctors urged the medical community to step in. In 2017, Dr. Stuebe chaired the American College of Obstetrics and Gynecology Presidential Task Force on Redefining Postpartum. The college called for a shift in the perception of postpartum care, from a single checkup to an ongoing recovery process similar to confinement but led by doctors.

"Following birth, many cultures prescribe a 30–40-day period of rest and recovery, with the woman and her newborn surrounded and supported by family and community members. Many agrarian cultures enshrine postpartum rituals, including traditional foods and support for day-to-day household tasks. These traditions have been sustained by some cultural groups, but for many women in the United States, the 6-week postpartum visit punctuates a period devoid of formal or informal maternal support," the college wrote in a statement. Doctors, Dr. Stuebe believed, were best placed to change the culture.

In place of the single six-week checkup, the college called for a full physical, social, and psychological assessment to cover emotional well-being, contraception, sleep and fatigue, disease management, recovery from labor, and general health maintenance. An initial assessment of the postpartum woman should occur three weeks after birth. Visits should continue after the postpartum period, with doctors handing over the patient's care to a general practitioner.

To address an information deficit felt by many patients, the doctors created a free online portal to connect postpartum women around the country with healthcare providers, doulas, and other mothers in their community. The site newmomhealth.com encourages women to create a postpartum care plan that spells out the support they need—cooked meals, groceries, or visits from friends. On the site, postpartum women can read articles on breastfeeding, sleep training, and even dealing with unsolicited advice. They can watch videos from other moms on intimacy and sex after birth and learn what symptoms to watch out for after labor.

The site also has tools for clinicians to better serve postpartum women, including webinars and training sessions on trauma, best practices, and lactation support.

"Healthcare should be a resource, not a place of last resort," Dr. Tully told me. "Instead of a one-off six-week visit, it should explicitly be intended to be ongoing, comprehensive care."

Dr. Tully's platform offers a digital, scalable postpartum recovery alternative for American moms. Much like the nurses I met in China, she is ensuring that patients are surrounded by a network of support as they recover from birth.

I realize now that that's what my mother-in-law was trying to do for me as well. By boiling strange soups on my stove, she was participating in a chain of care that stretched back hundreds of years. Her silent labor spoke volumes. It said my physical recovery was important, not a burden to be rushed or to bear unsupported. Years later, I realized that she was communicating love and solidarity the way women in her family had for generations: with soup. Had I known, I would have finished every drop.

## BRINGING IT HOME

What can confinement teach American parents? I'm certainly not suggesting new mothers skip showers or hire expensive nurses. But here's how you can DIY your own postpartum confinement, taking aspects of the Chinese tradition that work for your family:

1. **Take Stock:** Part of the difficulty in planning for postpartum is that it can be hard to know the kind of care you will need and want ahead of time. Karla Pippa, the cofounder of NYC Birth Village, encourages her clients to take stock of their stress and triggers before birth. Consider the following:

   - Does postpartum depression or psychosis run in your family? Do you have preexisting mental health issues? If so, seek a licensed therapist ahead of time and make appointments. Schedule at least one appointment before your birth so the therapist is familiar with your history and any issues that may be triggered.

   - How has sleep deprivation impacted you mentally and physically in the past? If you are sleep-sensitive, focus on obtaining support that will help you get a full night's sleep, like a night nurse or relative who can care for the baby while you rest.

   - How much support do you expect to receive from your partner? If your partner or support system is only available for a few days or weeks after birth, prepare ahead of time by asking in-laws or friends to step in to fill those gaps and ease the transition.

   - Are you an introvert or an extrovert? Introverts may like the idea of home confinement and call on their village to come to them, while extroverts may find postpartum isolation draining. In that case, pre-schedule coffee dates or outings as mental health buffers during the first few weeks. You can always cancel if you are not up for it once the baby arrives.

2. **Confine Yourself:** Consider a self-imposed confinement. I don't mean shutting yourself out from the world. Rather, like confined women in China, consider bringing your village to you. Prepare to

clear your plate for the first forty days after you give birth and let all the stakeholders in your life know it. Think through your duties at home and at work and assign them to others for the time. Even parents who are unable to take parental leave can make it clear to their spouses, bosses, friends, and family that they are actively recovering and cannot take on any additional tasks. Do not give in to the pressure to resume your work or social life as quickly as possible. When it comes time to emerge from your confinement, add activities and duties back in one at a time when you feel ready.

3. **Shower the Parent, Not the Baby:** For many Americans who grew up on strict values of self-reliance, asking for help can be intimidating. A baby shower is a wonderful time to point well-meaning friends in the right direction. Instead of a gift registry, consider asking ahead of time for a hand with laundry, meal trains, or extra childcare. One friend of mine made it clear that all gifts at her son's baby shower should be for her, not the baby. She asked for gifts she knew would encourage her to maintain self-care she saw as foundational for her mental health, like massage vouchers or gift cards to restaurants. Trust me, that fancy baby monitor or expensive stroller will be of little comfort six weeks postpartum when all you crave is a long shower, a ready-made meal, or a long talk with a friend.

4. **Bring the Village to You:** Before you give birth, build a network of professionals you can tap in case you need support. Get in touch with lactation consultants and find out what kind of physical therapy may be covered by your insurance. Call up a postpartum doula in your area and schedule a visit for one week after birth. Find a pelvic floor specialist whose number you can have on hand if needed. Have a therapist or postpartum counselor

you can call for advice and support. Budget for these services and schedule them ahead of time. You can always cancel if they are unnecessary. Doing the research and finding someone you can connect with takes time and energy. Don't wait for the situation to get dire before you get help.

5. **Find Your Bridge Builders:** Postpartum is a period of transition for the whole family, and because of that, it can be an emotionally volatile time. Family roles are changing all around—parents becoming grandparents, partners becoming parents, and younger children becoming big brothers and sisters. Talk through these transitions and iron out your expectations. Like Sunny's nannies, consider adding bridge builders to your life, people whose presence exudes positivity and peace, who can give you perspective amid the emotional rollercoaster. Call on them as needed.

6. **Don't Wash Your Hair:** In the weeks postpartum, don't be afraid to show up as you are, mess and all. When friends and family come over, remember you are not hosting. Don't worry about having the dishes—or your hair—washed. The point is precisely to invite the people you love into the emotional and physical chaos of the postpartum period. Allow them to witness the transition in all its disarray, then ask them to walk through it with you. There is no faster way to build intimacy and strengthen the bonds of our friendship than by showing up imperfectly and asking others to love us anyway. In the process, we also normalize postpartum recovery as a communal endeavor.

# Let Your Baby Sleep Outside

ON A CHILLY MAY EVENING IN 1997, ANNETTE SØRENSEN, A thirty-year-old Danish actress visiting New York, parked her sleeping baby girl in a stroller outside a barbeque joint and went inside. For more than an hour, she sipped margaritas with the baby's father, keeping an eye on the stroller from the window.

After the restaurant staff called the police, Sørensen found herself strip-searched and arrested for child endangerment, and her fourteen-month-old daughter, Liv, was taken into foster care. She spent thirty-six hours behind bars and eventually, the charges were dropped.

The case made headlines in New York and Copenhagen but for different reasons. In New York, Sørensen was the negligent mother who endangered her baby's safety for a drink. In Copenhagen, she simply left her daughter to sleep where babies nap best—in the cold.

Danes believe that letting babies sleep outside, especially in the winter months, elongates nap times and can even boost a child's immune system. This practice starts when the baby is about two weeks old and continues for as long as the child naps.

The tradition isn't exclusive to Denmark. Letting babies sleep outside is a hack Nordic parents have sworn by for generations. Guidelines for parents in Finland as far back as 1920 advise parents to let children sleep outside to prevent diseases and increase blood circulation in the nose and mouth. The practice is still common today. Ninety-five percent of Finnish parents surveyed in one study thought there were no disadvantages to letting kids sleep outdoors. Most reported that outdoor naps made their children more active, better eaters, and healthier. They may be on to something. The study found that when children napped outdoors, most did, in fact, sleep longer.

But sleeping outside is not just good for babies. Parents benefit too. Danes routinely leave babies in stroller parking lots and sidewalks while shopping, dining, and grabbing coffee. The practice smoothes the transition into parenthood, enabling adults to hold on to parts of who they used to be even as they become parents.

My babies never slept outside, and perhaps yours never will either. But I decided to travel to Denmark to learn how the practice creates space in parenthood for both mothers and their children.

## The Chill Parents

Fariah Raziani was digging into her salad at a Copenhagen cafe when a flutter outside caused her to pause mid-bite. On the other side of the restaurant's window, her seven-month-old baby was starting to fuss. She slipped out the door to check on him. A few rocks of the stroller later, the baby fell asleep outside, and she settled back into her chair across from her sister. Fariah loves these nap-time lunches. They have become a sacred self-care routine during her maternity leave. "It's time for myself," she explains. Her son comes along for the ride but gives her some space.

These bite-sized moments of separation have helped Fariah hold on to her pre-baby identity. Watching the scene unfold, the memory of the dueling desires for closeness and space, the unconditional love for the baby, and the grief for the life I left behind returns to me like muscle memory. Though rarely talked about, it's a tension all new parents feel, especially in those nebulous first weeks of parenthood.

Yet rather than labeling a desire for separation from their baby as taboo, Denmark facilitates it. Movie theaters in Denmark offer special showings for parents of newborns. Sleeping babies are deposited in the lobby and monitored by an attendant while their parents watch the film undisturbed. Theaters use a ticket system, like a coat check, to return the baby to the correct parent if they start crying mid-movie.

Iben Dissing Sandahl, a psychotherapist and author of *The Danish Way of Parenting*, credits these programs as essential to smoothing the transition into motherhood. "You were young, doing whatever you wanted, and then you became a mother. Suddenly, you have to leave all of that behind, which can be very isolating," said Sandahl. "But [in Denmark] we can keep feeling that we are ourselves. We have been working at something important and beautiful, but we can combine that with our social life as well."

Parents don't have to erase the rest of their lives the minute they bring their baby home. Instead, they are encouraged to reintegrate into society. Government-facilitated parent groups ensure that new moms know there is a place for them both inside and outside the home. For every four to six babies born in a neighborhood, the state creates a parents' support group that meets regularly through pregnancy and birth. Initially intended for mothers, the group is now open to all parents. The programs, beloved by Danish parents, foster lifelong friendships between neighbors with kids of similar ages.

Parents in Denmark still suffer identity crises, postpartum depression, and career challenges like the rest of us. But crucially, they are not isolated and left to figure it out by themselves. Ina Nørgaard had a thriving career working long hours as a doctor in a hospital in Copenhagen. But when she gave birth to her daughter at thirty, she felt like the dreams she had been chasing all her life no longer made sense. "When I went back to work, it felt like a heartbreak," she said. Ina started to resent the job she once loved for keeping her from her daughter's bedtime. Standing in the hospital bathroom in the middle of an eighteen-hour shift, pouring her pumped breast milk down the sink, she knew she needed a change. "I used to be really ambitious. Now, it was difficult for me to prioritize work."

Like so many mothers, Ina's identity was shifting. Her friends who didn't have children couldn't understand why she would give up a career she had worked so hard on. Neither could her husband, a PhD student, who didn't feel the changes. But the moms in her parents' group immediately got it. With them, she didn't have to put on a happy face. "Now I'm not really sure what I dream of. All my feelings are muddled," she told them.

With their support, she decided to take a job as a general practitioner at a hospital nearby that didn't require a night shift. At these meetings, parents like Ina are allowed to remove their cheerful masks and get real. "Even though we weren't friends before, we could talk about the most private things, all of the feelings that come with being a mother—not just happiness."

## Meet You at the Disco

Denmark also ensures that new parents have places to gather and learn how to stimulate their children as they grow. Every week, the government hosts free "open sessions" at indoor play areas staffed with motor skills specialists who can advise parents on their children's development and encourage their growth. These sessions are designed for children from infancy to twelve years of age and include obstacle courses, ball pits, craft rooms, and even animal sanctuaries where the kids can interact with turtles and hamsters. Crucially, they also serve as spaces for parents to work and socialize while their kids play. One Thursday morning, the session is packed with children of all ages. They carefully remove their shoes before entering the indoor play area, which is complete with a life-size pirate ship, zip line, and soccer field. Some parents take meetings in a coworking space outside, while others actively participate in their kids' play, diving into the ball pit and kneeling next to them to color.

As fun as these sessions are for children, they serve an even greater purpose for parents. Instead of waiting for problems to fester, open sessions give parents access to experts who lead lectures on developmental delays, help spot concerns early, and connect parents with other government services when needed.

"It's a good way to get parents into contact with the rest of society and to dialogue with them. We will talk to people about anything. If they are laughing, we will laugh with them. If they are stressed, we will try to relieve them," said Mikkel Georg Shultz, a pedagogue expert who runs one of the open sessions in Copenhagen. To Shultz, the sessions are one more way Danish society tells parents they aren't alone in navigating the new territory of parenthood.

Open sessions also serve as a social meeting place where parents can trade notes on their kids' development, discuss their return to work after parental leave, and bounce ideas off each other. For Shultz, that's the point. "If you want to meet a sexual partner, you go to a discotheque. If you want to meet other parents, you come here. It's a way to meet others in the same situation as you are right now."

## Developing Your Intuition

Perhaps it's unsurprising that these public programs, combined with universal healthcare, free education, and general safety, help foster more secure parents.

Annie Samples, an American mother of four, experienced the difference firsthand when she moved from Portland to Copenhagen. "I don't really hear mothers here talking about how they lost themselves," she said. She credits this partly to the extensive support the country offers new parents. "It feels like I have a village. I don't have to handle the judgment, the pressure, and all the choices I have to make in one day, alone."

Parents in Denmark are entitled to six visits from a registered nurse to screen for postpartum depression, help mothers with lactation or sleep problems, and deal with mental or physical complications from birth. "Our role is to discuss their concerns and put their worries to rest. The whole family must be healthy. We cannot help the baby if the parents are unwell," said Sus Kornerup, a public pediatric health nurse.

But the nurses don't just teach new parents the best position for breastfeeding or how to swaddle a baby. They also, importantly, try to teach them how to develop their own parenting style. Nurses, parents' group facilitators, and doctors emphasize that parents are largely capable of deciding what is best for their baby. A pacifier, screentime, or naptime coffee run won't ruin their child; they assure new parents. It's a take that runs opposite to the constant fear and anxiety coursing through much of American parenting advice. "Parents are very insecure. Everything is new, and many don't have family around. They lose trust in their own abilities, and social media becomes a big influence," said Sus. "I try to explain to them that there is no right way to do it. Try to feel. Look at your baby. What do you think your baby needs?"

Sus calms their fears that they will damage their child irrevocably by experimenting with one parenting philosophy over the other. To deepen their sense of intuition, She tells new parents to disconnect from social media for six months and avoid googling answers to their questions. Instead, she urges them to slowly start to look to themselves for answers. "Don't copy anyone else. You need to find yourself in parenthood."

As all parents learn, parental intuition does kick in with time. The skin on the back of your hand will eventually be able to discern a fever from night sweats. You will be able to sense a cold coming from a mile away and know when to take a child to the doctor or wait it out. You'll notice the slump in your child's back that signals a tough day at school. The trick is allowing yourself enough space for that intuition to flourish.

## Fractured Trust and Fraying Ties

Of course, in most countries, children cannot be left unsupervised on the sidewalk, and the kinds of extensive social programs Denmark offers to support new parents are not coming to America anytime soon. But we can learn a lot from the way Danes approach the transition to parenthood, including how to make room for our pre-baby identities even as we trade nightclubs for playdates.

Childbirth and pregnancy have a way of shattering our ideas of who we used to be. Often, our identities, not just our bodies, have to be stitched back together after labor. Many of us emerge from it with priorities, ambitions, and traumas alien to our pre-parent selves. The biological, hormonal, neurological, and psychological changes as a woman becomes a mother rival adolescence in speed and scope. Dads, too, undergo physical and emotional changes with the birth of a child. We urge parents to be patient when dealing with adolescents undergoing rapid change, to allow room for mistakes as they experiment with who they want to become. But new parents can't seem to catch a break even as they undergo a similar biological and social transition.

And unlike the Danes, many of us in America are transitioning to parenthood in isolation. More than half of American adults believe that most people "would try to take advantage of you if they got a chance," according to a 2019 Pew Research survey. Not exactly the kind of folks I'd want walking past my sleeping baby.

When our trust in society erodes, we naturally isolate ourselves. Instead of parenting in public, we stay home. Instead of relying on relatives or neighbors, we navigate these changes alone. For parents still building their new identity, this self-reliance can create a dangerous vacuum.

Once constrained to television screens and advertisements, the ideal parent now stares at us from inside our phones. Over the last decade, performative motherhood has taken over social media feeds. There are an estimated 4.5 million mommy influencers in the United States. Too often, their accounts portray a vision of high-stakes motherhood that forges too direct a link between parental decisions and long-term outcomes. In this world, breastfeeding can increase SAT scores and skipping vaccines can prevent autism. But in addition to sponsored swaddles, what the accounts are really selling is control. It's not just a benign ideal. Their version of "intensive parenting" catastrophizes even the most minor parenting decisions, sometimes with little science to back it up.

The world of intensive parenting calls for the space between mother and child to be minimized. A sleeping baby does not belong outside, and his mother does not belong away from him, having lunch with her friends. Baby-wearing, feeding on demand, and homeschooling are the modus operandi.

In the mommy-blogger world, there are no grape juice spills, tantrums, or identity crises. But of course, this idealized version of motherhood leaves everyone falling short.

"No terrible twos with this sweetheart," mommy influencer Amber Fillerup assures her audience in the caption of a photo of her next to her daughter in matching pink dresses.

Motherhood in the mommy blogger universe is nearly always described in gushing, pontifical captions. Consider homemaker and influencer Megan Wells, cuddling with her newborn in an Instagram post. "I'm grateful for every second as a wife and mother," she exclaims. "After years of flaunting & owning my independence & pride, I can assure you there is nothing more peaceful and 'right' than leaning into nature as God designed it... I've never felt more in tune with my children, more empathetic towards others & more patient, gentle & soft than I do in these postpartum days."

That's certainly not what postpartum looked like for me and for many new moms looking at her content. A feed of similar posts day after day batters the new parent, whose experience is inevitably not as immaculate, uplifting, and fulfilling as the one on their screen.

The motherhood these women are selling leaves little space for hobbies, careers, or interests outside the home. Homemaking and the unpaid labor that goes with it is a singular vocation; they insist—one that should be your top priority, or else.

Life before motherhood or outside of it is irrelevant in these spaces. The woman on the screen is first and foremost, a mom.

These artificial depictions of motherhood have real psychological consequences and can ultimately corrode parents' trust in themselves. One study of 464 new mothers in the United States found that social media posts depicting idealized versions of motherhood provoked increased envy and anxiety.

A 2022 study of 125 first-time mothers in America revealed that the more time women spent on social media, the higher their cortisol levels. Anyone who has spent time in online parenting groups knows how quickly a simple question can devolve into a collective stoning. So while the Danes are constantly being told that they are capable parents fully fit to care for their kids, the message American parents often receive online is that they are not measuring up, that their instincts are not only wrong but dangerous.

Alexandra Sacks, a reproductive psychologist and expert on the maternal transition, a process known as matrescence, saw firsthand how faulty expectations set women up for disappointment in motherhood. Over decades of treating postpartum patients, Sacks saw a pattern. In a viral TED Talk, she described the phenomenon.

> It goes something like this: a woman calls me up; she's just had a baby, and she's concerned. She says, "I'm not good at this. I'm not enjoying this. Do I have postpartum depression?" So I go through the symptoms of that diagnosis, and it's clear to me that she's not clinically depressed, and I tell her that. But she isn't reassured. "It isn't supposed to feel like this," she insists. So I say, "Okay. What did you expect it to feel like?" She says, "I thought motherhood would make me feel whole and happy. I thought my instincts would naturally tell me what to do. I thought I'd always want to put the baby first."

What the women were experiencing, Sacks found, was not depression. Rather, they were coming face to face with the ambivalence of motherhood—the pull and the push as we fall in love with our babies but try to retain the parts of us central to our pre-parent identities.

"This is the emotional tug-of-war of matrescence. This is the tension the women calling me were feeling. It's why they thought they were sick. If women understood the natural progression of matrescence, if they knew that most people found it hard to live inside this push and pull, if they knew that under these circumstances, ambivalence was normal and nothing to be ashamed of, they would feel less alone, they would feel less stigmatized, and I think it would even reduce rates of postpartum depression."

It is clear from the many social programs offered to new parents and even from traditions like letting babies sleep outside that the Danes understand this. Instead of shaming mothers for grieving their former identities, for loving their children but also needing space from them, they leave a little room in everyday life for the natural ambivalence of parenthood. Unfortunately, I found myself far from Denmark in my first few weeks of motherhood.

## The Baby Bible

In the weeks before Oliver was born, my aunt handed me a thin book with a pale pink border. "Here," she said. "The Bible." *The Contented Little Baby Book*, by Gina Ford, she explained, was responsible for getting my cousin to sleep through the night at eight weeks. If I wanted to get any bit of my life back after baby, this was the key.

I was in the market for a holy book. Standing at the brink of motherhood, I was desperate for guidance. Ford was not shy about providing it. In the book, the British former maternity nurse promises to teach readers how to get a baby, any baby, to sleep through the night by eight weeks using a series of military-strict schedules. The schedules contain caregiving tasks assigned to specific blocks in the day, freeing up parents to visit their former lives during predictable daily nap times.

Since it was first published in 1999, the *Contented Little Baby Book* has become a parenting Rorschach test. Mentions of Ford's method can elicit disgust or delight, depending on the audience. While controversial ("I suggest avoiding eye contact at 10 p.m. and during night feeds to help you show your baby gently that this is not playtime," she says), Ford has also emerged as a patron saint of the exhausted parent. Here was someone who understood that parents, not just babies, needed rest. I read through the book and looked down at my ticking time bomb of a belly. Given the all-consuming nature of parenthood, I liked the idea that sleep was something that could be tackled and tamed.

So, I highlighted the key passages, memorized the baby schedules, and printed them out for good measure. The book assured me that if I did my part, so would my baby. The rest of my family was horrified. Who ever heard of putting a baby on a schedule? Like a cult follower, I explained that the rules weren't up to me. The book instructed parents to abide by the sleep schedule at all costs or risk sleepless nights. If that meant ripping Oliver from the arms of his great-grandmother at 2:44 p.m. sharp to get him into his bassinet in a pitch-dark room no later than 2:45 p.m., so be it. To my mother's horror, I'd also wake Oliver from a deep slumber at Ford's appointed time to keep him from staying up at night. Ford's instructions extend to the parents as well. She even tells them when to eat breakfast and wash the baby's bottles. For some, that might sound patronizing, but the truth is, in those hazy days of early motherhood, I was grateful for the orders, even if they came from a yellowing, dog-eared book. With my world turned upside-down in the weeks after I gave birth, I craved Ford's British sense of structure.

I clung to Gina Ford's book with the fanaticism of a zealot. Part of my despair came from the sudden realization that my breast milk did not come with a side of maternal intuition. For nine months, Oliver and I had been a seamless entity. My body knew when to make his kneecaps, grow eyelashes, or give him more legroom. But now that he was out, I was clueless. I waited for the moment when I would nod knowingly at his cries, swoop in, and expertly comfort him, both of us speaking a language of our own. But the intuition didn't appear. What did arrive, uninvited, was anxiety, made worse by the conflicting advice flung at me from every corner. I learned nothing attracts unsolicited opinions faster than a mother looking unsure of herself.

As much as I loved being close to my family in Brazil, I had to learn to parse out the wisdom gleaned from the mothers with decades of experience on me, from the old wives' tales and fears. That knowledge would come in time, but as a new mom, I felt like every comment from a stranger in an elevator was confirmation that I didn't know what I was doing. There were endless and absolute opinions on everything I did and didn't do. Give a baby a pacifier, and he'll have lifelong dental problems. Don't give it to him, and he will never learn to self-soothe. It's freezing out; that baby needs a sweater. Don't keep him so bundled. He'll never get any vitamin D. The only clear message in it all was that I was a terrible mother.

The Internet was no help. All articles about newborns seemed to shout at mothers in the same condescending, impatient tone. Remember, fed is best! Don't starve your baby just because you are not good at breastfeeding! They screeched. But also, formula kills! Don't you know powdered milk can have arsenic and lead?

Soon, like many new parents, I started sequestering at home, where I was safe from the judgmental stares. But the isolation began to eat away at me and my anxiety mounted. The reporter who prowled the city in search of a story was gone. Now, all I saw was danger. Something deep in me believed that Oliver was doomed to vanish as suddenly and quickly as he arrived.

So I gave all of myself to my baby and he soaked it in. The more I offered the more he wanted. I'd go to bed at the end of the night feeling depleted in a way I never had before. My days, nights, laughter, and tears all revolved around this twenty-inch human.

When, three months after Oliver was born, my editor assigned me a three-day reporting trip across Brazil, I found myself relieved. An exit strategy, some space away from my new, all-consuming role. But the relief was immediately followed by a wave of shame.

I looked at Oliver, his drooping cheeks, miniature nose, and rolls of baby fat mounting on his legs. For three months, he had been my world. He was perfect. But he wasn't enough. I realized then that he was never supposed to be. Motherhood was not a totem to be worshiped, an identity to erect my life around. It was a responsibility, a relationship, and on my good days, a calling. But there were other parts of my identity I loved, bits I wasn't willing to leave behind.

Ticket in hand, I kissed him and Rudy goodbye and drove to the airport. Sitting at my gate waiting to board, I caught my reflection in the window and took a deep breath. "Oh," I thought. "There she is."

## BRINGING IT HOME

The transition to parenthood can be fraught. But here are some tips from the Danes on how to carve out space for your identity even as you expand into your new role (without ditching your baby on the sidewalk).

1. **Integrate All Your Identities:** Don't segregate your home life. Bring your whole self to parenthood. Introduce your children to who you are outside of them. Let your coworkers meet and hold your baby. Show your kids your office and share with them your projects and goals for the year. Once in a while, when appropriate, let them tag along when you go for a drink with a friend. When you do, don't let them monopolize your time and attention. Let them watch what a playdate looks like for you. Explain other roles you play like sister, partner, and friend. Showing them that you are a whole person, not just a parent, will set a great example and give them permission to share the different versions of themselves with you, too.

2. **Visit Your Former Self:** Invest in what made you happy before you became a parent, even if it's scaled back. Whether it's in the books you are reading, the podcasts you listen to, or the conversations you have, try to integrate interests outside parenthood into your everyday life. Carve out at least 10 minutes a day for these soul-filling activities. The role of the parent can, especially in the early months, overshadow all others. But watering your interest, even the slightest bit, helps ensure there are other versions of yourself to return to when you're ready. Walking a mile when you used to run a marathon feels dispiriting, but as childcare demands recede (and they will!), you'll have a practice in place to grow.

3. **Take a Mommy Moon:** My friend Gabi has lived in half a dozen countries and loves to travel as much as I do. When she became a mom, she made it a point to take herself on "mommy moons," where she honors part of her identity that has been neglected since she became a mother. "Of course, motherhood is a gift, and there is a lot of joy and an incredible amount of love that comes with it. But there is also a loss," she said. "I realized I wanted to reconnect

with these other roles. I don't identify as only a mom. These other aspects of my life are also important. I felt like I couldn't give that up. It wouldn't be true to my identity, to who I am as a person," she told me. The practice benefits her whole family. Gabi comes back from these trips recharged and grateful. She also is setting a great example for her daughter of a motherhood that is expansive, instead of self-sacrificial. Mommy moons don't have to be expensive trips to the other side of the world. They can be as simple as spending the night at a friend's house or taking yourself out for an afternoon off. As you contemplate what this might look like for you, reflect on what parts of your pre-parent life you find yourself missing most. What facets of your identity are being placed on hold during the day-to-day rhythms of parenting life?

4. **Parent in Public:** Instead of shutting yourself in, bring your kids out. If your baby is small, keep it simple. Why not do nap time out of the house today? While they sleep, grab a coffee or go for a walk with a friend. For toddlers, start small, taking them to a few non-child-centered places each week. Let them run errands with you and explain what appropriate behavior in these settings looks like. Include lots of praise for good behavior. Once they get the hang of it, expand your settings. Introduce them to ways to self-entertain while you fill your cup. Bring coloring books to a coffee shop and let them do their thing while you do yours. Sometimes these excursions might end in a meltdown, cold coffee, and frustration, but try to let go of the Instagram-perfect standard of parenting you may have in your head. Learning to build a life and identity that includes your children but is not centered solely around them takes time—be gentle with yourself and your kids as you both figure it out.

5. **Create Your Own Parents Group:** There are plenty of apps connecting expectant parents with others due around the same

month. If you already have children, look for other parents you can connect with at the playground or park or through online parenting groups. Be sure to take the conversation offline. Find people willing to meet up regularly and trade notes. They will be a great resource as you navigate the shifting tides of parenthood. Like Ina in Denmark remember to show up as you really are, masks off. Talk about the struggles as well as the joys of your new role.

6. **Embrace the Ambivalence:** Accept the push and pull of parenthood for what it is—evidence of the complex, lifelong relationship you are building with another human being. It was never meant to be perfect or easy, despite what your social media feed wants you to believe. (I'm still working on this one. It's a daily practice!)

7. **Turn Off Your Phone:** Follow Sus, the Danish nurse's advice. For the first six months of parenthood, experiment with turning off social media. Silence feeds telling you what to think or how to parent. Instead, use the space to develop your own vision and style, however imperfect it may be. Imagine your children, at twenty, describing you to a new significant other. What are the words you hope they will use when talking about how you parented? Use that as a guide.

8. **Tap into Your Intuition:** Before rushing to consult experts or influencers on how to deal with a problem, test out your own theory. Give your intuition space to weigh in before the experts do. Turn to your gut before turning to Google. When in doubt, ask the people around you, those familiar with you and your baby in real life, for opinions. Remember, babies are resilient, and, for the most part, common sense can be as good a guide to your baby as any book.

## RULE 4

# Develop the Paternal Instinct

### The Newsroom Sieve

It's an unspoken rule in journalism that female reporters are solo agents. If they have partners or children, they leave no evidence in the office. Newsrooms are old boys' clubs where women fight not only for a seat at the table but, often, for the last one on a plane to a dream assignment. As more newspapers around the country close, the competition is fierce, and the opportunities are limited. So, while male coworkers display their growing families in smiling portraits on their desks, female journalists, myself included, try to mention our personal lives as little as possible. I've seen a journalist lie about a pregnancy to secure a fellowship and watched a star reporter conceal her growing baby bump behind increasingly bulky sweaters right up to her due date.

This self-censorship makes sense when you consider the culture of many American workplaces. One of my editors inadvertently summarized the way many bosses feel about maternity leave: "It's a pain in the ass," he said, speaking of the weeks a colleague was taking off after her baby was born. I made a mental note, adding maternity leave to the list of things that would make me a difficult employee or more likely to be targeted for a layoff in a crumbling industry.

Motherhood is like a sieve, quickly straining women from the newsroom. By the time they are in their forties, many female reporters either scale down to part time or leave altogether. Some migrate to public relations, drawn to the softer deadlines, predictable hours, and generous maternity leave policies.

Journalism is not unique in this way. Women in every field pay a price for motherhood, which can often force a career break that puts mothers at a comparative disadvantage to childless women and men. Every child she has dents a mother's hourly salary by up to 5 percent. For all the advancements in gender equality over the last twenty years, our paychecks have precious little to show for it. In 2022, women still earned an average of 82 cents for every dollar earned by men. That's just 2 cents higher than it was in 2002. The gap is even more pronounced for women of color. Hispanic women earn just 65 cents and Black women make 70 cents for every dollar earned by a white man.

What would it be like, I wondered, to live in a country where my decision to have children could happily coexist with my career? Where parenthood brought genders together instead of pitting them against each other? There was only one place to find out.

## Babes in Barbieland

Sweden is home to the most generous parental leave policy in the world, a whopping 480 paid days off per child. The policy is gender-neutral, meaning both parents have the right to take the same time off to care for their children. Perhaps more surprising is that they actually take it. Over 80 percent of Swedish fathers use their leave. In America, by contrast, 70 percent of fathers are back at work full time less than two weeks after the birth of their child.

Because parental leave in Sweden is equally doled out, fathers are also expected to be on duty. That means mothers don't have to choose between caring for their children or falling behind male coworkers at the office.

For the first 390 days of leave, the government pays up to 80 percent of the parent on leave's income, depending on their salary. During the remaining 90 days of leave, parents receive a standard stipend of about $16 a day, regardless of income. Any unused days of parental leave are valid until the kid turns eight, so many families save a few for emergencies or holidays throughout the child's early childhood.

When parents do go back to work, they define the pace. Employees reserve the right to scale down their hours through the child's eighth birthday, working part time for example, for part-time pay. This allows parents to be present for their children's early childhood without having to exit the workforce entirely.

The policy enables Sweden to maintain one of the world's highest female labor participation rates and allows women to see motherhood as compatible, rather than in competition, with their careers.

Of course, most countries, including America, are far from the Swedish reality. But there are lessons to be learned from its successes and failures for all of us, even those struggling to piece together a few days of leave. In this chapter, we'll look at how

Sweden's parental leave policy transformed gender norms, family life, corporate culture, and even maternal health. But we'll also examine where even the friendliest parental policies in the world clash with long-ingrained gender norms.

The next few pages will mainly explore heterosexual gender roles, where the tension between caregiving and working outside the home has been historically fraught. However, the experiences here apply to caregivers of all genders trying to divide the taxing work of raising little humans in a way that feels fair and sustainable. As we will see, tensions between primary breadwinners and primary caregivers can be found in almost every relationship. Luckily, our Swedish friends, who have been experimenting with these negotiations longer than the rest of us, can offer some insight and tips on how to navigate them.

While I had read extensively about Swedish parental leave, I did not expect to see the implications of the policy so visibly when I landed in Stockholm. Walking around the city feels a bit like landing in Greta Gerwig's Barbieland, a place where the patriarchy doesn't exist and gender norms are reversed. One crisp autumn morning, I walk past a row of fathers in the park pushing their children on swings. A red-faced dad suddenly pops out of a metal slide, a grinning baby on his lap. Across the street, a father carts his toddler on a stroller while balancing a scooter on his shoulder.

Underneath a pavilion, a line of fathers are gearing up for lunch. Diaper bag slung across his shoulder, Joe, thirty-two, squeezes into a picnic table with his thirteen-month-old, Vigor. He is three months into his parental leave, which he shared equally with his partner, and these trips to the park have become a cherished part of his weekly routine. He pulls out a Tupperware of pasta mixed with cream cheese and peas, "a guaranteed hit," he tells me. Vigor, wearing mismatched clothes and a skull bib, bounces in delight. The scene was exceptional precisely because it was so ordinary.

Just as striking as the presence of men at playgrounds was that of women elsewhere—they were the pilots on my flights, the guards standing in front of the royal palace, and the train conductors on the metro.

Still, it's not all perfect, said Niklas Löfgren, an analyst for family economics at the Försäkringskassan, Sweden's agency in charge of administering parental leave benefits. Women still take more parental leave relative to men and make slightly less than men for the same jobs. There are other inequalities as well. "Fathers tend to choose to be home from May to August, when it is a little bit more sunny outside," Löfgren explains.

Right. So how did this country the size of California get to a place where gender equality is measured down to who has to zip up the winter coats?

Today Sweden is considered one of the world's most gender equal countries. Nearly as many women as men work outside the home, and the gender pay gap is one of the smallest in the developed world. But in the 1960s, only 1 percent of Swedish fathers contributed to caring for young children, according to Swedish government data.

Driven by a desire to bring more women into a tight labor market, Sweden began expanding parental leave rights in the 1970s. In 1974, the government introduced the world's first gender-neutral paid parental leave policy, granting both parents the opportunity to care for their babies full time for up to six months.

It didn't work. The country found that women were still taking 99.5 percent of leave. "Men just didn't want to be home," said

Löfgren. Given the option of six months of leave, dads would promptly transfer their days to mothers, the cemented primary caregivers. To encourage a more equal distribution of leave, the country introduced a "use it or lose it" policy in 1994, which assigned thirty nontransferrable days of leave to each parent.

The change was immediate. When fathers could no longer pass the time off to their partners, they began using all their allotted days themselves. The government expanded the policy, increasing nontransferrable leave to sixty and now ninety days.

Swedes watched as decisions about parental leave spilled over into all aspects of life. When fathers took time off, their relationships with their partners and children became more stable and fulfilling. Also, surprisingly, when dads took leave, moms became healthier. A 2012 change in the policy that allowed both parents to take leave simultaneously caused a marked reduction in postpartum anti-anxiety prescriptions, hospitalizations, and antibiotic prescriptions *for mothers.*

Because almost all fathers were now taking time off, parental leave became an expected part of Swedish employment. Companies vying for workers started to offer expanded parental leave benefits, topping up government pay and offering flexible schedules for parents. "It changed the discourse on what is normal and what is not," said Eleonora Mussino, a demographer at Stockholm University. The policy also had the unintended benefit of buoying Sweden's fertility rate even as that of its European neighbors declined.

In time, Swedes started seeing parental leave as less of a cultural battleground and more of a right they don't want to leave on the table. "We want a system that can make it possible for both parents to have a job and a family at the same time. No one should have to choose between that," said Löfgren.

# Fatherhood on New Terms

While Swedish parental leave is unlikely to come to America anytime soon, the policy offers valuable insight into what happens when we allow fathers to contribute meaningfully to childcare.

Many families felt the biggest shift in dynamics at home. That was the case for Soheil Abjoudani, a business developer on parental leave with his two children. Leave has forced him to carry not only the physical but also the mental load of caregiving single-handedly. Up at 6 a.m., he makes breakfast for the family, feeds and changes the kids, and escorts the oldest to daycare, baby snug on his chest. His wife, Emma, an elementary school teacher, is at work for most of the day, leaving him in charge of school drop-offs, playdates, and trips to the park. Before he leaves the house, Soheil has to think about whether the baby has eaten enough and check the weather to see if his daughter needs a coat. The planning, worrying, and communicating that goes into childcare, even if only for a few months, is squarely on his plate.

The responsibility forced Soheil to develop his own parenting style, applying the attention to detail he was used to bringing to his job to his family. He puts the children on a tight schedule and keeps tabs on feeding, diaper changes, and developmental milestones. The experience taught him he was as capable of caring for the kids as his wife. "It's empowering to be able to say, actually, I can do this."

It also shaped his relationship with his children. "I connect in a completely different way with them when I'm the one taking care of them," he said, digging through a diaper bag. He produces a tub of applesauce and ten-month-old Mateos coos with delight. "Now I don't want to spend one more hour at work than I have to. I know I won't get his time back."

The parental leave policy meant a new generation of fathers could be present for their children in a way their own fathers never had.

Andreas Schennings is a system developer at a startup. Like most men of his generation, he grew up with a father who left for work early and came home late. His mother was the primary caretaker from day one.

"I love him a lot, but he rarely played with me. He never put me to bed or sang songs with me. Those are things I try to do with my kids, and I know my friends try to as well."

Unlike his father, who got just a few weeks off when he was born, Andreas split his 480 days of parental leave equally with his partner Klara when their son was born in 2020. He's noticed a similar shift in his male friends too. Many don't have close relationships with their fathers but are trying to break the cycle with their own children. To them, that starts with taking equal parental leave.

## School for Dads

Parental leave made active fatherhood not only viable but visible. Active fathers were everywhere: at school pickups, playgrounds, and parks. Now, the government has given them something to do together.

Nestled inside a playground in downtown Stockholm, the sloped-roof farmhouse looks plucked straight from a fairytale. It is painted storybook red, with white trimmings and a flower-lined windowsill. Inside, a dozen toddlers thump rhythmically under a disco light to the itsy-bitsy spider as a teacher sings along. While they play, parents gather around the coffee machine like coworkers, discussing the latest demands of their unrelenting bosses.

Welcome to Öppna Förskola, Sweden's open preschool, where parents on leave can bring their children any weekday to be entertained for free, no sign up necessary. This open preschool, one of forty-eight in Stockholm, offers instructor-led activities for babies and toddlers, like dancing, story time, and obstacle courses, all funded by the government. The schools come fully supplied with toys and snacks—for kids and parents.

"The best part is someone else makes the coffee," said Jonathan, here with his one-year-old daughter, Livia. The forty-two-year-old magazine writer, on his third month of paternity leave, is exhausted, and he's got the dark circles under his eyes and dazed stare to prove it. But notably, he's not doing it alone.

As much as we talk about how isolating motherhood can be, fathers can find it challenging to maintain friendships as they age. Friendship circles are shrinking for everyone in America, but especially for men. The percentage of men with at least six close friends fell by half since 1990, from 55 percent to 27 percent, a steeper decline than for women.

Parental leave and open preschool offer parents like Jonathan an opportunity to not only redefine the gender norms of his family but to expand his support network for this new phase of life.

Sweden's parental leave policy guarantees that a handful of dads in the same boat are also in the same place. After starting his leave Jonathan made a new group of friends—twelve other fathers also on leave. "We found each other in the playground," he said. Now, the dads meet weekly at open preschool, the park, and, after their partners come home from work, at the pub.

## Dad on Duty

While many Swedes welcomed these changes, shifting gender dynamics at home is not always easy. Elias and Mandella's apartment looks like the picture of equality when I visit one Saturday morning. While Mandella is at work, Elias sits with eight-month-old Minoo in a bright yellow kitchen. He has just finished making a batch of porridge with pumpkin seeds, and Minoo, wearing a gender-neutral gray onesie, scarfed it down.

After months of parental leave, it is clear the two speak the same language. Hanging from the doorframe is a swing that he knows will cheer the baby up when she's fussy. In the corner of the living room stands a guitar that Elias has been using to play original lyrics to classic lullabies. When he picks it up and starts strumming, Minoo babbles along in a heartwarming father-daughter duet.

Later that morning, Elias is cleaning up breakfast when Minoo's bright eyes narrow, and her brow furrows. He doesn't miss a beat. In one move, he sweeps her up and places her on a potty. Minoo relieves herself, and he's ecstatic. "I'm so proud of you!" he says, as she looks up delighted. "Sorry, sorry, I won't disturb you," he adds.

Toilet training the baby is the latest project of his paternity leave, which will stretch for a total of fourteen months. Mandella, who studies and works full time, smiles from the picture frames around the house but is otherwise nowhere to be seen. Elias is in charge, and he's found his groove. He does sit ups while Minoo poos, fixes the door handle while she plays, and hems his pants while she naps.

But sitting under posters of feminist painter Frida Kahlo in his living room, Elias explains that the journey to equity has not been easy. Growing up, Elias, forty-one, describes his father as the one in the Tom and Jerry cartoons—just legs that would walk in and out of the frame.

When his girlfriend Mandella got pregnant, they were determined to infuse equality into their parenting and rewrite the gender roles that they grew up with. "We wanted our home to feel like we were sharing everything fifty-fifty. It felt like an opportunity to change gender dynamics."

Elias decided to take fourteen months of leave, longer than any of his friends and nearly double the amount his girlfriend would take. For over a year, he would be in charge of feeding and caring for Minoo while Mandella worked and studied.

But after Minoo was born, both he and Mandella found that the gender roles they had long rejected resurfaced. Mandella's breastfeeding kept her literally attached to the baby, forcing Elias to orbit around them, squeezing in where he could. She quickly fell into the role of family project manager, a job both of them came to resent. She constantly worried about Minoo and struggled to trust Elias to care for her. Mandella would chase after him before every walk, reminding him what to pack before he left the house and interpreting the baby's cries for him. "The hardest part of taking care of a baby was my backseat driver," said Elias, laughing.

One day, he decided to take the baby along on a ten-kilometer walk with some friends. Halfway through, he realized he had forgotten the baby's pacifier. Minoo was inconsolable and could not sleep without it. He had no choice but to call Mandella. "It was a call of defeat," he said.

It could have been a moment for Mandella to gloat, asserting her superiority as the more responsible parent. But instead, she learned to bring Elias into the fold, even if it meant letting him fumble.

So she started letting the baby cry long enough for Elias to figure out what Minoo wanted. Now, he internalized a checklist instead of having her shout it out as he walked out the door.

"It is very important for women to see their own part in this. If you don't want to project lead, you have to give up that ambition and let us make mistakes," he said.

Parental leave also allowed the couple to test the limits of equality in spaces outside their home. Even living in Sweden, Elias constantly found himself the only father in Facebook groups for parents trying to decipher early potty training and best practices for reusable diapers. Even his social media algorithm was confused. He started following parenting content only to be fed pages about motherhood on social media. There was, it seemed, no space for involved fathers, even on the Internet.

Out and about, they notice the ways in which, for all its advancements, Swedish society still has room for growth. On the subway, the reactions of others were telling. "When I enter a public space, I get so much encouragement. 'Oh, you're so amazing.' they say. I get a pat on the back for everything. But the minute she cries, every other woman comes up to me and tells me, 'You should do this. Comfort her like this.' There are still structural obstacles," he said. "The change doesn't happen overnight."

Same-sex families in Sweden offer a unique insight into how parental leave can be a time to disrupt patterns that don't serve you. Untethered from the scripts that shape some families, many of these couples find themselves free to craft their own roles and rules. Fredrik and Felix had been together for nine years when their son Elliot was born. Fredrik took parental leave for the first year and then swapped with Felix, who took the next nine months. Like the straight couples they knew, Fredrik and Felix also had to learn to ask for and accept help from each other.

"But there was one very big difference," Frederik told me. "Nobody breastfed."

That meant that there was nothing Fredrik could do that Felix couldn't. The baby was not biologically tethered to one parent, freeing them to swap places as needed. Fredrik considers this a vital lesson for all parents struggling to divide caregiving labor fairly. Mixing some formula into your feeding plan can go a long way to sharing both the joys and the responsibilities of parenting.

"Yes, breastfeeding is important, but it is also important for you as parents to have close bonds with your children," he said. "I wouldn't want to make Felix a secondary parent. It gives me too much responsibility, and it deprives him of that closeness."

FELIX AND FREDRIK'S JOURNEY REMINDED ME OF THE REHASHING that happened in my own home in the nebulous days after Oliver's birth. From the very start, Rudy and I had different approaches to parenthood. I tackled pregnancy with the zeal of a new journalism assignment. I rushed to the stationery store, picked out a thick-bound notebook, and began researching what lay ahead. I took breastfeeding preparatory courses (a complete waste of time), read consumer reports about the best kinds of strollers, and practiced working a car seat. Rudy, on the other hand, seemed to be in denial. Being a father was a life experience he wanted, he was pretty sure. But not something he dreamed about. He ignored my growing belly, had no opinions on the nursery furniture, and, during one particularly stressful dinner during my third trimester, snapped, "Can we please talk about anything but this baby??" I added Rudy's parenting skills to my list of worries and dropped the topic. My mom reassured me these things take time. I still had weeks until Oliver's due date.

But a few weeks later, Oliver arrived early, and I was confined to my hospital bed, recovering from surgery, unable to stand on my own for more than a few minutes at a time. Rudy found himself looking into the eyes of a baby that, up until that point, he hadn't thought much about.

Alone with Oliver for hours on end in the NICU, Rudy fell into a love so deep I barely recognized him. I watched as the time they spent together morphed him from reluctant father to adoring dad. He talked to Oliver, sang to him, fed him formula from the hospital bottles, and would find any excuse to convince the nurses to pull him out of his incubator so he could rock him.

When we arrived home a few days later, Rudy scoured the nursery. "Where did you put the diapers and wipes? What stroller did we get? Are you sure it's safe?" I laughed so hard my stitches hurt. Rudy was the first to recognize Oliver's cries. He taught me how to change Oliver's diapers and clean his umbilical cord the way the nurses did.

To this day, Oliver and Rudy have a special bond. The unspoken conversation they started in those first days in the NICU continues. With just one look, Rudy can tell if Oliver is anxious, scared, or sick.

I often wonder what would have happened had Oliver not gone to the NICU those first few weeks or had I been more available to help care for him. Being Oliver's only available caretaker for the first few weeks of his life forced Rudy to step into an active parenting role and stay there. More importantly, it kept me out of the way. Because I wasn't there to rescue Rudy, he had to figure out his own way of parenting without my input, critiques, or breasts.

## State of the Parental Union

Sweden offers a powerful example of how policy changes can alter our most intimate relationships. But in America, parental leave laws are lagging far behind. We are the only industrialized country in the world with no mandatory paid maternity leave policy. In that context, paternity leave can feel like a pipe dream. While most fathers take some days off after the birth of their children, only 13 percent receive pay. Most leave is cobbled together from vacation and sick days.

Yet we know that the benefits of leave are long lasting. Even small amounts of paternity leave lead to happier, more stable marriages and better relationships between fathers and their children long after dads go back to work. Research from 2019 shows that American kids whose fathers took at least two weeks of paternity leave feel closer to their dads than those who didn't nine years later.

But men who do take leave in America are punished for it both professionally and socially. Studies show they are viewed as feminine, weak, and considered less productive employees. These perceptions can have real consequences on the job. In order to mitigate the professional risks of paternity leave, norms have to change. In some sectors, the shift is already happening. Tech giants like Netflix and Google and banks like Morgan Stanley have started to offer extended gender-neutral parental leave. But most American employers lag far behind.

A move to the Swedish model of gender equality would require mass policy changes in governments and companies. America can't pass a modest paid family leave act—forget 480 days and reduced work hours for years thereafter.

The good news is we don't have to wait for these policies to pass to start changing accepted gender norms. Mindsets must shift in government, to be sure. But they must also change at home. We can spark that change ourselves by taking a hard look at areas in which we've let lack of experience solidify gender roles that don't work for us.

The paternal instinct needs to be nurtured. We may believe that in theory fathers can care for babies as well as mothers. But, especially in a world of unequal leave and long-ingrained gender roles, it is common for mothers to feel more empowered when it comes to childcare. Sure, Dad can wake up to soothe a screaming baby in the middle of the night, but often Mom knows where the medicine is, has the pediatrician on speed dial, and remembers how long it has been since his last feed, poo, and vaccine. Quickly, Mom becomes the expert, while Dad is, at best, a sous-chef waiting for instructions.

This results in a vicious cycle in which the more caretaking tasks the mother takes on, the more efficient she becomes at them, so the easier it is for her to take on additional responsibilities. To break the cycle, we need to give partners space to problem-solve themselves.

When we were sleep training Oliver, Rudy, and I learned of the French philosophy known as Le Pause, where parents take a moment to let the baby soothe himself back to sleep before intervening. I recommend those in the primary caregiving role take a similar beat. Is the impending crisis actually an opportunity to nurture the parental instinct? Like Mandella, give your partners a chance to learn the ropes and develop some solutions of their own.

## Men in the Kitchen

The Swedish case study offers a look at how small changes in policy can alter the norms that govern our most intimate relationships. But these changes can happen from the bottom up as well. Even in places like America, with a fraction of Sweden's government support, small changes in our daily lives can nudge social norms.

To see this in action, I went to a place that is in many ways the opposite of Sweden: Japan, where husbands do less housework and childcare than their counterparts in any developed country. But as birth rates plummet to record lows, the government has recognized that in order to make child-rearing more appealing for families, there must be a shift not only in government policy but also at home.

Strict gender roles have governed domestic life in Japan for generations. Some men retire without ever gripping a knife or washing a dish. Those who lose a spouse to death or illness often find themselves unable to do basic chores. An old Japanese saying— *Danshi-chubo-ni-hairazu*, or "men should be ashamed to be found in the kitchen"—spooks many husbands from housework. Even those who want to help often lack the skills.

To try and lure more men into the kitchen, the government began offering free housework courses in community centers geared at men. Cooking schools also took note. After avoiding the kitchen for most of his life, Masahiro Yoshida was ready to cook. The sixty-five-year-old hung up his suit jacket and pulled a pink apron over his starched button-down shirt.

Yoshida's mother had prepared all his meals until he got married. Then, his wife took over. When he retired four years ago, his wife proposed a change. Why not share meal prep every week? Yoshida agreed, but he got lost making even the most basic dishes. He went online but found YouTube tutorials confusing.

Still, instead of throwing in the kitchen towel, Yoshida decided to do what a growing number of Japanese men are doing. He signed up for cooking school. Over six months, he learned how to mince garlic, chop mushrooms, and shop for meat.

"I had no idea how complex the cooking process was," he told me one afternoon at a cooking class outside Tokyo. Other men in his class were sent to cooking school by the women in their lives, who were desperate for a change in the gender roles that had governed their homes for decades. One man in the class said he was on a "scholarship" paid for by his adult daughter, who agreed to fund the course as long as he started contributing more at home.

It's a mindset shift that can have a multigenerational impact. By collectively rejecting incompetence as an excuse for their lack of contribution at home, these men are sparking a change that can alter future generations' ideas of accepted gender roles.

Home economics classes would certainly not undo decades of structural inequalities in the United States. But, as we see in Sweden and Japan, policy and culture are in constant conversation with one another. Changes can happen on Capitol Hill, but they can also happen in your own kitchen.

It was the case for my friend Lianne, whose partner Fábio had barely cooked before getting married. The two were determined to rewrite the gender dynamics in their own home in Philadelphia. After the birth of their son Teo during the pandemic, they had nobody to rely on but each other. Rather than plead incompetence, Fábio skilled up. He called Lianne's mother for recipes and learned his way around the kitchen, and Lianne learned her way around a toolbox. Today, Fábio takes on most of the family's cooking. Teo, of course, is watching Mom and Dad. "It was important for him to see that Dad can cook but also that I can handle drills and a hammer and fix his bike," Lianne said.

## BRING IT HOME

As we build a family culture, we get to choose which norms to accept and which to toss. We can and must think critically about how the dynamics in our own homes reflect the values we want to pass on to the next generation. The good news is that we don't have to wait for year-long paternity leave to invite fathers into an equal partnership. Here's how you can ensure that the gender dynamics at play in your home reflect your family's values.

1. **Max Out Your Leave:** As we learned from the Swedes, parental leave can set up a foundation for a fair partnership that lasts long after you return to work. If you are lucky enough to have parental leave, use it. Not only will your family thank you, but you will be paving the way for families of all kinds to use their leave too.

2. **Spell It Out:** Caregiving and the labor that goes with it can often be invisible. To ensure both partners are sharing the load, the first step is laying out the work. For one week, log all the

recurring household and childcare duties both partners conduct in the house. (Don't forget to add those project manager tasks like buying Christmas presents or scheduling doctor appointments!) At the end of the week go through your lists together and evaluate if your current division of labor is working. Remember the goal is not to keep score, but to recognize the work being done and find a balance that is sustainable for your family in this season of life. This will help make the workload visible, prevent chores from falling through the cracks, and, crucially, keep you from rehashing the workload every few weeks (or days!).

3. **Assign an Owner:** Distribute recurring tasks in a way that feels fair to both of you. Be explicit about who owns what childcare times and tasks. Remember, if you fail to spell it out, most chores will default to the primary caregiver. When handing the reins over to your partner for a task, ensure they are responsible for it from start to finish—including research, communication, and follow-ups. That means adding them to the email threads and chat groups with parents, friends, and teachers (and then leaving the chat!). Single-thread ownership allows each of you to specialize in a given task from start to finish, helping your home to run more smoothly and prevent you from stepping on each other's turf.

4. **Step Away:** Once you are aligned on the basics, follow the advice of the Swedes and step away from your partner when they are on duty. Allow them to devise their own systems and methods for childcare. Even if they aren't caring for the kids the exact way you'd prefer, invite them to contribute early and often. When things fall apart, and they most certainly will in the first few months of parenthood, resist the urge to step in. Give your partner a couple of chances to figure it out. Mistakes can be uncomfortable, but they teach lessons fast. Plus, you may be pleasantly

surprised by the creative solutions your partner brings to the table. If you catch yourself micromanaging, try to look at the big picture. Mismatched clothes or lumpy purees are not the end of the world. Skip the snide remarks and offer them encouragement instead. As long as a basic standard of care is maintained, does it really matter how a baby gets fed, entertained, or put to sleep?

5. **Conquer Your Domain:** For partners who have little leave or don't know where to start, take ownership of one aspect of parenting and expand from there. Own and specialize in one routine. Master mealtimes or make bath time your domain. Remember, an equitable division of labor does not necessarily mean you must do everything your partner does or share all household tasks fifty-fifty. As you find your groove in parenting, each of you will develop distinct styles and specialties. This is where a partnership can really flourish. Give each other the room to flesh out your unique roles in your family with the talents and interests that you already bring to the table. It will make parenting and partnership much more fun.

6. **Skill Up:** Where possible, improve on the skills you need to contribute fairly, whether that means taking a course or watching tutorials online. Take the time to teach your partner any relevant skills you have mastered. The upfront costs of teaching them how to change a diaper or sterilize a bottle may seem high at the moment, but remember; it will save you time, effort, and a lot of bickering in the long run. Best of all, it sets a tone of equality in your home that can last well beyond childhood.

7. **Find Your Buddies:** Do not underestimate the power of peer pressure. Expand your circle of friends to include parents who are also trying to share responsibilities equally at home. Like-minded peers can normalize male caregiving and support partners as they try to break generational cycles.

## Troubleshooting
## WHEN YOUR PARTNER IS NOT ON BOARD

Conversations about gender roles and division of labor at home are inherently difficult. They can be especially triggering to partners who come from traditional backgrounds or cultures and are struggling to recalibrate. Some may be reluctant to take on additional duties at home because they are burnt out at work or because they don't have the skills necessary to step up. If that's your family's situation, don't lose hope. A counselor or therapist can help you navigate these conversations. But here are some tips to get you started.

1. **Curiosity Counts**: Approach your partner with curiosity about how they grew up, rather than judgment or hostility. The way your partner's family assigned roles at home will likely inform their vision of family life. Even the most gender-equal families I spoke to in Sweden found themselves sometimes slipping into the patterns they saw as children. Asking your partner to analyze their background can help them to identify and break unhelpful patterns. You can start by asking, "How did your parents split up childcare, housework, and work outside the home in your family? Were there any tensions that arose, and how did they handle it? How do you think our goals and values differ? What is your vision for how our family will handle these duties?"

2. **Invest in Learning:** Sometimes partners shy away from responsibility because they don't feel as capable in certain areas. Take a page from the Japanese and help them improve their skills. Cooking classes, sleep seminars, and nutrition webinars make great gifts for the well-meaning but ill-prepared partner. Be sure to introduce the topic gently. "Now that our family is growing, I'd

love to level up our homemaking skills. I'm going to sign up for a class on home repair. What do you think of taking a cooking course to learn some basic dishes?"

3. **Bridge the Gap:** If your partner's vision for how you will balance family and work life differs substantially from yours, it's time to put pen to paper. If you are the primary caretaker, add up the hours required to keep the house clean, the children fed, and your job secured. Numbers are harder to argue with. Chances are your spouse does not realize just how much time and energy go into caretaking. Start by acknowledging the tasks they already take on before sharing how you feel. "I know how important our family is to you and appreciate all you do. Still, I'm overwhelmed by the amount of tasks on my plate. How can we better divide up these responsibilities in a way that's more sustainable?"

4. **Source More Support:** If your partner is still unwilling or unable to step in, it may be time to have a conversation about hiring help. "I know you feel like you can't add anything else to your plate. But mine is overflowing too. Before we both burn out, what tasks can we outsource to free up some time for us?" See chapter 8 for more tips on outsourcing help.

## WHEN YOUR COMPANY IS NOT ON BOARD

If you find yourself working for an employer who does not have an adequate parental leave policy, here are some steps you can take to advocate for yourself and other parents.

1. **Read Up**: Find out what rights you already have. All Americans working for a company with more than fifty employees in a seventy-five-mile radius who have been at their job for at least 1,250 hours a year are eligible for twelve weeks of unpaid

time off. This applies to families of all shapes and sizes: Married, unmarried, LGBTQIA, with adopted or biological children. Some states offer family leave programs and partial wage replacement benefits for pregnant women. Temporary disability insurance is also available in certain states to pregnant people diagnosed as disabled by their doctor. Recovery from a difficult birth counts!

2. **Schedule a Chat**: Before your baby comes, schedule a time to speak to your boss. Emphasize your commitment to the company and the contributions you've already made. Frame any time off as an investment in the sustainability of your career at the company. Have a detailed plan of who will take over your duties and how you will ensure your team does not suffer. Be precise about how you will ease the transition before you leave.

3. **Find Strength in Numbers:** Real change requires company-wide concessions. Consider gathering other parents looking for leave benefits and approach HR together. Make a detailed list of why parental leave is a priority for these workers and align on the changes you'd like to see. Share studies showing that paid leave helps companies retain talent and diversify their workforce. Research the parental leave policies of competitors in the industry. Tackling the issue together is less intimidating, and will ensure the message to the company speaks to more than the needs of a single employee.

4. **Look Beyond Leave:** If your company is unwavering, fight for other concessions. Gender-neutral policies are an easy way for companies to take a stand on equality without expanding the total number of days parents have off. Flexible hours and work-from-home benefits can also help parents stay in the workforce and redistribute the burden of caregiving more equally. Be creative in thinking of benefits that will allow you to be there for the moments that matter, even without leave.

# RULE 5

# Love Thy Nosey Neighbor

I DISCOVERED I WANTED TO BE A FOREIGN CORRESPONDENT THE DAY Pope John Paul II died. My father and I, seated side by side in his silver Toyota, were listening to the news on the radio just like we did every day on the way to school. But that morning, Campbell Brown, the NBC reporter, was not presenting the headlines from her desk in New York City. She was reporting live from the Vatican, thousands of miles away, where the pope's funeral was under way, and the selection of his successor was imminent. "Wait, that's a real job?" I asked my dad. "You can just travel where things are happening and tell others about it?"

"That's journalism," he answered.

I was hooked. Some ten years later, fresh out of journalism school, I boarded a plane to Mozambique for my first assignment. The story I was chasing wasn't quite the death of a pope. I was there to report on a discovery of coal and gas reserves that had caught the eye of international investors. They were preparing to pour billions of dollars into the projects. The investment had the potential to serve as a ticket out of poverty for a country scraping the bottom of the Human Development Index.

It was a long-awaited turning point for Mozambique, which was still recovering from a fifteen-year civil war. Evidence of the violence was everywhere, long after the last shots had been fired. In central Mozambique, local post offices and general stores were poked with bullets. Landmines still dotted the hills, killing scores of children and livestock every year. A resurgence in violence between the two main political parties had everyone wary.

Assignment in hand, I moved to Maputo, the country's quiet capital on the shores of the Indian Ocean. It was a city of contradictions. During the day, the vast, tree-lined boulevards overlooking the ocean looked like paradise. There was a breezy, Latin vibe to the city that reminded me of Brazil. On Sundays, hymns and songs would waft above churches, the congregants' voices traveling for miles. But at night, the city was silent and dark, save for the flames lit by squatters on the sides of the road and in abandoned buildings. I was alone, really alone, for the first time in my life. Far from family and friends, I had to build a life from scratch.

I rented a studio on the edge of town and got to work settling in. During a meeting at the US embassy in my first week in Maputo, I would meet the handsome diplomat who would eventually become my husband. But first, the basics—I needed to set up a bank account. Like everything else in Mozambique, just getting to the branch was an adventure of its own.

A busy road stood between my house and the bank. There were no bridges, sidewalks, or stop lights to stem the traffic. For ten minutes, I tried in vain to cross the road, but the flow of cars and trucks blowing clouds of orange dust was unrelenting. That's when I noticed the other pedestrians around me holding hands. Suddenly, the woman beside me gripped my wrist, and lunged at the moving cars. Together, we stopped traffic. It was my first lesson in the power of collective action, a force that shapes daily life in Mozambique.

## The Neighborhood Net

As money poured into Maputo, the city developed markers of cosmopolitan life. There were bars serving expensive bottles of champagne, concerts, and fashion shows. But I knew that just outside the city center, life was very different. When I drove to the remote coal mines on the edge of the country's border, I passed whole villages made of mud and straw houses, where people were living the same way they had for generations.

I will not romanticize the levels of poverty and desperation I saw on these trips. Life without electricity, indoor plumbing, and basic healthcare was ruthless. Most families had to travel to access potable water to drink, bathe, and farm. It was not an idyllic society by any means, especially not for women and children, who often bore the brunt of these social ills.

Yet Mozambique offered me a masterclass on the power of community. Here neighborly ties were essential for survival. Communities had alternatives for all kinds of social safety nets I took for granted in the States. Instead of banks, there were village savings schemes, where groups of ten to twenty people contributed monthly to a joint savings account and received an annual lump sum payout. In the place of insurance, social funds were set up with monthly contributions that could be cashed in during emergencies.

Unsurprisingly, childcare solutions were also collective. Neighbors joined forces, caring for dozens of kids so their parents could work, teaching older ones skills to contribute to village life, and even breastfeeding each other's children when necessary. They also disciplined each other's kids, sharing the responsibility of teaching them the community's common values. This practice, called alloparenting by sociologists, was just part of everyday life.

I'm not suggesting the Mozambican model can or should be copied and pasted onto American society. As countries develop, many of these ties naturally loosen. You don't need to rely on your neighbors to survive in a country with free public education systems, extensive healthcare, and public libraries. But have we lost an essential aspect of our community even as we gained these critical services?

In developed countries, money can bandage gaps in community. Instead of seeking advice from family, we pay therapists. We prefer to hire our kids a tutor than ask a neighbor for homework help. Instead of calling on friends to babysit, we pay a professional. Especially in the West, we favor reliable, clean transactions that leave no debt behind. In asking for help, many believe we lose face, independence, and control. But when our village shrinks to the people in our homes or on our screens, do we lose more than that borrowed cup of sugar?

In the Malhazine neighborhood north of Maputo, Rosa Alberto Maziove stands surrounded by a posse of children outside her house. Only two are biologically hers. "But the rest are mine too," she assures me.

Rosa acts as a *mae de rua* or street mother, watching a gaggle of kids while their parents work. When children are hungry, she feeds them. When they are sad, she comforts them. She is also there in case anyone gets injured. Last week, she had to race to get ice for a toddler who gashed his forehead open while his mom was at work. "The pain of a child getting hurt is the same, no matter who they belong to," she said. In exchange for keeping an eye on her neighbors' kids, the children's parents give her a *refresco* or small tip of a few dollars a week.

In Mozambique, families are tied not by blood but by action. This distinction is evident even in language. Deciphering biological relations is difficult because children called all older women who take part in raising them "Mom." Cousins are referred to as "sisters" and neighbors "cousins."

Family is not necessarily the people who gave you life but those invested in your survival. Over the last three decades, one of the world's worst AIDS epidemics orphaned 1.3 million children in Mozambique. Many orphaned children were adopted not by relatives but neighbors.

That was the case for Albertina Afonso Matlhonhane, who was nine when both of her parents died. Her neighbor, Evelina Nkuku, adopted her informally and raised Albertina alongside her four biological children. Now that she's an adult, the tables have turned. Albertina financially supports her adoptive mom in her old age with money she makes working at a banana factory. In return, Evelina watches Albertina's three children while she works.

"Albertina is acting as my daughter in a way my own children are not. Caring for her children is a way to thank her," said Evelina. "It is small, but it comes from the heart." In this way, families are tied together in a never-ending web of aid. Every crisis averted brings them closer together. Every social debt accrued and paid deepens the friendship.

Community, not family, I learned, was the first line of defense when things went wrong. And in Mozambique, they often did. That was the case for Almira, who left home at fifteen to marry a much older man. Five years and three children later, he left her for a job as a builder in South Africa and stopped answering her calls. Alone with a basic education, she had to find a way to provide for her three children, Milena, Foguive, and Sebito.

It was an all too common story in Mozambique, where 48 percent of women marry before eighteen. So common, in fact, that Almira decided to turn to her childhood neighbor, Elena, who was in a similar predicament, for help. Elena Silvestre Tila had grown up living next door to Almira in a small town in central Mozambique. Walking side by side to collect water at the village well, the two became fast friends. Like Almira, Elena married young. At seventeen, her family pushed her to settle with a man double her age. In exchange for ten heads of cattle, she became his third wife. But the marriage was short-lived. Two years later, her husband moved to South Africa to work as a driver, abandoning her to raise her young son with no income.

As her savings vaporized, Elena faced a harrowing choice. If she returned to her parents, they might be forced to pay back her dowry, a prohibitive expense for her family. But staying and finding a job proved impossible, and she resorted to begging for food. Dismayed by her lack of options, she was desperate for an alternative when her phone rang.

Her childhood friend Almira said she had just been offered a job as a housekeeper but couldn't take it unless someone cared for her children. She thought back to her childhood friend and asked her to move in. "I wanted someone I knew I could trust, who would treat the children like they were her own," she said. Together, the two mothers created a new kind of family. The kids are being raised as siblings, and call both women "mom." Elena cares for them, ensures they attend school, and cooks their meals, while Almira works and provides for their expenses.

Elena said she quickly developed maternal feelings for Almira's children. "I don't differentiate the care I give to the children based on who came from my womb. They are all my kids," she says, stroking Sebito, Almira's youngest, as he curls into her arm for a nap. The two women forged a new life with the help of their neighbors who provided them with all the support they needed to keep going. Local women who had also broken out of difficult marriages came over to welcome them when they moved in. "They taught me to keep my head up, that this is not the end," said Elena. When a thief tried to break in, Elena called not the police, who are notoriously corrupt, but her neighbors. They chased the intruder away and tried to track his footprints until they lost him.

Joana, down the street, keeps an eye on the kids when Elena has to run to the market. Zito, two blocks down, stops by once a week to help them with homework. It's a system of collective child-rearing that has enabled Elena to make a life independent of her husband. Plus, she said, it benefits the children, who are literally being raised by a village.

"A child must learn from many people. You send kids to school knowing that their teacher, a stranger, will impart their knowledge to the children. Why wouldn't you trust a neighbor you see daily to do the same?" Elena asks. "We are all trying to make them better."

I think of life in the United States, where my interactions with neighbors were limited to tight smiles in hallways and elevators, where I was reluctant to look anyone in the eye, let alone ask for help. If I were falling through the cracks, I'm not sure my neighbors would look up long enough from their phones to notice. I probably wouldn't either.

Of course, Elena and Almira's situation is bred out of necessity, not choice. The adversity and injustice they've faced is vast and not every element of their setup is enviable. But their family offers an example of what happens in societies where community is woven into daily life.

During an afternoon at their house, I'm astonished by the sheer number of social visits the family receives. A rotating cast of neighbors is constantly dropping in. The front yard serves as a semi-public place, with friends parking themselves under the mango tree for visits that sometimes last hours. As Elena and I speak, her friend Taira stops by unannounced, silently pulling up a chair as we talk. Soon, a teenage boy shouts into the front yard, asking if twelve-year-old Foguive is home. A friend of eight-year-old Beyoncé stops by to ask her to go shopping for coal.

That's not the only difference I notice at Almira's house. Being part of such a tight-knit community teaches the children that they must contribute, not just consume. Everyone has a role to play in the functioning of the neighborhood, including them. Between games of tag and soccer, the children do chores—unprompted. As I approach the house in the early morning, I spot Foguive holding a gallon of water to bring home for the family. At twelve, he knows how to cook basic meals for his siblings. If Elena needs to go out, he can make cornmeal and sauté sweet potato leaves for the other children. He is also in charge of bathing his brothers every night.

Later that morning, Beyoncé is playing a clapping game with her sister Milena when she sees it is almost noon. Unprompted, she walks over to an iron stove with two burners sitting in their front yard. She brings it inside to the kitchen on her own. Carefully, she spreads a bed of coal on the burner. Noticing that there are no matches left in the box, she asks Elena for a coin and walks two blocks to the general store to buy some. Back at the house, supervised by Elena, she lights the match and uses paper to kindle the fire. Five-year-old Milena watches attentively. She is eager for the task to be passed down to her. For now, she is in charge of gathering sticks from the backyard and feeding them to the flames. There are no sticker charts, prizes, or allowances. The reward is lunch.

Yet this added responsibility hasn't stripped the children of their childhood. In fact, they roam the neighborhood in a pack of friends my kids would envy. They play seamlessly, moving from yard to yard, digging tunnels in the earth, kicking soccer balls against the walls, and building cars out of bits of plastic. Walking up to Almira's house, you hear the neighborhood children before you see them, bursts of giggles and squeals that get louder as a gang of kids meanders from house to house. Today, one group of friends is attempting a three-legged race. Tied together, they wobble down the street until they inevitably crash in a plume of dust. Their laughter is a siren call to the neighborhood kids, who pop out of their homes to join the game. The kids are free to explore the neighborhood until dusk, when dinner calls them back.

## Isolation Nation

The women in Mozambique faced challenges even the most strained American mother likely doesn't encounter daily, like lack of access to basic food and sanitation. These are hardships that no one should have to face. But over and over again during my time in Mozambique, the way I saw communities come together around women in times of need inspired me.

I thought of them often when I returned, a year later, to the capital of awkward elevator smiles, New York City. But it turns out life in America wasn't always this lonely. Community ties in the United States have weakened swiftly over the last fifty years with psychological and civic ramifications that continue to ripple through society. Memberships in clubs, unions, and community boards, once staples of American life, are withering. For the first time, less than half of Americans say they belong to a religious organization. And as much as a chat with your neighbor about politics or religion may sound excruciating, these conversations once served an important purpose. They were vehicles that exposed Americans to people outside their immediate bubble. Churches, volunteer groups, or parent-teacher associations, once gathering places for Americans to discuss political life, have atrophied.

Social media is a poor substitute.

Early Internet defenders lauded the technology's ability to connect people who shared common interests, especially those who struggled to find a place in analog communities. In chat groups, message boards, and blogs, many found a sense of belonging that evaded them in real life. These were, and continue to be, essential vehicles of information and social belonging for many marginalized communities.

But they also established a blueprint for social media as a place where people grouped themselves together by identity. It was a sharp change from the days when newspapers would try to appeal to as wide a base as possible. The resulting echo chambers have contributed to a polarization not seen in the last fifty years.

And despite having more people's perspectives at our fingertips than ever, Americans feel increasingly alone. In 2019, 61 percent of Americans said they were lonely, up from 54 percent the year before. Young people are even more likely to feel isolated. Seventy percent of millennials and nearly 80 percent of members of Generation Z reported being lonely, according to the survey.

And while many Americans chat with their neighbors interactions tend to stick to the surface. Only 14 percent of Americans who know their neighbors get together with them monthly.

Many friends I've spoken to want to be more connected to their communities but don't know where to start. When you're the only one doing it, asking for help from neighbors can feel like an insurmountable hurdle. But, as I saw in Mozambique, leaning on our neighbors is an excellent way of strengthening ties. Proactively building up a social debt ensures your neighbors feel comfortable relying on you when they need it too. There will be plenty of time to pay the favor forward.

Some Americans got a taste of this kind of community living during the pandemic when forced to rely on their neighbors for childcare, transport, and groceries. As the pandemic raged, many schools shut down and parents united to find a childcare solution. By August 2020, over 30 percent of American parents with school-aged children participated in a pandemic pod or an informal childcare setup.

That was the case for my friend Melody, a content developer in Los Angeles trying to survive the pandemic with a baby and a three-year old. When her friends who had kids the same age started a pandemic pod, she decided to move across town to be closer to them. Dubbed the "Tiny School," the pod was a rotating childcare system where neighborhood parents took turns caring for their preschool-age children while isolating themselves from the virus. The pandemic forced Melody to socialize in this child-care circle almost exclusively and she watched as her friendship with the other parents and their kids deepened. It's a bond that has endured beyond the pandemic. Melody also found that reciprocity was key.

"There's this very American mentality of you take care of what's yours, and I'll take care of what's mine. But our kids' friends were constantly opening their homes to our children. And as a result, I started thinking, maybe I should offer that too." When her neighbor invited Melody's daughter to sleep over so that she and her husband could have a night out, Melody felt indebted. It started a cycle of mutual care that continues to this day. When she is stuck in traffic and running late to pick her daughter up from school, she knows she can count on her parent friends in the neighborhood. She says they feel the same, and know they can help each other out with carpools and afterschool care.

"They have become like extended family to us. We are just very real about the fact that we are doing the best we can and that we need help. It has been very life-giving for me and my husband."

## The Suki Solution

My memories of Mozambique stayed with me long after I moved away. As much as I admired the parenting I had seen in Mozambican villages, it felt far removed from my own reality by the time I found out I was pregnant back in Brazil.

Until I met Suki.

Suki grew up in Hong Kong but lived in Brazil with her Italian husband and three-month-old daughter, Esme. She had a global upbringing and spoke a mile a minute with an American accent she had picked up at international school. She was intense, passionate, and had an appetite for life that I found especially appealing in my exhausting third trimester.

In many ways, Suki was my foil as a mother. While I made Rudy memorize sleeping schedules, Suki lay Esme to sleep on an armchair she placed against the wall for the first few months of her life because she couldn't be bothered to buy a crib. "We just never got around to it, I guess," she told me. But where I tore through baby books to learn how to manage each phase of Oliver's development, Suki navigated motherhood innately. While taking her baby on a walk, she would get close to the bushes and let the leaves tickle Esme's leg. She was the most popular mom at the park and would bring water balloons in her baby bag and roll them down the slide, splashing the kids on the landing. One day, I came to her apartment to find Esme playing in a cardboard box full of cooked, rainbow-colored spaghetti that Suki effortlessly threw together that morning.

Mothering with Suki was magical, and I wanted a piece of it. There was an empty apartment directly above us up for rent. So, when her lease was up, I saw an opportunity. One day, during a playdate, I blurted out. "Move in upstairs! We could do it all together," I told her. "Motherhood, but with a friend."

As the words came out of my mouth, I realized how crazy I sounded. What grown woman invites a friend to live above her? What if it was too close, too fast? What if we didn't get along as neighbors? What if this ruined our friendship?

But Suki wasn't spooked. She looked me straight in the eyes. "I'm in."

Suki moved in, and our lives changed forever. Our friends responded in surprise, tinged with envy, as we took turns hosting playdates and washing each other's dishes. Sometimes, at night, the doorbell would ring, and I would open the door to find a large bowl of cooked pasta. "Dinner is ready," she would text me.

As an expat in Brazil, Suki didn't have an established network of friends. But I watched up close as she stitched together a community for us from scratch. Every trip to the playground was a chance to get to know more people. She would routinely bring home new moms she met out and about, like a puppy gathering sticks from the neighborhood. Soon our group of friends swelled. Her place was always a mess, with dishes in the sink and clothes scattered all over the furniture. But anyone who came over would be greeted with a mug of tea and an invitation to stay for dinner. Suki didn't bother weeding out moms we didn't especially connect with. She wasn't looking for a best friend, I realized. She was building a social foundation for the neighborhood, and everyone was invited.

I always thought of hosting as a formal, labor-intensive activity that required days of planning. But Suki showed me it didn't have to be. She braided it into our daily lives. She kept activities simple and invitations open. Everyone was welcome to join us for whatever we were already doing that week. To coordinate communication, she created a group chat that grew to two dozen moms. But unlike so many of my other chats, which became substitutes for offline socialization, this one was strictly a vehicle for planning real-world interactions. On it, she would announce our plans for the day in case anyone wanted to join. A simple trip to the park or walk around the block would quickly become a group outing. Others followed her lead, and soon, we found ourselves with a vibrant, offline social life.

As much as she did for the neighborhood, Suki also had no qualms about leaning on others. Our arrangement quickly extended to life beyond playdates. When the plumber was over, and she couldn't understand his Portuguese, she would message the group asking for a translator. I supervised more than one trip to the bank when she needed help accessing an account and negotiated with the electrical company to keep her lights on when a bill accidentally went unpaid.

By leaning on us, she made it okay for us to ask for help too. One month, I was called to go on the reporting trip of a lifetime. A tribe in the heart of the Amazon rainforest was fighting for its survival. A proposed hydroelectric plant would flood the tribe's historic land, and the tribal chief had agreed to an interview. The trip would be brutal, and I'd be without communication for at least three days while I trekked through muddy roads and up a river to the remote village for the interview. But it was too good an opportunity to pass up. So, I went to Suki. Could she step in for three days to help Rudy while I left? "Go," she said. "The commune will provide." That line became a running bit we employed whenever we had a tough week and needed the other to step in unexpectedly. Our little commune always did provide, and because of it, I could jump on work opportunities I might have had to pass up had it not been for the alternate mother waiting in the wings. At night, exhausted by the dawn of the terrible twos, we would recover with popcorn and mocktails, binging endless episodes of *Gilmore Girls*.

Over two years, we were there for the moments that our own extended families missed. When Suki was pregnant with her second child, my phone rang in the middle of the night. "I think it's happening. I'm going into labor," she said. She was over a month early and alone. Her husband had gone on a last-minute work trip across the country.

"I'm coming," I said and raced over, leaving Rudy to watch over Oliver and Esme.

She labored through the night while I held her hand and talked her through contractions. As day broke, her son, Max, was born. "Ten fingers and ten toes!" I called out to her as the nurses sewed her back up.

It wasn't perfect. There were moments when our parenting styles differed, our foibles got on each other's nerves, or we felt like one person was taking more than giving. But the independence I had to give up to create our little commune was the best parenting trade-off I ever made. When Suki's husband was transferred to Spain a few years later, I was shattered. So was the neighborhood. But our experiment taught me that I didn't want to do motherhood alone again. Luckily, I wouldn't have to. Suki taught me how to create a community wherever I went.

## BRING IT HOME

Maybe convincing your friends to move to your neighborhood seems like a pipe dream (though I recommend it!). But you can start by leaning on the people already there. What would happen if, instead of rolling our eyes at our nosey neighbors, we invited them in, opened up, and asked for help? You may find that the support you craved was right across the street, and you'll also be contributing to a significant cultural shift in how we relate to our communities. Instead of keeping up with the Joneses, let's check in on them.

1. **Utilize New Beginnings:** It may be cliche, but a great time to get to know your neighbors is during a transition. Take advantage of the first few months after you move in to introduce yourself

to as many neighbors as possible. After all, "I just moved to the neighborhood" is an easy opening line that won't always be available. Take the opportunity to get to know new families moving in as well. Welcome new neighbors within a week of their arrival. A neighborhood tour or a list of suggestions of your favorite local restaurants creates a segue for more hangouts.

2. **Find a Fresh Start:** Even if you've lived across from your neighbors in silence for years, it's never too late to strike up a friendship. To make things less awkward, look for a fresh start. There is no shame in hiding behind your children. Setting up a lemonade stand or neighborhood Easter egg hunt can reheat a stale friendship or spark a conversation with neighbors you haven't spoken to in a long time.

3. **Find Your Suki:** Community building does not follow a straight line. In all likelihood, the people you first meet won't be the ones you click with immediately. That's okay. Not everyone you meet has to be your best friend. Look for people who can serve as a connection to the community. In the beginning, quantity over quality is key. You must build a social carpet to walk on first. Once you have a good network, look for the sparks that can lead to deeper friendships.

4. **Ask, and You Shall Receive:** The best way to forge ties with your neighbors is to lean on them. Take a tip from the Mozambicans and start a debt cycle. Ask for help with something small. A request to water plants while you are on vacation is a great way to start a conversation you can continue after your bags are unpacked. If you hesitate to ask for help, remember that most people crave deeper connections with their neighbors. Of course, don't let the debt become too lopsided. Thank them for any help with an invitation to dinner, or an ice cream outing on you to keep the

hangouts going. Be sure to offer them support as often as you can. If your neighbors are hesitant to ask for help, pull a Suki. A bowl of pasta or cookies at the door will almost always be welcome.

5. **Take It Offline:** Online neighborhood groups can be a great way to scout for friendships. Like with parents' groups, be sure to take the interactions offline as soon as possible. You don't even have to host something at home if you don't want to. A girls' night out or meetup at a local coffee shop works just as well as a way to connect offline. I like to offer at least two invitations to take conversations offline before I move on. If asking directly feels too scary, remember you don't have to reinvent the wheel. Announcing your plans for the day on a small group chat is a great way of opening an invitation to anyone who feels like coming.

6. **Volunteer Your Skills:** Keep a finger on the pulse of the neighborhood. What are the greatest needs of the families around you, and how can you contribute? When families casually mention a difficulty or trial, don't just listen. Proactively think of ways you can alleviate their plight. If you are a math whiz, let parents know you are available to help a teenager struggling with fractions. If you love cooking, making an extra plate of food for the harried family next door is an easy way to show support. Your experience, not just your skills, can help. A word of support from someone who has been through sickness, trauma, or divorce and emerged on the other side can encourage those currently walking through those challenges. Remember to bring your kids along for any offers to help. Maybe an elderly neighbor needs a weekly grocery delivery or tech support. Another may need help shoveling snow. Taking the kids with you for these activities and encouraging them to participate will teach them that they are not only consumers but contributors to the community.

7. **Look for Teachers:** The flip side of the coin is to consider what your neighbors have to teach you. Do they have any skills you'd like your children to learn? Shadowing a neighbor as they engage in their hobbies can be a fun way to introduce diverse interests and abilities to your kids. Some may be available and even excited to help with school projects, mentor a teen, or teach a skill and help you connect in new ways with the families around you.

8. **Find a Front Porch:** It is not a coincidence that the front porch is a staple of Southern hospitality. Like the front yards I saw in Mozambique, front porches serve as an intermediary space between private homes and public streets. Even if your house doesn't have a front porch, look for semi-public areas where neighbors gather. Apartment lobbies and nearby parks can serve a similar function. Interactions in these places offer a low-commitment way to test the ground for fertile friendships.

9. **Have an Open-Door Policy:** Allow your home to become a hangout space for neighbors and their kids. Consider investing in your front yard instead of your backyard. Swing sets or toys placed there attract neighborhood kids and start conversations with families nearby. They also encourage kids to socialize and see themselves as part of a broader neighborhood. Remember, your house doesn't have to be pristine to be the neighborhood hangout. Aim for hospitality, not perfection. Your kids certainly won't notice, and, in all likelihood, your friends won't care. As I learned from Suki, a cup of hot tea and a listening ear make more of a difference to your neighbors than an immaculate kitchen.

10. **Share Your Traditions:** Holidays and traditions are opportunities to connect with your neighbors. Opening up your home for a dinner of your family's ancestral food or celebrations is a bridge to intimacy. Not only will these events strengthen ties, but they

can also serve to educate neighbors about cultural differences and promote tolerance. If major holidays feel too private, consider including neighbors in traditions leading up to the celebrated day. Decorating Christmas cookies can be even more fun if you include a neighbor's child.

11. **Be a Superconnecter:** Opening up your network to those around you can help strengthen ties throughout the neighborhood. A biannual "invite-a-friend" dinner is a great way to expand your circle and connect with your neighbors. Invite five people who must each bring at least one new friend. These events can help introduce neighbors to people they might otherwise never meet. Remember, someone may not be *your* soul sister, but she could be exactly what another parent is looking for. When hosting events or introducing neighbors, offer to connect them with others who share similar hobbies, skills, or family structures. This can help create a web of mutual support that extends beyond your family.

12. **Take It Further:** If you feel a spark with a neighbor, it's time to deepen the relationship. Sometimes, after many social encounters, you may notice conversation gets stuck in small talk or, worse, kid talk. Follow up a simple "How's it going?" with a specific question about their week to get the ball rolling in the right direction. Being vulnerable is another shortcut that communicates the trust and value you place on the relationship. Practice making the first move by sharing a recent struggle or breakthrough. It will also give the other person permission to do the same. The back-and-forth will deepen your relationship and make a friend out of a neighbor.

## RULE 6

# Propose to a Friend

### The Sour Taste of American Parenting

Over sushi one night, Rudy and I began casually tossing around the idea of having another baby. We always wanted to give Oliver a sibling, and a year and a half into parenting, it seemed like we were finally in a good place. I didn't rush to the hospital every time Oliver sneezed, and my strict sleeping schedules had loosened into suggestions. Breastfeeding, which we struggled through for four painful months, was (thankfully) over after my milk supply dried up during a reporting trip. Most of all, our lives felt stable. If we were to introduce another ball into this juggling act, now felt like a good time.

A few months later, we were pregnant with a daughter, Dahlia. True to her personality, the pregnancy and birth were blissfully smooth. Even breastfeeding went off without a hitch.

Then, two months after she was born, the COVID-19 pandemic struck. I was scheduled to fly with Dahlia to northern Florida and cap off my three-month maternity leave with a visit to my parents.

"Just don't go to Disney World, and you'll be fine!" her pediatrician in São Paulo told us. "This thing will go away in a few months."

So we hopped on a plane and landed on a different planet. While Latin America was just waking up to the realities of the pandemic, with a few cases popping up here and there, the United States was in full panic. "You shouldn't be in this crowd with a newborn," an American immigration officer scolded me when we landed in the airport as he pulled us out of line.

Outside, supermarket shelves were emptying, and the stock market was tanking. I called Rudy, who was still in Brazil with Oliver. "I think we should be together. This feels... big."

He bought tickets that night and left with Oliver on one of the last flights out of Brazil. We extended my trip for a few weeks and squeezed into my parent's place, with the kids sleeping in the hallway and Rudy taking work calls in the living room. Two months later, we were still at my parents' house "waiting out" the pandemic when Rudy got a call. His company's division was closing, and a long-awaited promotion vanished.

By that point, Brazil was in chaos, with one of the world's highest daily death tolls, a president who was shrugging off the virus as a "little cold," and hospitals packed with people dying in hallways. Not the best place for a newborn.

We decided to stay put, and I got my first taste of American parenting. But parenthood during a pandemic, I would learn, was a whole other level. In addition to reporting for the *Post*, I took on a second job working part time in public relations to give us health insurance in the United States while we waited for the pandemic to pass. With no vaccines in sight, my parents, who were in their early sixties, eventually fled to a separate apartment as the virus spread across the United States.

Slowly, I started to lose it. "Is this what a mental breakdown feels like?" I asked Rudy, six months in. My hair was falling out in clumps. I started counting the hours until bedtime at noon. I felt simultaneously exhausted and bored. Even the aspects of motherhood I used to love, teaching Oliver his letters, building Lego towers, and taking him for scooter rides around the neighborhood, now felt like chores. I was juggling two jobs while caring for a toddler and a newborn and like so many other parents during the pandemic, Rudy and I were doing it alone.

Underlining the exhaustion was the ever-present anxiety of navigating the pandemic. Every trip to the park, every grandparent visit felt reckless. At the same time, two-year-old Oliver was desperate for friends. So we walked the tightrope between fear and social famine, venturing to the park only to come home panicked if anyone got too close. Thinking back to our life with Suki in Brazil, I felt a near physical longing. But how could I build a Suki-style network with the virus raging around us? Would it be possible to re-create our little commune somewhere else, we wondered.

## Singapore Seeds

Rudy and I had always dreamed of living close to our best friends, Jeremy and Melissa. The four of us became inseparable years earlier when we were neighbors in Washington, DC. At the time, Jeremy and Melissa were the US correspondents for a Singaporean newspaper on a three-year stint to cover the 2016 election.

Jeremy, an incredible cook, would invite us over for noodles and curry with sauces he brought over from Singapore. We quickly hit it off and would talk late into the night, trying to make sense of the political changes sweeping the United States. Our debates always came back to discussions about the differences in culture and values between our two countries. Singapore was tiny but mighty, an island-nation that stunned the world by the speed and scope of its development. It boasted one of the best education systems in the world, a jaw-dropping skyline, and was so safe people left their cars unlocked—with the keys inside. When Jeremy and Melissa spoke of life there it was with a pride and optimism I hadn't heard in America in a long time. Their tales piqued our curiosity and before long, Rudy and I started dreaming about what it would be like to one day join them there.

Right off the bat, ours was a different kind of friendship. We would fall asleep on each others' sofas, pick each other up at the airport, and burst in Kramer-style, no knocking required. We joked that we were living in a real-life '90s sitcom. Anytime I would try to make things too formal, asking for a drink instead of opening their fridge, or calling before coming over, Rudy would remind me to protect the intimacy that made our relationship special.

For over two years, we would meet up several nights a week to vent about our days, complain about difficult bosses, and binge-watch TV shows. It felt like we had known them forever. By the end of their stint in DC, the four of us vowed to one day live close to each other again.

A few years before the pandemic we visited them in Singapore where they had a son Oliver's age. We joked about how fun it would be to raise our kids side by side. "There are economies of scale to be had!" Jeremy insisted.

But at the time, we shrugged off the idea, thinking Brazil was our last stop before growing up and settling down in the United States, where our extended families awaited our return. Now, experiencing American motherhood for myself, I wasn't so sure.

One day mid-pandemic, after he found out his company was closing its division in Brazil, Rudy pulled me aside. "What if this is our chance? What if now's the time to go to Singapore?"

Rudy didn't need to be convinced of the merits of moving next to our best friends. For as long as I had known him, he had been a fan of communal living. He had roommates long after it was socially appropriate or economically necessary. As a diplomat, alone in embassy houses built for families, he would constantly offer up his home to anyone willing to visit. A few friends made trips to Latin America and Africa, but most didn't. Still, he always kept sheets on the bed in his guest room, just in case. Whenever anyone was short on housing, between leases, or didn't feel like driving home at the end of the night, he would offer up his place. When we started our little commune in Brazil with Suki, he was an immediate supporter. But to him, Brazil was just the beginning of what was possible.

Still, moving to Singapore was a crazy idea and he knew it. COVID was shutting down borders around the world and everyone was staying put. This was not the time to orchestrate a cross-continental move. But the pandemic sharpened our desire for community. In that moment, it seemed what we needed most were our people.

So Rudy started looking for jobs on the other side of the world, staying up all night to interview. When he got an offer from a Singaporean tech company, we jumped on it.

Our decision to move continents away to live closer to Jeremy and Melissa unsettled our friends and family. Some saw it as a sign of immaturity. Who upends their lives to live closer to friends past the age of twenty? Others saw it as a display of arrogance. What kind of people think their careers can survive a move like that? There was a bit of truth in both of those interpretations. The closeness of our friendship was the stuff of middle school—slightly embarrassing to admit and challenging to explain. And our careers would suffer more than we expected as a result of the move.

Still, having to spell out to everyone time and again why we were moving, only to be met with puzzled or judgmental looks quickly became exhausting. Jeremy and Melissa also got tired of having to explain to their parents and friends why this American couple was moving to a foreign country not for a job or for their kids' schooling, but to be closer to them. Trying to assess just how weird we were, people would ask, hopefully, whether we were related. Eventually, we settled on the line, "We're moving to be closer to family." It was a shorthand that felt true to us.

After the two-week mandatory quarantine, we arrived in Singapore shell-shocked. We gaped at the crowds shuffling through malls and eating at restaurants. Singapore was a country virtually untouched by the pandemic. Using contact tracing, social distancing, and isolating patients, it had been able to stamp out all cases for months.

We went straight from quarantine to Jeremy and Melissa's, where we would be staying while we sorted out our housing. Sitting on their couch, drinking whiskey while our kids played, we finally felt like we were home.

## Experimenting with Communal Living

Our idea, though different, was not original. Experiments in communal living have been around for as long as human beings have been thinking critically about the best ways to live. In 530 BC Pythagoras, the ancient Greek philosopher and father of utopian thinking, founded a colony where "all things were common and the same to all." In 375 BC Plato conjured his Republic, a utopian city ruled by guardians whose children would be raised communally to help their parents look out for the common good and prevent them from being sidetracked by their families' individual needs and ambitions. The Greeks weren't the only ones who blurred the lines between friends and family. From monks in French monasteries to Israeli farming Kibbutzim, communes have historically agreed on little, except for the idea that a life lived in community with others is superior to one lived in isolation.

And while for millions of years, people of different cultures and religions have lived together in close quarters, today, the marker of successful adulthood in America is the move away from home. There are over ninety million single-family homes in the United States, triple the number of multifamily ones. That privacy comes at a price. Only half of Americans have meaningful in-person interactions on a daily basis, according to a 2018 survey. Add toddlers to the equation, and the white picket fence can start to look an awful lot like a jail cell. According to a 2021 study commissioned by The Cigna Group, 69 percent of mothers and 77 percent of single parents in the United States report feeling lonely.

While it's clear that for many, the single-family home is not ideal, communal living can feel like a radical solution.

However, certain communal lifestyles are accepted and even cherished parts of American culture. The roommate, for example, has long been a cornerstone of the college experience and gives Americans a first taste of what is possible when we eliminate the walls that separate us. While I can barely recall what I learned in class, my formative university education happened over late-night debates in our college dorm rooms, where we tried new ideas on for size.

Of course, communal living is about more than just cohabitating. It requires sharing not just physical but emotional and intellectual real estate. Cohabitating can be a state of convenience, while communal living is often the opposite. It can require a level sacrifice and intentionality of life's closest relationships.

There is a certain intimacy that comes with sharing bathrooms and kitchens that can be hard to replicate post-college. Voluntarily choosing a communal lifestyle in adulthood, certainly after marriage—where the couple's relationship is meant to take center stage—is considered suspect. But that leaves families and parents isolated at a time when many crave community.

"We often measure closeness with others by the rooms we are willing to share with them," American ethnographer Kristen Ghodsee writes in her history of communes, *Everyday Utopia*. What would our living structures look like if we did away with the social norms that have isolated couples and families for decades? What rooms would we be willing to share with our friends?

For many, this kind of reimagining brings up images of the hippie movement, when thousands of disillusioned Americans chose to "drop out" of society and into communes that challenged social norms, espoused free love, and promoted anti-capitalism. Some three thousand of these communes sprouted in the United States in the 1960s and 1970s, most of them short-lived and radical. Famous examples, like the Kaliflower Commune in San Francisco, promoted group marriage, the use of psychedelics, and free labor. Other communes morphed into cults, with free-love practices members would later disavow. Communes often struggled to generate the resources necessary for their survival and many lacked a sustainable economic model. As the 1970s wore on, the Summer of Love soured and thousands of groups disbanded. But communes left an enduring legacy: they gave Americans permission to rethink the structure of their most intimate relationships.

At the same time, a growing gay rights movement was redefining definitions of family. In her book *Families We Choose: Lesbians, Gays, Kinship*, anthropologist Kath Weston explores how LGBTQ+ communities have expanded the concept of chosen family. For many, friendship networks emerged as an alternative family structure in cases of familial estrangement due to their sexual orientation. These groups were some of the first to articulate the concept of "chosen family," long before it became a toast at your yearly Friendsgivings.

It feels like we are at a similar inflection point in American society today, a place where we can rethink whether nuclear family ties should dictate everything from our living arrangements to our schedules. Faith in institutions is at a historic low. Nationwide protests on abortion, war, and police brutality echo the calls of the civil rights movements in the 1960s. As Americans seek alternatives to economic and social isolation, many are going back to the drawing board and reimagining the family unit. Communes have also resurged. The number of intentional communities in the United States nearly doubled between 2010 and 2016 to roughly twelve hundred, according to the Foundation for Intentional Community.

Yet many people curious about communal living get spooked by the stigma associated with communes of the past.

For those of us who don't want to shave our heads or open our marriages, the options can feel few and far between. The very thought that we might be lumped in with those extremes is enough to forgo going beyond past hallway hellos. But the reality is that most people have versions of communes they're already a part of. If you ask your neighbor to get your mail or a friend to care for your dog when you're out of town, those are the embers of a community. Experiments in communal living can be as radical and self-sacrificial as you want them to be. You get to decide how far to push those boundaries and what structure works for your family.

A "light" commune can bring together people trying to solve a single problem. For example, I've witnessed tight-knit pet-sitting communities, where members are happy to step in and take care of their friends' pets free of charge when they travel or have an emergency. The communal aspect of these groups is limited, but cherished. Unlike other clubs or groups with loose ties, members trust that at least when it comes to their pets, their values align. There is a standard of behavior expected of everyone, that includes putting individual freedoms aside for the collective good, even if only in this sliver of life.

Others are scared by the idea that communal living poses a threat to their individual freedom. But that dichotomy is false. Pursuing what's best for yourself, by yourself, can actually limit your potential in the long run. Paradoxically, working with others can ultimately expand your freedom by allowing you the flexibility and resources to do what's impossible on your own.

For example, as Rudy and I looked for a home in Singapore, we knew that to create a true communal living situation with Jeremy and Melissa we would have to live as close as possible to them. But I didn't particularly love the neighborhood where they lived. Their building bordered a major street and had no parks close by.

If Rudy and I were to have prioritized our individual freedom and chosen a place based on what was best for our nuclear family, we would probably have looked at a more central, green part of the city. But the area was close to Jeremy's office and allowed him to commute by bike. It was also zoned for the school where they hoped to send their son, Jay.

Living in their neighborhood meant an individual sacrifice for our family, but it turned out to be a communal gain for everyone. It meant that Oliver and Dahlia had a built-in best friend. Spontaneous hangouts, advice, and emergency babysitting would be steps away.

That's just one example of the thousands of decisions that we made daily to prioritize the group. Living in community takes effort, intentionality, and, often, sacrifice. Taking someone else's needs, preferences, and schedule into account does not always come naturally. The skills needed to live in close proximity with others—cooperation, empathy, and patience—too often atrophy post-college when we no longer need to convince our roommate to wash the dishes. But I've found that the returns often tower over the investment and that, done right, communal life gives more than it takes.

Still, our little commune was still a complete anomaly in the larger world. I wondered what would it be like to live in a society where communal living arrangements were not only encouraged, but the norm.

## A Sleepover with the Headhunters

The Iban tribe in Eastern Malaysia are known mainly for two things: their jungle dwellings called longhouses, where up to forty families live together, and headhunting—as in, the severing, storing, and collecting of human skulls.

One muggy August afternoon, my Iban guide Chris, his machete, and I venture deep into the Malaysian rainforest to see how the tribe's centuries-old experiment in communal living has endured. The trip is intense. We hike all morning, crossing five rivers holding our gear above our heads. As we advance deeper into the forest, Chris explains his tribe's traditions.

"Collecting heads was a sign of bravery and one way to gain respect and admiration in the tribe," he says.

"You mean, like enemy heads, right?" I ask.

"No, just anyone," he says with a smile.

We comb through the lush mountains, wade through fog, and hop over bent tree roots, stopping to snack on mangos we find along the way. Suddenly I notice a prick on my wrist. A leech has gripped my artery. When I feel another latch onto my ankle, I start to wonder if this could have been a Zoom meeting.

As I struggle uphill, I learn that the trip is arduous on purpose. The isolated longhouse is located under the shadow of the Mountain of Last Resistance, the place where, after much fighting, the Iban capitulated to British invaders in 1861. But the Iban left a lasting impression as fearless fighters. The British would later tap them to orchestrate guerrilla attacks against the Japanese during World War II. In fact, many of the human skulls adorning Iban longhouses today are said to be Japanese.

We reach the longhouse in the early afternoon. The structure is one of three thousand Iban longhouses in Indonesia, Brunei, and Malaysia. It looks like a cross between a barn and a warehouse, with long wooden walls fenced by a porch. Built in the early 1950s, the house consists of a shared hallway about the length of a soccer field, with individual rooms spanning the sides. Inside, the decor is bare. Save for a few hanging machetes; some with human hair tangled on them, the walls are bare.

True to its name, the house is, in fact, long. Sixteen families live here, hunting wild boars and bats and farming pepper to survive. The families sleep and eat most of their meals in their individual apartments but share the outside large common area. As night falls, the families slowly pour in from their hunts. As they retreat to their individual rooms for baths and dinner, I wonder if this life is really all that different from apartment living in the United States.

Then, around 9 p.m., one by one, the adults emerge from their apartments to the common area. They lay down on hammocks strung up between poles in the living room or sit on straw mats and smoke cigarettes. Some weave baskets made of ginger leaves, and others just chill.

The scene is immediately familiar: it's a hangout. There's that college dorm room vibe, with people coming and going as they please, being together with no purpose other than to be together. Soon, laughter echoes through the hall as conversation picks up. They chat about politics ("Who do you think will win the elections in western Malaysia?"), gossip ("Did many people show up to the funeral of the elder from the tribe next door?"), and work ("I see that new bat trap worked well for you today!").

And while the conversation topics are familiar, something feels different. For hours, through lulls between stories and moments of boredom, nobody reaches for their phones. I can't think of the last time I saw two dozen people hanging out with no distractions for this long. By 10:30, I am starting to get tired, but it is clear the Iban don't want the conversation to end. These daily hangout sessions, I learn, are integral to their communal life.

## Longhouse Rules

To my surprise, there are strict rules separating private life and communal life at the longhouse. Each family has their own electricity meter and contributes exactly one lightbulb to the common room. The families buy their own groceries, plow individual plots of land, and trap animals for their own consumption.

Other aspects of life are shared. When the men go hunting for big game together several nights a week they divide up the proceeds evenly amongst the tribe. The Iban take turns caring for the communal areas of the longhouse and hosting visitors. They elect a tribal chief, who receives and distributes welfare from the state.

But more than space and money the Iban are expected to share each other's time. Unless members are ill, nightly hangout sessions, which can stretch late into the night, are all but mandatory. Nobody texts to cancel at the last minute.

With so many adults living in such close quarters, childcare is also more accessible. Bonds with children are not exclusive to parents here, and it is typical for aunties and uncles to take turns soothing, playing with, and even disciplining children.

Children are the "kings" of the longhouses, Chris explains. "Whatever they want, they get away with." Children are so integral to Iban relationships that adults are known by their relation to their children. When a child is born, the parents are no longer called by their first names. Instead, they are called "so-and-so's parent," a title they will only update to "so-and-so's grandparent" when the time comes.

It's easy to see how children are central to Iban life on my first night at the longhouse when an eighteen-month-old named Danish (pronounced Dah-NICHE) toddles out of his apartment to hang out with the adults. Wearing a Tigger T-shirt, he goes from his grandfather's to his aunt's lap, before finally settling on an uncle, his head resting gently on the uncle's belly.

Danish has been living in the longhouse since he was a newborn. At this point, he is closer to the adults in the longhouse whom he sees daily than to his mother, who works during the week in a lab in a city six hours away. The adults take turns chiding him, playing with him and making faces from across the hall. Danish laps it up and makes faces back, engaging his playmates. But the adults also reprimand him. Tonight, he is engaged in a battle with one of the many cats who live in the longhouse. As he pulls the cat's tail, an echo of "tisks" spreads throughout the common room. One auntie finally pulls him aside and demands he stops. When he doesn't, she picks him up, takes him in her lap, and holds him tight to the relief of the poor cat.

"We do scold the kids," says Langguan Anak Jubin, a sixty-year-old resident of the Longhouse.

"Not too hard!" clarifies his wife, Rena. "Just to teach the kids not to do it again. The parents don't mind."

After all, teaching the children how to live in harmony with others is integral to their development and long-term future at the longhouse. And it must happen early. At six years old, the children spend the week at a boarding school paid for by the Malaysian government. They return to the longhouse for weekends and vacations, but the time to prepare them for future longhouse living is when they are still toddlers.

Because harmonious coexistence is essential at the longhouse, for everyone's sake, there are many unspoken social pressures. People are encouraged to limit gossip and always keep their word. Those who don't are asked to leave, though it is rare for someone to get kicked out.

Still, living in close quarters, everyone's business is in everyone's business. The walls between apartments are so thin that people interject in their neighbor's conversations, correcting them as they tell stories from the apartment next door. People have an opinion on the details of everyone's life, because it will inevitably affect them too. One day at breakfast, one family is debating whom another one of the residents should marry. "That girl is too young for him. The other one is nice, but she is not a good worker," one of the women says, shaking her head. The potential bride, after all, represents not only a new neighbor but an extra pair of hands at the longhouse.

The tribe's seventy-three-year-old chief, Siba Anak Laba, likes to remind the residents that the only way for their ancestral lifestyle to survive is if the tribe is united. "We must remember to mix properly," the chief tells the tribe at every festival. He has seen neighboring longhouses fall apart at the mercy of cliques and gossip. "Sometimes at night, those people don't even come out to talk," he tells me, shaking his head. "They just stay inside all night." Sounds like New York, I tell him. That won't happen here, he says. Not in his longhouse. Not while he is still chief.

## Longhouse in the Big City

Back in Singapore, our budding commune resumed the daily hangout sessions we loved in DC. At night after work, Rudy and Jeremy discuss the best strategies for dealing with difficult colleagues while Melissa updates me on a friend's love life. We're naturals, I think to myself.

Unfortunately, creating a longhouse of our own proved to be more problematic. We considered pooling our incomes and finding a place we could all share. But a longhouse in the big city, we learned, was hard to come by. Legally, there were other hurdles we couldn't cross. No landlord in Singapore was keen to lease a place to two unrelated families of four adults and three kids. Even architecturally speaking, it was hard to find a home that would accommodate our needs: large, shared spaces but bedrooms distant enough that we would have some privacy.

We decided on an arrangement that would allow us to live separately but close enough to maintain a sense of community, an apartment across the street from each other, just like we had in DC. We called our little commune a Kampung, Malay for village, and tried to reap the financial, psychological, and educational benefits of a communal house, from separate homes. This time, however, we merged more of our lives together. We split bills, babysitting, and dinners. We put the kids in the same preschool and carpooled to extracurriculars. During school holidays, we took turns ferrying the kids on little field trips to the zoo and the aquarium. Socializing with each other was our default schedule. Every Wednesday, the adults went out to dinner while the kids ordered pizza. We took turns cooking for each other on Sundays and supervised sleepovers for the kids once a month. A few times a week, when we worked from home, we would set up shop together on someone's dining table or at a cafe and keep each other company through the slog of meetings.

The ratio of kids to adults meant that we, like the Iban, had more hands on deck at all times. I took the kids to Chinese classes on Thursdays and hosted playdates on Fridays to free up Melissa to work as a director at the theater company she started. On Saturdays, Melissa often organized a homeschool science lesson that gave me precious weekend time to myself. Rudy was our head entertainer. He played with the kids on an equal level, inventing scavenger games, teaching them to swim, and building forts in our living room. Jeremy was our tribal chief, taking care of the adults so we could care for everyone else. He set the tone for the commune, made sure we got over every argument, and showed up to dinner. He called us out for flaking, kept us from watching too much trashy TV, cooked for us, and fixed all of our tech problems.

But my favorite part of living in the commune was when we were able to show up for the unexpected. One day, when Melissa fell sick while Jeremy was out of town for a work trip, I rushed her to the hospital. When the nurses wouldn't let me go in with her, I explained I was family. When life with small children got overwhelming, as it inevitably does, and I needed to cry or vent, Melissa was there to pour me a glass of wine or take the kids out and give me a few hours of peace and quiet.

We were each other's emergency contacts but also the first people we called to celebrate new jobs and raises. We showed up at opening night for every play Melissa directed, and she brought champagne over to toast our promotions.

Perhaps the biggest beneficiaries of the commune were the children. Ollie, Jay, and Dahlia shared toys, books, and scooters that flowed freely between houses. At night, exhausted from a day of play, they said goodnight to each other across the street through walkie-talkies we set up for them.

Part of what made the arrangement feel like family is that we kept things from getting too polite. Several times I've walked into my living room surprised to find Jeremy and Melissa sitting on my couch or laying out snacks for themselves on our table as they waited for us to finish a phone call or wrap up work. One morning, a friend visiting Melissa looked horrified when Rudy and I dropped the kids off to play with Jay and spontaneously went on a date. "But... when will they come back?" she said. Melissa hadn't bothered to ask.

Like the Iban, we would sometimes yell at—or gently scold—each other's kids. While our discipline styles differed, our values were aligned. I trusted Jeremy and Melissa as parents and knew they were pointing my children toward kindness, compassion, and patience. It felt vulnerable to parent in front of others, but I found the practice to be a marker of the intimacy of our ties and an important opportunity for the kids to learn social fluency—that every house has its rules and that respectful and kind behavior matters everywhere.

Even our parents became pseudo-grandparents to each other's children. On Chinese New Year, Jeremy and Melissa's parents presented each of the children with a red packet full of money. When my mother came to visit, in the pile of presents for my children, there was always something for Jay.

We also argued. A few times a year, we would step on each other's toes. Words came off harsher than intended; amends had to be made. But our daily hangouts inoculated us and, crucially, allowed us to store up enough goodwill to weather the unkind moments. In some ways, those episodes and the reconciliations that follow became defining ones for us. No matter the fight, we always came back to each other. There were dinners to be made and children waiting to be dropped off to piano class, after all. We never once regretted our little Kampung. Jeremy described our arrangement in a column in the local paper: "I'm aware that this is nowhere near approaching normal." But, he wrote, "our lives are richer for it."

# BRINGING IT HOME

Not everyone will be able to implement a joint living situation like ours. But many are trying. People around the world are rejecting the isolation of modern life in favor of communal lifestyles. Co-living startups have tried to capitalize on our craving for company creating dormitory-like housing with ample amenities. Many of these buildings come with built-in hang-out sessions, like weekly movie nights for residents, to foster a sense of community.

You can also, however, create your own community. Across the United States, single parents have joined forces in platonic communes to raise children and split the load. When her marriage fell apart, Kristin Batyke-fer found herself homeless and unemployed. Together with three other women, she decided to create a "mommune," a commune for single moms. Batykefer's videos detailing life in the mommune have been shared millions of times. When she's sick, the other women step in to help with childcare and make her snacks and vegetable soup. When it's her hus-band's weekend with her daughter, she goes to concerts and parties with the other moms. While mommunes like Batykefer's are rare, there is noth-ing stopping parents from fostering communities of our own.

A commune is less a physical space than a relationship status. If the thought of living together spooks you, remember, you can take it as far as you feel comfortable. Even if you skip moving in next to your friends, you can experiment with elements of communal life. You can integrate another family or person into your life in a variety of ways, depending on what works for your unique situation. Here are some ground rules to consider as you begin:

1. **Define Your Search:** Before exploring communal living, it may be helpful to define what level of interconnection you are looking

for. Are you seeking an emergency contact, a childcare swap arrangement, someone to help you with your weekly meal planning or something more? Consider which areas of your life feel overwhelming or like they could benefit from more hands on deck. What are you able to help with? Are there areas you are not willing to compromise your individual needs or vision?

2. **Find Your Tribe:** Like in dating, look around before settling down. You can start a community with anyone—friends, family, or even coworkers. The better you know them, the higher the likelihood of success. Your commune comrades don't have to share your parenting philosophy, have kids the same age, or even send their children to the same school. The most important element is finding people *you* love being around and respect. Look for those who can make even the most challenging experiences more fun merely with their presence. People who you would want to hang out with, with or without your kids present. Shared values and a sense of humor is always a plus.

3. **Test It Out:** When you think you've found the right people, test it out. Invite them to show up when you need help. Drop off your children at their place with little notice and see what happens. Can you exchange babysitting on date nights? Carpools? Take turns making dinner or hosting playdates? Evaluate the chemistry between all parties. Their presence should make your life less stressful, not more. If someone's personality grates on you, keep looking. Unlike a more casual friendship, communes require investment, so take your time finding the right match.

4. **Propose:** When you have zeroed in on your comrades, it's time to make a move. This can happen organically, as you rely on each other more and more, or you can propose it formally over dinner. Skip defining the relationship as a commune if the term will freak

everyone out. Explain the benefits you're hoping to tap into. Ask them what pain points they want to alleviate and see how you can help. Compare schedules and see where the other people in the commune fit in. Generally, these rules become more flexible with time. But as with all aspects of communal life, it's better to start small and scale up as you feel comfortable.

5. **Prenup Rules:** Communal living requires sacrificing some independence for the greater good. You must be okay with giving up bite-sized pieces of control, whether it's over your family's schedule, diet, or parenting style. But just because you live communally doesn't mean every aspect of your life is available for sharing. Like the Iban, decide which areas of your life will be communal and which will be private. As a general rule, if you are creating a commune with people whom you are still getting to know, spell things out more clearly. It is up to you whether your commune will share time, food, lodging, finances, or childcare. Iron out the nonnegotiables. The rest will naturally settle as you implement the commune.

6. **Show Up for the Hangs:** Like the Iban, show up for the moments big and small—the nightly chats are just as important as yearly festivals. Create predictable times where you can hang out as a commune with no agenda, whether it's a weekly dinner, playdate, or lounging to catch up on your favorite TV show. Over time, these hangout sessions will deepen the relationship and give it a closeness that's difficult to come by otherwise. It's very hard to keep up performances when you see each other so often. Stay present through times of boredom, discomfort, and even pain. Think of these moments as a chance to build your social muscles. Remember, these will be the people whom you will eventually want to vent to, cry with, and turn to for advice.

Aim for a fall-asleep-on-their-couch, dig-through-their-fridge kind of intimacy. Even if it doesn't start off that way, weekly hangouts will help you get there. While it's important to show up for the hangs, don't expect everyone to show up with the same amount to give every night. Energy spikes and lulls are to be expected. Be generous in redistributing. Lighten the burden of those around you whenever you can.

7. **Carry the Sick:** When one of the Iban falls sick, their fellow tribesmen carry them on the two-hour hike down the mountain to the closest road to get medical attention. Carry the sick in your commune too. When a fellow comrade is down, take the kids off their hands, offer to cook, or just drop off a meal at their house. Keep track of important dates when your fellow tribesmen may be overwhelmed. If someone has a big work presentation coming up, watch their kids for the afternoon. Draw a safety net around your commune to catch members when they fall.

8. **Give and Receive:** Think of the strengths you bring to your commune. Are there aspects of parenthood that you love? Distribute those talents to everyone in the group. Love cooking? Make a little more for your tribe. Taking the kids to the park? Offer to bring their kid too. I love planning parties and celebrations, for example, and quickly took on that role for all the kids in the commune. I would stay up late, blowing up balloons and coming up with themes, hosting parties, and ordering cakes. I also worked from home, so I could host more playdates than Melissa. She's a fantastic teacher and always came up with science experiments and lessons for the kids. Rudy, on the other hand, loved playing with them. He gladly came up with activities for birthdays and outings. Jeremy put his cooking talents to use for the group, scrounging up meals when we were too tired to cook for ourselves.

9. **Forgive and Move On:** As with any relationship, be prepared to work through moments of friction. When they arise (and they certainly will), handle them with care. Remember that when you are seeing each other this much, there are bound to be misunderstandings. Like in any intimate relationship, you will discover soft spots in your comrades. Take note of things that trigger each other. Step gently around past traumas. Avoid quick judgments and give each other the benefit of the doubt. Deep relationships take time, stamina, and second chances. Take a step back when you need to, but always come back to each other.

## RULE 7

# Make Granny Nanny

### Silver-Haired Pickups

Something was off at the preschool pickup. We had been in Singapore for a month, and every day, I was the only mother waiting outside the school for her kids. Instead, the parking lot was filled with silver-haired grandparents standing ready to shuttle the kids to after-school activities or take them home for a nap.

Around the world, grandparents provide one of the oldest networks of support for new parents. But these ties are eroding. As families become smaller, more mobile and independent, relationships with grandparents become more casual.

In the United States, where nuclear families are the norm, we often ignore grandparents as potential caregivers. Though some parents want and need help, family members often live too far away to be able to count on each other.

However, many grandparents thrive when given a recurring role in their grandkids' lives. Singapore, where grandparents are the

137

primary caregivers to thousands of children, offers an interesting experiment. What happens when you take an island full of grandparents and give them time and access to their grandchildren? The data shows that they naturally step in to help care for kids.

Grandparents are the primary caregivers to half of all Singaporean children at eighteen months old and one-third of children at three years old, according to a 2019 study by the Singapore Children's Society. In the United States, by comparison, grandparents are the primary caretakers of just 4 percent of children.

Over 20 percent of Singaporean grandparents live with their grandchildren. But even those with a place of their own often take over daily childcare duties while parents work. Instead of sitting the kids in front of the TV, many also assume educational responsibilities, helping kids with homework and taking them to extracurriculars. I wandered through Singapore's leafy suburbs one Monday afternoon to watch this play out in person.

It's 4 p.m., and the giggles are flowing. In a brick house under a mango tree in western Singapore, two-year-old Ava Valliani and her seventy-year-old grandmother Irene are dancing and singing, arms open and legs hopping in unison. It's a ritual that kicks off their daily afternoons. Irene reads books to Ava, pointing out all the animals and imitating their sounds. Intently, she watches as Ava finishes several puzzles, clapping in praise when she gets a piece in, pinching her cheeks lovingly when she gets something wrong. Once a week, Irene accompanies Ava to a mommy-and-me Mandarin lesson.

Ava enjoys quality time, and importantly, it's a lifesaver for her parents. Mom Hanyan Goh works sixty hours a week as a policy director for the government in Singapore. Her husband Amir puts in as many hours as an executive at a telecommunications company, plus weekly travel to neighboring Malaysia and Indonesia. Without grandparent help, Amir and Hanyan could never keep their demanding jobs and care for their three kids, ages four, two, and six months.

For Irene, grandparenting is a full-time job. She takes six-month-old Kian to her house for tummy time and cuddles in the mornings. In the afternoons, she picks up Ava and her four-year-old sister Maya from preschool and spends the afternoon reading to them in her native Mandarin and taking them to activities. In return, Hanyan helps her parents pay for household appliances, accompanies them to doctors, and helps them file taxes every year.

Spending time with grandparents is a staple of Singaporean childhood. Even before she had children, Hanyan knew her parents would be intimately involved in their care. She herself grew up in her grandmother's kitchen, playing with her cousins and learning how to make curry puffs while her parents worked late into the evening. Like many young Singaporeans, when it came time to find an apartment of her own, she chose one within walking distance from her parents, knowing that they would need to rely on each other.

While they have disagreements, the mutually binding ties ensure both sides have a stake in keeping the peace. "My parents might say something as a suggestion, but if we reject it, they abide by our decision. It makes it much easier for us to welcome their help because a high-tension situation would affect us both equally," she said.

As much as the after-school care benefits the Vallianis, Irene also loves the time with her grandchildren. The lessons have given her, a former schoolteacher, a purpose.

"Before, I thought I would spend my retirement doing tai chi or taking classes in the community center," she said. But she jumped in when she saw her daughter's packed work schedule left little time for the kids. "Life has gotten more complicated; the demands they face are much more difficult. I'm their help."

The arrangement allows her to get to know her granddaughters more intimately, but it has also strengthened the bond with her daughter: "If I wasn't involved in childcare, seeing her would depend on whether they are busy. They might only visit once a week, and we would not be so close," Irene said.

For Irene, stepping in to care for her granddaughters wasn't a decision she grappled with. Rather, it was expected. The hours she spends planning lessons, chauffeuring, and playing with her grandchildren mean she cannot hold a part-time job or develop hobbies. She has had to sacrifice peace and time to herself to be there for them. But, like so many grandparents in Singapore, she sees it as part of the job. "Of course I do it. You must do your part as a grandmother," she said.

## The Island Test

Grandparenting in Singapore is serious business, partly because there are a lot of them—18 percent of the country is over sixty-five. Grandparents live longer in Singapore, where the average life expectancy is eighty-four years. The country's low fertility rate means all those grandparents can focus their time and attention on a small number of grandkids. Singapore is also tiny. The entire country is roughly the size of New York City, making it easy for grandparents who want to be involved to pick kids up from school and participate in their daily routine. All this makes it indisputably different from most places in America. But, Singapore offers a valuable example of how one country has helped parents tap into their existing family networks for support.

In Singapore, the government underwrites the relationship between grandparents and the nuclear family with cash. It provides housing grants of up to $15,000 for adults who live within three miles of their parents and has created intergenerational public housing where extended families can live together. Singaporean mothers who turn to their parents, in-laws, or other relatives for childcare help are also eligible for a tax subsidy of up to $2,700. These programs show that policies don't always have to reinvent the wheel. By reinforcing existing family relationships, Singapore's government supports its growing elderly population while deflecting childcare costs.

Families certainly need the help. Singapore has one of the world's highest rates of women working outside the home. Grandparent care is a widely accepted childcare solution. Of course, just like in America, there are tensions and disagreements. Parents in Singapore also worry that grandparents are spoiling their children or not giving them enough stimulation. But because parents in Singapore understand that life would be a lot more complicated without grandparent help, they are flexible. Grandparents are so central to the daily functioning of the family that they were even excluded from Singapore's COVID-19 social distancing laws, some of the strictest in the world. During the peak of the pandemic, the government even limited the number of guests allowed per household. There was one exception: grandparents.

Grandparents benefit from these arrangements in more ways than one. Their visits are not limited to once-a-year holiday dinners. Instead, they braid their grandchildren into their daily lives. Their grandkids visit markets with them, get to know their friends and attend religious services together. They watch and learn as their grandparents play games like mahjong or cards with friends. The time together offers a crucial opportunity to pass on hobbies, customs, and even languages to the next generation. In Singapore, there's also a financial benefit. In return for childcare, parents often pay grandparents a monthly stipend of 10 percent of their income to help with expenses. Some studies show that up to 80 percent of Singaporean elders receive this financial stipend. The Singaporean government does not leave this practice up to the goodwill of its citizens. Adults who refuse to help their elderly parents with expenses can be sued in court.

Many in America would balk at the notion of being forced to pay Grandma a weekly allowance to watch her grandkid. But in Asia, the stipend contributes to a cycle of reciprocal exchange that continues for generations. Grandparents who provide childcare in their sixties are often repaid through eldercare in their eighties. Children who receive care in childhood become caregivers as adults.

Or as a 2019 study on intergenerational solidarity in Singapore put it, "The physical and emotional support from grandmothers by taking care of their grandchildren and the economic support to the grandmothers from their children shows [a] mutual exchange of services."

This dynamic can be traced back to the time of Confucius. The Chinese philosopher argued that each generation has a responsibility within the family. To this day, the cultural expectation that elders hold the family together instills a sense of purpose that Singaporean grandparents do not take lightly.

## Made to Grandparent

The role of grandparents in Singapore may seem like an anomaly to many American parents, but it would make sense to our hunter-gatherer ancestors. In fact, researchers have found that the transfer of resources from older to younger members of society was essential to our survival as a species.

In 2022, anthropologists Raziel Davison and Michael Gurven were trying to answer a delicate question. What was the evolutionary purpose of grandparents? Unlike other primates, humans continue to age well beyond reproductive maturity. Why did these men and women, no longer able to reproduce, survive to old age?

Analyzing hunter-gatherer societies, they found that the contribution of older adults was so crucial to group survival that it may have caused the human lifespan to adapt. Elderly members of hunter-gatherer communities trained other members to forage for food more effectively. They shared their own surplus food with more vulnerable members, improving fertility amongst women and the survival of infants.

"Because intergenerational transfers of adult surpluses can increase the fertility and survival of others (especially the young), these indirect fitness contributions could drive selection for survival well beyond ages of reproductive cessation," the researchers wrote in a 2022 paper. Grandparents, in other words, survived because their contributions were essential.

The reciprocal sharing of food, resources, caregiving, and information between generations is still widespread among hunter-gatherer societies. Even today, most older peoples in Asia, Africa, Latin America, and the Caribbean—populations that emphasize the collective over the individual—live with children or extended families. It makes logical sense: as our ancestors understood, sticking together and pooling our resources helps us survive.

But in the United States and Western Europe, where independence is prized, we sequester ourselves in nuclear-family households and retire elderly family members from our communities. We turn to Google for knowledge and let hospices care for our elders in old age.

Even those who aren't sent to a home are often isolated from the rest of their families. The United States is one of the most mobile countries in the world, with nearly a quarter of Americans reporting in 2013 that they have moved at least once in the last five years.

Not only does that force the 30 percent of elderly Americans who live alone to fend for themselves, but it leaves young parents in a bind. As we chase careers that take us far from home, we often are forced to choose between our wallets and our families. But the career ladders we climb as young adults can turn on us when kids enter the picture and we find ourselves isolated from our support networks. Too often in these cases, parenthood becomes a one-person job.

## A Word on Boundaries

For many Americans, the idea of having grandparents involved in the daily care of their children seems like it would produce more conflict than it's worth. But part of the problem is that Americans have little training on how to live in extended communities with people of varying opinions, habits, interests, and, of course, ages. Accommodating the values of different generations takes flexibility and compromise, hard skills to master, especially when we don't get much practice.

That's truer now than ever before. Nearly one-third of Americans are estranged from some member of their family. In fact, American parents are twice as likely as their Israeli, German, and Spanish counterparts to have contentious relationships with their adult children.

If a family member or friend disagrees with our beliefs or lifestyle, we are quick to cut them off or label them toxic. We can filter out friends who don't share our interests online and replace them with virtual communities that align with our political and social identities.

The problem is that an online sense of belonging does not translate into real-world support. In other words, your Subreddit is unlikely to take care of you when you're sick, old, or, in the case of new parents, overwhelmed.

"In the United States, we are working so hard at developing our identities, and who is in and who is out, cutting off toxic people, establishing our boundaries, and not being triggered. My feeling is that it has, in general, been a loss for society," said Josh Coleman, a psychologist specializing in family estrangement. "We are becoming more and more atomized, more torn apart, and I think the high rates of loneliness, depression, and rising rates of mental illness are a testament to that."

I'm not suggesting you should bring grandparents into your daily family life at all costs. Of course, sometimes cutting grandparents out of the picture is the best option for your family. Multiple studies show that increasing contact with grandparents who don't share an affinity with their grandchildren is psychologically harmful. Plenty of people have children only to rediscover unsavory elements of their own upbringings that they have to work through.

Even for families that have not dealt with trauma and abuse, grandparent relationships can be turbulent. The sheer number of ties at play, compounded by existing emotional history, makes grandparent relationships hotbeds for conflict. But understanding how to separate your relationship with your parents and in-laws from your child's relationship with them can help salvage the bond.

Many people grandparent better than they parented and thrive when given a second chance to be involved in a young person's life.

Here again, we can learn from Singaporeans who have succeeded in this balancing act for generations. Boundaries are important. In fact, according to Singaporean grandmothers, they are pivotal to maintaining good relationships. But in Singapore, setting boundaries is not synonymous with cutting people out. Rather, it means knowing how to maximize love and devotion and minimize conflict.

"I never interfere with taking care of [the] children even though I am a doctor. If I want to give running nose medicine to [my] grandchild, [I] will call my daughter-in-law and ask her permission, can I give? I try [my] best to follow," said Sara, one Singaporean grandmother cited in the 2019 study on intergenerational solidarity. "I learn[ed] it's the best way. As a grandmother, my job is to be happy with them, play with them, [I] don't want to discipline them. We just want to be happy." Sara knows where her role as a grandmother begins and ends. She does not make parental decisions or overstep.

Not all grandparents are as astute. I've heard horror stories of grandmothers who want full control over grandchildren's lives and make parenting decisions that should be reserved for primary caretakers. One friend of mine sat across from me at lunch a few years ago, distraught because her mother-in-law insisted her grandchildren call her "mommy."

My own conflict-prone mother-in-law has a hard time accepting our parenting style and sometimes scolds my shy kids for not speaking to her—a form of discipline I believe is harmful to them. At first, I thought our only option was to take away our yearly visits. But taking a page out of the Singaporean grandparents' handbook, I have tried to maximize the good and minimize the bad. Rather than look away or cut her out of our lives completely, we now make visits short and stay at a hotel so that we can leave whenever we feel the situation is devolving. I send her photos and videos of the children and call her so they can chat whenever possible.

My parents and I have also had our share of conflicts. Every year while we lived in Singapore, for three months, we pack up our lives and return to Florida. Inevitably, within a week, the kids fall into all sorts of habits they never have at home. As soon as they wake up, they race downstairs, spending over an hour watching cartoons while my parents cuddle them. Nearly every morning, my mom makes them pancakes drenched in syrup, with sprinkles on top as an added insult. It's a far cry from their oatmeal and yogurt breakfast in Singapore. By the time we get home, all of us are addicted to sugar, have a few extra inches on our waist, and rely more on screen time than I would prefer.

At first, these differences would blow up into major fights. I reasoned that I could not spend nine months out of the year protecting my kids from preservatives and Peppa Pig only to throw it all away when the holidays came. I was tired of being the bad guy, but determined to parent consistently; someone had to look out for the children.

One summer, I decided to stand my ground and issued a blanket ban on screens and sugar. It's hard to say who was more disappointed as I lay down bowls of plain yogurt in front of the kids. The cartoon binges disappeared, but so did the cuddles.

By the end of that summer, I learned my lesson. Instead of trying to force the other adults in the children's lives to follow my rules, I let them love my kids in the ways they know how.

For my father-in-law, love looks like drilling the kids on Chinese flashcards and helping them with their homework. For my mother-in-law, it's phone calls and short visits where she brings out Rudy's old Legos and watches the children play in her living room.

Of course, I always step in when I think something is dangerous or wrong. I never force the kids to do something they feel uncomfortable with just to appease the adults. Still, slowly, I'm learning when to look away, step back, or avoid a lecture when a word will do. Most of all, I've learned that generally, when I prioritize my children's bond with their grandparents, we all win.

Keeping the long-term goal of a strong grandparent-grandchild bond can help us find clarity in emotionally messy times. I try to follow up every no with a yes. No, we cannot stay over for three weeks, but come over for this three-day-weekend instead. No, we cannot watch five hours of television, but why not show the kids this educational program every morning. By proactively suggesting an alternative I am comfortable with, I can guide the grandparents' relationship while ensuring it continues.

After all, the benefits of the relationship to our children are so clear that experts call it "the Grandparent Advantage." Strong bonds between grandkids and their grandparents result in lower rates of depression for both parties. This is especially true for grandchildren raised in single-parent households.

Children who are regularly around older adults with dementia develop better emotional intelligence, including empathy and patience. Introducing multigenerational relationships into your child's life will also expose them to diverse perspectives and knowledge they might not otherwise come across. Community living, as we discussed previously, is a muscle that must be developed. Daily interaction with grandparents can teach kids how to navigate relationships with people of different ages, backgrounds, and beliefs. It also gives them some of their first lessons on caregiving.

Of course, the benefits of reciprocal care are not unique to Asia. In fact, I saw it firsthand when I moved back to Brazil and found that my teenage cousins, who grew up in daily contact with our grandparents, often accompanied them to doctor appointments and bank errands. They knew how to help them up from their seats to minimize their joint pain, fetched water for their medication, and knew their favorite snacks and TV shows. The relationship offered my cousins a crash course on intergenerational love that my American peers didn't learn until middle age, if ever.

Yet, getting the hang of parenting can be hard enough without grandparents coaching from the sidelines. As a gay couple raising two daughters in Florida, Khaleel and Kirk already felt like they were under a societal microscope. "There's this immense amount of pressure to not screw it up. If you do, it looks unfavorably upon everyone else who is coming after," Khaleel told me.

They live a few streets down from his parents' house. When he first brought his daughter Kaia home from the hospital, Khaleel's mom, a retired midwife, couldn't stop herself from criticizing his parenting. "I'd be changing a diaper looking over my shoulder like, 'lord, please don't let me mess this up,'" he said.

But he found that the more quality time the family spent together, the more his parents seemed to respect him as a father. "They saw she was fine, alive, well-adjusted, and happy, so they stepped back and let us parent."

When his daughter Kaia turned four, Khaleel started taking her to his parents' house for a weekly dinner and sleepover. It's a tradition his parents look forward to all week. They spend hours planning the menu, and shopping for her favorite foods and books to read.

"They are so grateful to have that time. I feel like, in many ways, I'm extending their lives by giving them this level of access to my kids. And I'm able to impart generational wisdom to my daughter, stories of me as a kid, or stories about my parents and their parents."

The sleepovers may actually be adding years to his parents' lives. According to some studies, childcare can improve grandparents' cognitive functioning and well-being and even make them live longer. In one study, grandparents who provided childcare for their grandkids lived 33 percent longer than grandparents who didn't. Keep that in mind next time you feel guilty asking Grandma for help.

Caring for grandkids also makes it easier for grandparents to accept help when needed. In fact, grandparents who only received caregiving or support but did not provide it reported more depressive symptoms than those who did, according to a 2016 study that looked at relationships between six hundred children and grandchildren over twenty years.

For many, the coronavirus pandemic brought grandparents back into the fold of the nuclear family. Parents seeking support as they attempted to juggle at-home learning with Zoom meetings often had to rely on extended families for support. Some families, squeezed by rising housing costs, decided to move back in with their parents. By 2021, a quarter of adults in the United States ages twenty-five to thirty-four were living in multigenerational households, nearly triple the rate in 1971.

Others asked grandparents to move closer to them to help with the load. That was the case for my friend Rebecca. When she was pregnant with her daughter, Maisy, her mother-in-law, Robbie, casually suggested she would love to move closer to help. "I was vehemently against it," Rebecca told me. She worried having her mother-in-law close by would only lead to conflict. Then came the COVID pandemic. The daycares that stayed open had three-year waitlists and cost a fortune. So Rebecca agreed to a trial arrangement, and her mother-in-law booked an Airbnb. After a month, she and her husband Chip realized the help was a godsend. Her in-laws agreed to sell their house and move closer to care for Maisy. In return, Rebecca and Chip compensated them with a $1,000 monthly stipend. Not only was this cheaper than any daycare they could find, but it quickly became clear that the quality of care Maisy was receiving from her grandparents was unbeatable. Robbie was invested in her granddaughter's well-being in a way that no daycare worker ever would be. "You know, I had all these fears about how it would go. Is she going to be like an employee of ours because we are compensating her? Will our relationship change to something transactional? But honestly, it's been totally fine," Rebecca told me, three years into the arrangement. When she gave birth to a second daughter, Quinn, her father-in-law also stepped in to help. Rebecca tries to keep the relationship peaceful by checking in regularly and ensuring communication flows. Do they need a break? Are they happy with the hours they are caring for the kids? When they do disagree on issues, like how much sugar the kids should have, they try to address it quickly and openly. "Our relationship has shifted. It's almost like we are a communal unit built around the girls."

## When Granny Isn't Available

Of course, not everyone has the option of living close to their parents. I know this struggle intimately. When we relocated to Singapore, we ended up moving our kids as far away from their grandparents as possible. Snuggles with Grandma were an eighteen-hour flight away. Watching the bonds between my parents and children strain over a video call broke my heart.

But even while we lived across the world, we tried to prioritize maximizing the time the kids shared with their grandparents. Every month, we saved money and counted airline miles to be able to afford yearly vacations back to America. Both our parents came for month-long stays whenever possible. Whenever a work trip took us away from home, they were the first people we called.

But remember, the elders whom you invite into your life do not have to be actual grandparents or even blood-related, for that matter. If having grandparents in your life is impossible due to choice or circumstance, you can craft an intergenerational chosen family. Consider adopting a "grandfriend" in your neighborhood. Most communities have a host of elders looking for connections who wouldn't mind donating some of their day to help parents squeezed for time. Neighborhood Facebook groups are a great place to find them. Many communities offer Big Brother and Big Sister programs that match an elderly volunteer with a child in need of mentoring or care.

It's clear families are hungry for these kinds of connections. In 2021, Greensburg, Indiana, desperately needed new residents to offset its shrinking population. It created a program called Grandparents on Demand to lure remote workers to relocate. Locals agreed to provide free babysitting services and even fill in for absent grandparents on Grandparents Day at school. In the first week alone, fifteen hundred people applied, according to the local paper.

Generations Child and Memory Care Center in Mankato, Minnesota, also understands the importance of multigenerational relationships for kids. The center combines caregiving for elderly people with dementia and childcare in one facility, with the understanding that both children and the elderly benefit from joint care. The center was inspired by the founder's grandmother, who suffered from dementia but loved being around children.

Many of the activities that are standard at daycares also help those suffering from memory loss. Arts and crafts, pretend play, and music lessons stimulate both groups. The idea was so popular that its infant care spots were filled before the center opened. Families in the "sandwich generation," those caring for elderly parents and young children at the same time, take advantage of the single drop-off while children get to learn how to interact with people of different ages. Today, there is a waitlist for all childcare spots at the center.

There are one hundred such daycares around the country, according to Generation United, a network of organizations that foster intergenerational relationships, but parents and caregivers are desperate for more. More than four in five Americans say if they or a loved one needed to be cared for, they would prefer a care setting where there are opportunities to interact with people of different age groups, according to a 2018 study by the group.

"There are people who will say, 'But I don't want anything to do with my grandparents.' That doesn't mean there can't be a positive intergenerational relationship to support you," said Sheri Steinig, the director of strategic initiatives at Generations United.

Building new intergenerational bonds can be a source of healing for families who are estranged from their grandparents. When creating a chosen family, consider reaching out to older adults who are also estranged from theirs. Sage, an advocacy group for LGBTQ+ elders, allows volunteers to host dinners with older members of the LGBTQ+ community, many of whom have been isolated from their own families and are looking for connection.

"In America, at least from our perspective, we are trying to counter this idea of rugged individualism and trying to do it on your own," said Steinig. "It's not healthy, and it doesn't help."

## BRINGING IT HOME

1. **Invite Them In:** Think through the pain points in your day. Are there times when you could use an extra pair of hands? Whether it's daily school pickups or babysitting for the occasional night out, tap grandparents for help. Start small and scale up. One friend of mine put her father-in-law in charge of brushing her daughter's

teeth before bed. Within months, he took over her entire bedtime routine. Now he stays for dinner.

2. **Map It Out:** Think through the rules and customs of your house. Only involve grandparents in nonnegotiable aspects of parenting once you know they will respect your stances. Steer clear of asks that are time-sensitive, controversial, or too complex. This not the time to convince Grandpa of the benefits of baby-led-weaning or co-sleeping. Some grandparents may see such tasks as an invitation for lectures or criticisms about your parenting style. Instead, opt for simple chores like cooking, cleaning, or laundry. If you ask for help with a task, do not micromanage how it is done. You cannot ask your mother-in-law for help making dinner or shopping for groceries and maintain detailed control over the menu or the brand of ketchup. Be generous in thanking them, and pay them back with lots of cuddles, playtime with the grandkids, and maybe even some financial help now and then.

3. **Let Go:** Give grandparents the space and time to create their own systems of care. Maybe your mother, like mine, favors too much screen time during her visits for your taste. Maybe your father-in-law curses in front of the children. Sometimes, we have to choose what to let slide to both preserve the childcare arrangement and help foster precious bonds between grandparents and their grandchildren. At the same time, abide by the boundaries grandparents set in their own lives. Respect their hobbies, jobs, and activities. Work around their schedule when requesting childcare. Don't assume that they don't have other priorities just because they are retired or that you are entitled to their time.

4. **Encourage Reciprocity:** Having grandparents nanny is not just about childcare. As kids get older, their relationship with their grandparents also develops. Encourage grandparents to introduce

grandkids to their favorite activities and hobbies. Ask grandparents to bring kids along to meet friends or finish errands. Just as you can invite grandparents into your family's daily routine, you can also encourage older children to partake in their grandparents' lives. Give kids caregiving responsibilities early, starting with something as simple as bringing Grandma a glass of water or handing Grandpa his glasses. Ask older children to help accompany grandparents to appointments and keep track of doctors' visits. Digitizing stories or photographs is an excellent way for children to give back to their grandparents and learn about their lives. Remember to model this reciprocity yourself. Take care of the elders in your life. Help them set up routers, organize their medications, find activities, and file taxes. Teach children that the bonds of love and duty go both ways.

5. **Test the Waters:** Not all grandparent relationships are made equal. You are the best judge of the people you'd like to bring into your child's life; your children's psychological and physical safety is paramount. But remember that involving grandparents in childcare does not mean getting rid of all boundaries. For turbulent relationships, start small. A few hours here and there can rekindle a bond as you test the limits of the relationship. Fixing a bike, washing bottles, or doing the laundry are low-stakes asks that can help take the load off. If the children are old enough, put the grandparents on the phone and let them do the talking. Sending photos or holiday cards can go a long way in nurturing a grandparent-grandchild bond, even when you don't want to maintain a relationship of your own.

6. **Find a "Grandfriend":** If involving grandparents in your life is not an option, don't worry. Your children can still benefit from the "grandparent advantage." Start by looking where you are.

Multigenerational relationships can be found all around your community. Are there elderly neighbors who could use a few groceries or even a weekly dinner invite? Does a neighbor need a hand mowing the lawn? Asking older residents for a neighborhood tour is a great way to learn about the history of your area. Involving children in these activities can expand their social circle beyond their age group. Look past your immediate neighbors and see if your local assisted living facility takes volunteers. Children may relish the role reversal in reading a story at a nursing home or helping seniors navigate technology.

## When Grandparents Are Far

1. **Keep Them in the Loop:** Even if your child's grandparents live far away, look for opportunities to weave them into your children's lives. Weekly calls help both sides stay connected between visits. To keep the conversation from going stale, talk to your children beforehand about what they want Grandma and Grandpa to know about their week. Keep grandparents updated on the small milestones and make sure they know when ballet performances and math tests are coming up so that they can ask questions and follow up.

2. **Don't Discount Facetime:** Calls with grandparents don't have to be another item on your to-do list. Virtual caregiving is a reality for many families. Daily bedtime stories over the phone, for example, can give you a few extra minutes to clean up after dinner. With a little guidance, some grandparents can even supervise piano practices and help with homework from thousands of miles away.

3. **Be Strategic About Visits:** Consider the best timing for trips and visits. Some grandparents are happy to fly in when you have

to travel or be away from the children for extended periods. These trips give grandparents a little more freedom to care for children without a parent hovering over them, help bridge any gaps for the children in care, and give parents a much-deserved break.

4. **Celebrate the Big and Small:** Because my children lived far from their grandparents when we were in Singapore, we took every opportunity to celebrate when we were visiting. Birthdays became bashes, with as many balloons as I could blow up. We went fishing on the longest day of the summer and made gratitude trees at Thanksgiving and gingerbread houses every Christmas. Going all-out for these events helped maximize the memories from the time we had together and allowed children to feel their grandparents' presence during many important milestones.

5. **Build Traditions:** Whenever possible, keep visits consistent. Scheduling trips at the same time each year allows family traditions to take root and helps the relationship to build over time. Think of which holidays you can "assign" to grandparents and extended family. These don't have to be major ones to count. Children love traditions, no matter how small. Easter egg hunts, trick or treating, and even planting a tree on Arbor Day can become cherished annual celebrations.

6. **Consider Moving Closer:** Consider whether your current living environment serves you and your family. If decisions made in early adulthood no longer align with your needs and priorities, it's okay to walk them back. Sometimes, it is worth giving up career opportunities and investing in family networks that can support you for decades. Some grandparents are also open to relocating under the right conditions. If that's the case, facilitate the transition as

much as possible by helping them establish medical care, make friends, and find housing. Remember that these bonds are new. They take time, space, and, most of all, patience to nurture. But by bringing grandparents back into the fold of childcare, we are not only getting valuable help and support but also bolstering the foundations of a more interdependent society, where we take turns caring for one another.

# RULE 8

# Shout for Help

## Mary Poppins Arrives

One day, a few weeks after we moved, I went to Melissa's place to use her washing machine. Ours had inexplicably broken, and I was desperate for clean underwear. It was the last straw in what had already been a difficult few weeks for us. For all of its advantages, Singapore had the worst weather I'd ever seen. The country is smack on the equator, making it hellishly hot and humid year-round. A trip to the playground was excruciating. A quick stop at the local market drenched us in sweat.

Oliver was also struggling to adjust. Singapore marked his third move in as many years. He missed his friends, his room, and his toys. The expat life was not for him, he informed us through increasingly loud meltdowns on the street. Dahlia, meanwhile, was constantly crawling toward her death in a house that was not yet baby-proof. More than once, I looked up to find her trying to put her fingers in sockets, digging through a medicine cabinet, or climbing the furniture. But as Rudy dove into his new job, I had to wade through the bureaucracy of our new life—setting up bank accounts, getting local phones, and signing up for school.

One Saturday, Rudy had to work. Hoping to make some headway unpacking the suitcases, I parked the kids in front of the TV when I heard a strange whirl coming from the back of the apartment. The washing machine suddenly stalled and would not turn on. Already grateful for our little commune, I texted Melissa that my laundry and I were on our way.

Minutes later, balancing a load of dirty clothes in one arm, Dahlia in the other, and Oliver clinging to my sweatpants, I hit the buzzer with my pinkie. Melissa opened her front door and walked me into another dimension.

In a more civilized world, she was hosting lunch. "Guys, this is Marina," she said, eyes rising to meet my messy bun. Behind her, a handful of her glamorous Singaporean friends looked up, their legs crossed under silk skirts, wine glasses clinking. I waved hello and, on cue, Oliver peed on the granite floor.

"You need help, Marina," Melissa said sympathetically later that day. She wasn't just referring to the unwashed clothes, or for that matter, the unwashed children. Since the coronavirus pandemic, it felt like I couldn't hear myself think. I couldn't remember the last time I walked down a street alone with no diaper bag to keep track of or sweaty hand to grip.

The contrast between us was jarring. Melissa still felt like a whole person. She had a fresh haircut, restaurant recommendations, and political opinions. She was creative, overflowing with ideas for new directions to take her theater company. And God, did she have energy.

Watching her prance from school pickup to work to gallery openings was painful. She seemed to be exactly who she had been when we were friends in DC, whereas I felt fresh from a lobotomy. It wasn't always like this, she assured me. She suffered through postpartum depression and a recovery from birth so complex that it took months for her to be able to sit down without feeling pain. "I lost myself too," she told me. "But I guess when you have help, you find yourself faster." After a few months, with the aid of an extensive support system, she clawed her way back to herself.

The maternal fog hadn't lifted for me or most of the moms I knew. But I had dismissed the exhaustion as the price of motherhood. The fact that nobody was enjoying themselves seemed not just expected but, in some ways, sanctifying. Being miserable was a sign I was doing it right, giving it everything I had. Like many mothers before me, I was doing much of the work alone, even if I hated it. Melissa was not doing it on her own, and she had no desire to. Like so many parents in Singapore, she and Jeremy had a paid domestic "helper."

Children need care everywhere. Who takes on the cost of that care has been at the center of social debate for generations. In Europe, the state funds government daycare and public education. In Latin America, the Middle East, and much of Asia, inequality means domestic help is widely available, affordable, and therefore, socially accepted. For the many faults of these domestic worker systems, in the United States, where paid help is out of reach for most families, the burden of care falls squarely on parents and overwhelmingly on mothers.

But preventing Singaporean women from having to do it all by themselves was deemed a matter of national interest. In the late 1970s, the nascent Singapore government specifically introduced migrant visas to bring nannies in from neighboring countries and direct Singaporean mothers into the workforce. The recently independent nation had ambitions to grow into a global economic hub. They couldn't do that if half the population stayed home.

To lure women to the quickly expanding textile and electronics sector, the government created a subsidized daycare system and liberalized birth control policies. Mothers who worked outside the home received even steeper discounts on daycare programs and tax breaks when hiring domestic workers. It worked. Today, Singapore boasts one of the world's highest rates of women working outside the home. In Singapore, 64 percent of women participate in the labor market, compared to 58 percent in the United States. Women in Singapore are also much more likely, I found out, to be able to have and finish a thought.

Employing a helper let Melissa and Jeremy to work full time. But more than that, it allowed them to cherish their time with their son. Like so many parents in Singapore, they act as project managers, delegating the rote tasks of parenthood to focus on the areas where they each add the most value.

Their helper, Henny, takes on the household cleaning and ferries Jay to and from school. Henny does the grocery shopping, freeing Jeremy and Melissa up to do the parts of parenting that they love and excel at: taking Jay to parks and museums and helping him with his homework. Like any job, they still regularly have to do tasks they don't enjoy. But sharing the responsibility ensures that their time with their son nourishes rather than depletes them.

I, too, wanted a motherhood that didn't make me want to run away from my children. So, I asked Melissa to hook me up with one of Singapore's helper agencies. Later that month, Frelyn showed up at our door, a cheerful Mary Poppins with a Filipino accent. For $900 a month, Frelyn would help cook, clean, and care for the kids.

On her first morning, as I rushed around the kitchen, showing Frelyn where everything was, she ushered me to the dining room and sat me down with a cup of coffee. "What would you like for breakfast?" she asked. The question made me unexpectedly emotional. I realized it had been months since anyone, myself included, had asked.

## Blaming the Babysitter

Of all the topics I've researched and interviewed parents about, paying for help is the most fraught. In America, hiring paid help and talking about it is taboo for many reasons. First of all, caregiving is so expensive that in many circles, talking about it is an affront to families who don't have the option. Others feel that in paying for help, they are admitting defeat in parenthood or diluting their role in their families. Then there's the undeniable legacy of slavery and of forced domestic labor, which haunts the social discourse in America, and rightfully so. In this chapter, I will walk you through how I disentangled my own complicated feelings about domestic work and came to view hired help, when fairly compensated and protected, as not only morally acceptable but essential to how I parent, both in America and in Singapore.

By its very nature, paid caregiving can be a tricky business. As Americans we tend to look with suspicion on transactions that involve exchanging payment for affection. Love and care are meant to be given freely. Money cheapens it. The truth that many parents do not like to admit is that when paying someone else to change their children's diapers or read them stories, we are also often paying them to love our kids.

I learned that the American unease for paid caregiving has been decades in the making. In part, that is because, for much of American history, childcare has been invisible as far as the formal economy was concerned. Even as their own families were torn apart, enslaved Black women were charged with caring for their enslavers' children. In white Puritan families, young girls cared for younger siblings and cousins. In Latino immigrant families, girls known as "little mothers" cared for droves of siblings on city streets. In rural areas, mothers turned to extended family members for support. Childcare was plentiful, but at best unseen and unvalued, and at worst a product of slavery and forced labor.

But with the dawn of the twentieth century, families scattered across urban centers, and mothers began turning to a modern solution: paid help. In cities where people were plentiful, babysitting boomed. During the Great Depression and World War II adolescent girls and boys were hired to look after young children after school while 1.5 million American mothers ventured into the labor market.

By the 1950s, families jaded by the war traded city life for the stability of suburbs. However, many did not realize that leaving the city would mean shedding support networks integral to family life. The shift to the suburbs coincided with a baby boom that nearly doubled the size of the American family. More babies were born between 1948 and 1955 than in the previous thirty years. But who would care for them? Women were urged to leave their wartime jobs and, instead, work full time to optimize family life.

The professionalization of motherhood began. Advertisements at the time urged women to arm themselves with the right tools and products for the job, just like their husbands in the office. But many women found that "labor-saving" technology like washing machines and dishwashers did not, in fact, save them time. Refrigerators helped store food but raised the amount of time spent shopping for it. The dawn of washing machines increased the number of times clothes could be laundered per week. The better her tools, the more was expected of the housewife. Never was there a mention of coworkers available to help lighten the load.

In fact, despite technological advances, full-time housewives in the 1950s spent fifty-two hours a week on housework, an hour longer than their counterparts in 1920. Extra time not spent on housework was quickly filled striving for a new standard of parenting. Separated from their families, mothers began turning to psychology manuals rather than family for advice on how to raise their children. Experts urged women to follow strict schedules and take responsibility not only for their children's development but also for their academic and moral education, and leisure time.

It was a job that you dared not clock out of. The rise of intensive mothering was bolstered by a revolution in child psychology that placed a child's relationship with the mother at the center of their long-term mental health. The 1950s brought about the first studies on childhood attachment theory or the idea that a baby's earliest bonds with their primary caregivers created the blueprint for adult relationships.

British psychologist John Bowlby, one of the fathers of attachment theory, studied the family patterns of "pathological" children and found that broken maternal relationships were often to blame. Working with juvenile delinquents at schools in the

United Kingdom, Bowlby found that a third of young thieves experienced early and prolonged separation from a primary caregiver before the age of five.

While Bowlby focused his studies on delinquent children, his work upped the stakes for mothers everywhere. The absence of maternal love was found to have significant and irreversible mental health consequences, he warned. Therefore, mothers must be "an ever-present companion," he argued, providing "constant attention night and day, seven days a week, and 365 days in the year."

It was a punishing ideal that left little room for a babysitter. A good mother, the narrative went, would never jeopardize her children's safety to indulge in selfish pursuits. It was a job that could not be outsourced.

By the 1960s, isolated from their family networks and left without support, many women were losing it. Their only allies in childcare were paid neighborhood sitters. But the anxieties of the era would soon be projected on this new generation of entrepreneurial sitters. Men's periodicals began to warn families against the dangers of bringing these young, autonomous women into the family home. The babysitter began to be depicted in popular culture as either a vixen, intent on seducing her male boss, or a villain, ignoring the needs of the children to focus on selfish pursuits. "[B]abysitting became a magnet for anxieties about maternal adequacy that spurred exaggerated fears about teenage girls' expanding social, cultural, and sexual independence and authority," writes Miriam Forman-Brunell in her book *Babysitter: An American History*.

Depictions of manipulative or neglectful babysitters were stamped across books and movies. In the 1952 thriller *Don't*

*Bother to Knock*, Marilyn Monroe stars as Nell, an irresponsible babysitter who mentally unravels while caring for a little girl, Bunny. Over the course of the night, the babysitter tries on all of the mother's clothes while she's away, attempts to kill herself, and fights an urge to push the Bunny out a window when the child interrupts Nell with her lover. When the mom comes home, she finds Bunny tied and gagged in bed.

So, maybe skip that date night.

## Lost in Translation

Back in Singapore, Frelyn wasn't destroying our family. She was reviving it. There was a tangible shift after she arrived. Life before Frelyn was tense. Rudy and I were constantly rushed, bickering, and overwhelmed. My time with the children was not intentional and, if I'm honest, all that enjoyable. Like many parents, I was stuck in survival mode, which too often meant my interactions were laced with impatience and annoyance.

After Frelyn, there was less shouting. To my surprise, when I had time to shower undisturbed, run errands alone, or get some work done, I was much more patient and loving with the children. I had space to think through discipline approaches and energy to get through a bedtime story with their many interruptions. When my attention wasn't split between work, laundry, cooking, and cleaning, I started to see the kids less as problems to be solved and more as people to get to know. Over the next several months, our relationship flowered.

Creatively, I came back to life. After years of feeling burned out as a writer, I started having ideas again. I thought up projects and pitched stories. I had enough mental energy to start dreaming of new goals. The experience made me wonder how many books were left unwritten, how many businesses unfounded, and how many harsh words had been spoken, all because we expect parents to do it all alone. Employing Frelyn showed me what is possible when we stop treating motherhood as a solo job and invest in a support team.

As time passed, the chasm between my assumptions about paid help as an American and my actual experience of it in Singapore widened. It wasn't just our family who felt a weight lifted off their shoulders. One friend credited his promotion at work to his family's nanny and gave her a share of his bonus. I personally know of many children who would not have been born if not for their helper's contribution to the family. Many of our expat friends had a "Singapore-third," the third child you would never have in your home country because of the lack of help.

Even though we were thriving with Frelyn, we hesitated to tell our friends back home. Importantly, paid help is prohibitively expensive for the 43 percent of Americans who already struggle to pay for daycare. Still, even my friends who can afford some kind of paid help would sooner spend on the self-care aisle at Target than consider hiring someone to help ease their load. They aren't alone. The average American spends over $300 a month on impulse purchases, including clothing, shoes, and electronics.

I understand their reluctance. It's hard to convince cash-tight families to pay for something our parents and grandparents never had to. But, of course, the care previous generations received was never truly free. It was provided overwhelmingly by women who had little choice in the matter. The share of wives who make as much, or more than, their husbands has tripled in the last fifty years. And while gender dynamics at home and in the workplace have changed dramatically, women still bear the burden of childcare, according to a 2023 Pew Research Survey. On average, wives still do 2 more hours of childcare and 2.5 more hours of housework than their husbands. Even in marriages where wives are the primary breadwinner, they still take on a larger share of childcare and housework.

To see just how fried they are, look no further than the hospital fantasy. For those unfamiliar with it, the hospital fantasy lurks in the back of the minds of many moms. They daydream about being medically constrained. Nothing serious, they assure you. A minor procedure or car accident would do—just enough for them to be forced to rest in a hospital bed for a few days.

According to an ongoing online poll of over five hundred people conducted by Katrina Alcorn, author of **Maxed Out: American Moms on the Brink**, 77 percent of participants admitted to having a hospital fantasy. While revelations of the hospital fantasy stunned readers, many moms were not surprised.

"[F]or them to take a vacation or go to a hotel by themselves, is something they would never even consider. Instead, they dream of hospitals," Gabi Garrett, an occupational therapist and mom coach, explained to Today.com.

When revelations of the hospital fantasy first lit up Internet forums, a few of my friends confessed privately to the same daydream. To be clear, these people don't want a vacation—God, no, not one more thing to plan. They want to be in the only state where they won't be judged for rest, a place where they can have their needs taken care of without simultaneously caring for the needs of anyone else—a hospital bed. Must we be physically incapacitated to feel we deserve time off? Instead of waiting for a small car accident to put us out of commission or trying to shop our way to serenity, why not buy back some of our time?

Financial considerations can sometimes mask more complex hesitations when it comes to caregiving.

Even as I marveled at how much Frelyn helped our family, I struggled to shake off the shame that asking for help meant I wasn't a good mom or was lazy because I didn't want to do it alone. Yet we would never accuse a doctor who employed a team of nurses or a lawyer working with paralegals of negligence because they did not do it all themselves. We assume the opposite—their help allows these professionals to focus their attention on the most critical aspects of the job.

Before hiring Frelyn I worried that by offloading parenting and housework tasks to her, I would dilute my own role in the family. Looking back, that fear spoke volumes about how underwater I felt then. It's true that before she started working for us, my contributions to the family were chained to the daily cooking and cleaning that had to be done. But with her help, I was able to come up for air long enough to think critically about what areas of my life I could—and wanted—to give to my family.

I realized that these fears reduced my relationship with the kids to the chores I did for them. But the heart of our relationship was not the hours I spent doing laundry or cleaning the house. In fact, that labor was too often invisible to the children, who would much rather I spend my time playing, doing art projects, and reading with them.

Like many parents who avoid outsourcing childcare, I also worried that hiring Frelyn would interfere with my relationship with the children and that her love for them would compete with mine. I couldn't have been more wrong. Children always have the capacity to accept more love. When we got home from school, they would race to "Auntie Lyn" to show her their latest projects and tell her how their day was. She painted Dahlia's nails and helped Ollie build forts in the living room. Knowing that they were receiving her care and attention made me more peaceful when I couldn't be there to give it to them myself. Their lives and mine were undoubtedly better with her in it.

Financial transactions, especially in American culture, are meant to be impersonal and clean. But caregiving, it turns out, is made of the opposite. Quickly, as so often happens with paid caretakers, our relationship with Frelyn evolved into something more complex than employee and employer. We celebrated birthdays together, traveled, and cried to each other during times of stress.

The nature of the job practically ensures that love and work bleed into each other. But that's precisely why employers must take extra care to instill and respect boundaries and protections for their employees.

## Invisible Help

That Frelyn benefited our family was indisputable. But there were parts of the arrangement that did not sit well with me. According to Singapore laws, as a foreign domestic worker, Frelyn would have to live with us. We were responsible for her lodging, meals, medical care, and even providing for her personal needs, like shampoo and soap. I felt uncomfortable with the all-encompassing arrangement and unsure how to navigate the power dynamics that were not set up to protect her.

And yet for Frelyn, her salary as a helper in Singapore was triple that of a doctor in her hometown. With the money she made, she was working to break the cycle of poverty for her family. Her salary guaranteed financial independence that hopefully would provide for her family for generations. Within one year of working for us, Frelyn had saved enough to afford a house of her own, an apartment for her daughter, pay for her dad's medical costs after a stroke, and send a monthly stipend to her sister.

Though Frelyn had few protected rights as a foreign worker in Singapore, I knew there was a lot we as her employers could do to ensure she was treated fairly in our home. The caregiving dilemma was one that I had been wrestling with since I was a kid. In Brazil, like the United States, caregiving has a tortured history. Brazil was the last country in the Western world to abolish slavery. From the sixteenth century to the mid-nineteenth century, it produced the world's most extensive system of forced labor, receiving more slaves than any other country.

By the time it was abolished in 1888, slavery had shaped nearly every aspect of Brazilian life and culture. Formerly enslaved people entered into an increasingly unequal economy. With limited access to schooling and education, many of the country's freed Black women returned to the same work they did before the abolishment of slavery, cooking and cleaning in the homes of the wealthy, this time for a low wage. That dynamic continued through my childhood. Until the mid-2000s, live-in maids were so common in Brazil's urban centers that apartments were designed with shoebox bedrooms adjacent to kitchens for maids and their families.

In the mid-2010s a swath of laws were passed expanding the rights of these workers. These laws assured domestic helpers the same rights of employees in other sectors, including unemployment insurance, overtime pay, and workday limits.

When I moved back to Brazil as an adult, the change was undeniable. Though critics warned that the laws would make the employer-employee relationship more acrimonious than necessary, in my experience, the opposite was true. The limits clarified the scope of work for everyone involved. It also, crucially, protected Brazil's seven million domestic workers from abuse.

It is imperative that we protect the rights of the domestic workers we trust with what is most precious to us. Many organizations worldwide are trying to create safety nets for domestic workers and change laws to prevent their abuse. That fight is not theirs alone.

And while caregiving can be so much more than just work, it is a job. Respectful employers must remember that and honor the limits of the relationship as you would with any other employer. That means establishing regular work hours, pay, expectations, and conditions for advancement. That was essential for Judy, a Filipino helper working in Singapore. "I have worked with my employer for almost seven years. They respect my rights as a worker and never make me feel neglected. They show me the value I have for their family," she said.

Sonia, an Indonesian helper who has been working in Singapore for seventeen years, said she appreciated feeling like her employers supported her ambitions and pursuits outside of work. She suggested that other employers can take on a similar supportive role. "Ask them if they want to learn something or improve themselves in some way, like through a cooking class or other activities."

In my own home, I sought to treat Frelyn with the dignity and respect I'd want in a workplace. Some of it was basic. I stuck to a predictable, mutually agreed upon work schedule, making sure her weekly days off were sacred, and ensuring she had ample time for rest.

But we also tried to invest in Frelyn's career, researching opportunities to expand her skills, offering to pay for courses, helping her set up a savings account and financial goals.

Whole books have been written about the fight for rights of domestic workers around the world. This one chapter can't possibly do it justice. But given the complex history of domestic labor, and the abuses that often accompany it around the world, it is all the more crucial that we employ paid caregivers ethically and respectfully.

## BRINGING IT HOME

Paid help is a luxury, but one that should be reframed from an indulgence to an investment. It can protect our mental health, benefit our marriages, and propel our careers. Normalizing the idea of spending money on paid help would go a long way in helping mothers avoid burnout and exhaustion. This tradition, perhaps more than others in the book, is not one that is available to all families. But I encourage you to take a fresh look at your family's budget, minus all the stigma and taboos around paid help, and assess what kind of support you can tap into.

1. **Build Your Team**: Start by defining the term "help" as broadly as possible. Paid help can include not just nannies but someone to help you meal prep, cleaners, organizers, and even one-off personal assistants to help you tackle projects. If you don't have a natural village, there's no shame in paying for one rather than going it alone. This is especially important for families who do not have other systems of support around them. Parenthood is one of

the most draining jobs in the world. Like a surgeon in the operating room, set up a team to help you.

2. **Consider Your Narratives:** As we've seen in this chapter, the history of domestic help is complex and has often been exploitative. As you consider hiring outside help, in whatever capacity, it can be helpful to first process your own assumptions and concerns around it.

   - If your initial response to the idea of hiring outside support is "nope!," take a moment to process the deeper reason behind your hesitation. It could be anything from distrust of relative strangers in safe family spaces to financial constraints, but it's worth naming.

   - Did you grow up in a family or culture where domestic help was accepted, looked down upon, or simply not present? Are there taboos or historical legacies around domestic work that you struggle with?

   - Have you encountered (or lived through) instances of domestic workers being taken advantage of? In what ways?

   - Are you worried that hiring help detracts from your ability to be a good parent? If so, in what ways?

   - Do you feel guilt around hiring help? If so, is this because you feel you're "failing" in your role? Because the money could be spent elsewhere? Because you worry about how it would look?

3. **Clock Out:** Eliminate martyrdom as an option. Burning yourself out to take care of those around you does nobody any good. There is nothing selfish about hiring someone to care for your kids while you care for yourself. Add up how much time you need to invest in yourself to be able to best show up for those around you. Even if you aren't able to hire help to cover all those

hours, consider setting limits to your workday as a parent and make arrangements to ensure you have sufficient time off. Schedule times to take care of yourself as you would a work call. Put workouts, walks, and even reading time into your calendar. Show up for the meetings.

4. **Budget:** Paying for help does not have to mean handing your monthly paycheck over to a nanny. Hourly or one-off hires can help alleviate your workload without breaking the bank. If you hate cooking, is there a student chef you could hire once a month to batch-cook some freezer meals? If errands are the death of you, a personal assistant hired online can tear you from the car for a few hours a month. You can also look for options that can give you the benefits of a nanny at a discount. Nanny shares and au pairs can deliver a lot of value for money. Finally, think of domestic help not as a fixed monthly expense but as an investment you will make in yourself and your family for a fixed period. After all, the amount of direct care children require diminishes as they get older, but as older women in the checkout line at the supermarket love to tell you, they are only little once.

5. **Be Creative:** Hiring help in the traditional sense might be outside your budget, but there may be other options to make household labor more efficient and take some work off your plate. If cleaning is your nightmare, perhaps you spring for a one-time investment in a robot vacuum that can tidy while you're at work. Pay a little extra to have groceries delivered to save a run to the store. Or when the laundry pile is so overwhelming you can't imagine digging your way out of it, plan to drop the whole shebang off at a wash and fold. Even if these services aren't part of your regular weekly rhythm, you can keep them in your back pocket for times when work, life, and parenting are particularly

overwhelming. Consider your pain points and get creative about how you might be able to buy back your time.

6. **Define Your Goals:** When your identity and fulfillment are tied to parenting, delegating responsibilities to someone else can feel like you are diluting your role. But while a parent's bond is unique, the truth is that the daily chores and maintenance required to keep a house going can be done by anyone. Define your goals as a parent. What kind of relationship do you want to build with your children? How do you want to be remembered? What contributions do you find most meaningful? Paid help can allow you to carve out time for the important conversations, memory-making activities, and quality time necessary for that vision. Focus on those priorities and delegate as much of the rest as you can. Chances are, your kids will appreciate the time spent with you much more than they will the sparkling floorboards.

7. **Invest in Your People:** Take care of the people caring for you. That means fighting for a system where caregivers have more protections and better rights. It means paying them a fair wage and investing in them as employees. Draft contracts that specify vacation days, notice periods, and time off. Articulate expectations from the beginning and check in frequently to ensure both parties are satisfied with the arrangement. Be aware of the position of power that you hold as an employer and treat those who work for you with respect and professionalism—even (and especially) when they're deeply involved in your family's day-to-day living. Ask the people working for you, even if they are one-off hires, about their financial and career goals. How can you help them get there? When possible, invest in their education with training and courses, help them research new opportunities, build a portfolio or client base, and leave them positive reviews. Think of them not

as people performing a service for you but as members of your team, worthy of investment.

8. **Talk About It:** If you hire paid help, be radically transparent about it. It's past time we dismantle the illusion that we can do it all on our own and acknowledge, thank, and credit the people who help us along the way.

# Abandon Your Kids
# in the Woods

## The Activity Addiction

"Excuse me, ma'am–Don't take this the wrong way, but you gotta watch your kids." The security guard had approached me slowly, like I was an unpredictable animal he didn't want to startle. He did not want to be having this conversation. But he carried on, pointing to my kids. Their squeals of laughter had been echoing through the neighborhood that afternoon as they rode their bikes around a pond in front of my parent's house. Now, they froze, watching mommy get in trouble with the law. "There are some massive cars around here, and they are so little. They could get seriously hurt." As his words sank in, I felt the shame wash over me. Was my parenting so terrible that security had to be called, that a stranger needed to intervene? Had I put my children in danger, all in the name of giving them more freedom? "Wait, I can explain," I wanted to shout. "It's not like that! I'm a good mom! I'm just... I was just trying to do as the Dutch!"

You see, I was attempting to course-correct. Some people have a thing for expensive purses. Others are addicted to shoes. I collect extra-curricular activities. I couldn't see an ad for a kid's after-school class at the mall without handing over my credit card. Chinese theater, soccer, speech, and drama: you name it, my kids have tried it. "How could I say no to anything that could give my children a leg up in their education?" I would ask myself as I dipped into savings for yet another class.

I wasn't the only one packing my kids' schedules.

Today, 73 percent of American kids participate in at least one extracurricular activity. My afternoons were taken up shuttling the kids back and forth from activity to activity, trying to juggle work calls in the gymnastics school lobby or swimming class deck. And while the children learned how to recite Chinese poetry and play nursery rhymes on the piano, they lost a much more primal skill: play.

I started to notice that any time they were not partaking in a scheduled activity, Oliver and Dahlia didn't know what to do with themselves. During playdates or trips to the playground, they turned to me for directions. "What should we do," became a refrain in our house, one I didn't remember hearing in mine growing up. I would transition from driver to entertainer and back again, until I was exhausted.

We were overdue for a break. So, when summer vacation rolled around, I was excited to visit my parents back in the land of the free to give my kids a taste of a real childhood. After teaching them to stop and pull over whenever they saw a car, I let Oliver and Dahlia, six and four, bike around the neighborhood pond.

It was nerve-wracking. My heart jumped to my throat whenever I saw a car approaching. But they got the hang of it quickly, the adrenaline of their newfound independence carrying them through. They lasted approximately three minutes before the security guard came by. Defeated and ashamed, I brought them inside.

Across the world, a group of children were enjoying a very different kind of summer tradition. In the dead of night, a car stopped at the forest's edge, dropped off three preteen kids and sped away. Over the next four hours, the kids, armed with nothing but a map, had to find their way home.

What may sound like the beginning of a horror movie is actually a wholesome summer ritual known in Holland as a "dropping." Every summer, Dutch parents abandon their kids in the woods and drive away. Against all odds and with no outside help, the kids must find their way home.

Sometimes, a couple of parents will secretly trail the kids, stepping in only in cases of emergency. Others arm their kids with a flip phone, just in case. Some parents scout the trail ahead of time, leaving clues and/or breadcrumbs to help guide the children home in a real-life rendition of Hansel and Gretel. But more often than not, the parents try to make life harder, not easier, for the stranded children. They are known to hide behind trees and make spooky sounds in case the kids aren't scared enough.

If other adults see the children, they are expected to let them be. Allowing kids to figure it out on their own is part of the fun. The tradition is a cherished part of Dutch childhood—something closer to a scavenger hunt than a military drill. Kids participate in it year after year, and adults look back on their own droppings fondly.

A few years ago, journalist Genine Babakian wrote an account of her own children's experience that stuck with me. Her Dutch husband and his friend were taking their kids to their annual dropping in the woods when a cop pulled them over. "When the police officer looked into the car and saw five blindfolded children crammed into the back seat, he didn't raise an eyebrow," she wrote. "Oh, a dropping," the policeman laughed. "Have a good time!"

## Dutch Discernment

It's great to be a kid in the Netherlands—and forest droppings are just one reason why. A United Nations study of forty-one high-income countries gauging physical health, mental health, and social development found that children in the Netherlands had the highest sense of overall well-being. Even Dutch babies are happier than American ones. One study comparing babies in the Netherlands and the United States revealed that Dutch infants laugh, smile, and cuddle more than their American counterparts. They are also easier to soothe and less frustrated.

Why are Dutch children so much happier? "Childhood over here consists of lots of freedom, plenty of play, and little academic stress. As a consequence, Dutch kids are pleasant to be around," Rina Mae Acosta, an American mom living in the Netherlands, wrote in her book *The Happiest Kids in the Word: How Dutch Parents Help Their Kids (and Themselves) by Doing Less*.

The Netherlands also has a rich tradition of neighbors monitoring children in public spaces. Catch a teenager acting out, speaking too loudly, or being inconsiderate of those around him, and before long, you'll see an adult reprimanding them. "Doe normaal," a popular phrase that roughly translates to "be normal," is aimed at both misbehaving children and adults breaking social rules. While Americans would balk if their loud phone call on the subway was met with a demand to "be normal," in the Netherlands, the phrase reminds them of the behavioral standards expected of all citizens. It's a phrase of course, that can be weaponized against anyone who does not fit society's narrow definition of what's acceptable.

But it's also created a kind of neighborhood watch that, paradoxically, gives children a freedom American kids could only dream of. As we saw in Denmark, where babies routinely sleep outside, letting your kids off the leash is easier when you know that a whole neighborhood is looking out for them.

Dutch parents are also good at assessing risk, or what they call *relativeren*, without the paranoia and anxiety that plague parents in America. Instead of fretting over the possibility their children will get kidnapped on their bike ride to school, the Dutch save their worry for common, if deadly, risks like drowning and traffic accidents. In keeping with their practical, down-to-earth approach to most things, they dedicate time to arming their children with the necessary tools to dodge the most common threats and leave the rest to fate. It's a skill that increasingly seems to evade American parents, who can be scared to drop their kids off at school, let alone in the woods. But, it turns out there is a logic to American paranoia.

## Caged in America

Before you send your kids off into an American forest on their own, it's good to remember that there are reasons why droppings happen in Holland and not Florida. The Netherlands is an objectively safer place for kids. There, whole cities accommodate children's desire for freedom. Almost 75 percent of kids bike to school, compared to just 1 percent in America.

Biking is a matter of national pride for the Dutch. But the country wasn't always this safe for child commuters. In the 1970s, growing urbanization clogged its narrow medieval streets with cars. The increase in traffic meant more pedestrians dying on the road. In 1971, cars killed more than three thousand people, including five hundred children. The fatalities sparked protests around the country demanding the government *stop de kindermoord*, or stop the child murder.

In response, the Netherlands created interconnected cycling lanes in its major cities. Today, it is home to some twenty-one thousand miles of bike paths. There are even charities to fund bikes for kids who can't afford them and national education campaigns to keep riders and drivers safe on the road.

While cycling in the Netherlands has become safer, trends in the United States are going in the opposite direction. Traffic fatalities have been falling throughout the developed world, but in the United States, they are rising. Deaths involving vehicles reached a sixteen-year-high in 2021, a 10 percent increase from the year before. Even during the pandemic, when car travel fell around the world, car-related deaths rose in the United States. In 2020 alone, road deaths in America increased by 5 percent, while in the Netherlands, they fell by 6 percent. That Florida security guard was right. I do need to keep an eye on my kids—especially on US roads.

American parents are notoriously anxious. But they have reason to be. Compared to twenty of the world's wealthiest countries, the United States has the worst overall child mortality despite spending more on healthcare for children. Children in America are also at higher risk of injury, obesity, HIV infections, and teen pregnancy compared to their peers abroad.

And while gun violence at school is still statistically rare, it is more likely to happen in the United States than anywhere else. America has fifty-seven times the number of school shootings as other major industrialized nations combined. The mere possibility of it terrorizes parents year-round. Every incident is a reminder that kids are not guaranteed safety even in the one place designed for them—school. Minority kids, particularly Black children, face even greater threats, including from police who are tasked with protecting them. There is no shortage of valid reasons for parents to worry about leaving them unsupervised.

For all the talk of American freedom, children in the States are largely caged. American kids are spending less time outdoors than their parents or grandparents. They have an average of just four to seven minutes of unstructured outdoor play a day (but upwards of seven hours of daily screen time). Dozens of studies have linked time outdoors to better health, vision, immunity, and cognitive development. So why don't kids get outside more? One reason is fear. In a 2004 study, 82 percent of moms stated that safety concerns, including fear of crime, prevented their kids from playing outside more.

Parents are also worried their kids will fall behind academically if they fail to hit the books. Nobody likes to think of themselves as a helicopter parent. But in America, intensive parenting has emerged as a logical response, not just to safety risks but to rising inequality.

College graduates earn almost double the income of high school graduates. That adds up to an average of an additional $1.2

million over a lifetime. Who can blame parents for going over their kids' fifth-grade math homework when their grades weigh this heavily on their financial future?

Researchers have found that parenting styles across cultures are determined primarily by inequality. Countries where intensive, achievement-oriented parenting is the norm have more significant gaps between the rich and the poor. In other words, "Permissive parenting is less attractive when the stakes are high," economists Fabrizio Zilibotti and Matthias Doepke wrote in a 2014 study of the relationship among love, money, and parenting.

Parents understand this innately. So many have made it their mission to do whatever it takes to ensure their kids land on the right side of the income gap. Today, American parents spend twice as much time with their kids as parents did in the 1970s, a figure especially astounding when you consider that many more mothers are working outside the home now. Much of that extra time we devote to our children is spent on homework and educational enrichment.

As kids get older, when the arms race of college applications approaches, parenting tends to get more intensive, not less. What was once optional becomes essential. Extracurricular activities, SAT prep courses, and study abroad programs are all but mandatory for college hopefuls. It's a process that has parents across the economic spectrum on edge.

## Operation Varsity Blues

This kind of helicopter parenting is foreign to the Dutch, who don't need to calculate whether badminton or horseback riding looks better on a college application. Students don't exactly apply to college in the Netherlands; they enroll. If they meet a basic set of criteria, including graduating high school, they can snag a spot in one of the country's universities. Enrollment in majors that are widely sought after, like medicine, is determined by lottery. College is cheap and widely available, with an average yearly tuition of $2,500. The lack of stress trickles down, raising the level of happiness of kids from infancy.

In America, by contrast, college admissions represent the apex of helicopter parenting. A college acceptance letter can excuse all tactics and justify all means. A rejection, on the other hand, reflects a failure not just on the part of the student but, importantly, on the parent.

*U.S. News and World Report* began publishing college rankings in 1983, numbering America's universities by the most opaque of credentials, "prestige." But Americans took the rankings seriously. The achievement gap between your child and the neighbors' was suddenly measurable, according to an undisputed authority on the matter. Success was now a number, and parents were willing to go to extremes to climb the rankings.

Colleges asked for well-rounded students, and parents tacked on an extra after-school sport. They called for leaders, so parents pushed their kids into the student council. They sought community-minded volunteers, so parents secured seats for their kids on summer trips to build houses for the underprivileged in developing countries. When universities told kids to jump, parents asked how high.

Whole industries sprung up around the college admissions process. Private tutors, counselors, and coaches promised to help parents get their kids the coveted acceptance letter. Getting into college became an adult's game and one that parents were increasingly willing to play.

Look no further than the Varsity Blues Scandal to see just how far parents were willing to go to get their kids into a university. In 2019, federal prosecutors unveiled America's largest college admittance scandal. They charged thirty-three parents with paying more than $25 million in bribes to admissions officials, athletic staff, and coaches to secure their children's admittance to some of America's top colleges. At the center of the scandal was Rick Singer, owner of a for-profit college counseling business called The Key. The company promised to "unlock the door to academic, social, personal and career success." Singer funneled the parents' bribes to coaches and administrators who designated the students "recruited athletes," increasing their chances of admission, even though many played no sports at all.

Parents, including some celebrities, were accused of conspiring to commit felony, mail fraud, and money laundering, among other charges and some spent months in prison. The scheme was intentionally designed so parents could rig the admissions process while protecting their children's egos. Before the scandal broke, some of the children had no idea their parents had paid for their admissions. "You don't have to tell him a thing," Singer allegedly told one parent trying to get his son into the University of California, according to a transcript of the FBI's wiretap.

But the scariest revelation of the scandal was how relatable it felt to many parents. Of course, most of us aren't spending millions to bribe our children's way into school. But how far would we go to ensure our children's success? Would you call in a favor to secure an internship? Ask a contact to give them a leg up on an interview? After all, even in the adult world, connections are currency.

The scandal forced us to face what many knew to be true: that wealthy Americans, even those playing by the rules, have an edge when it comes to college admissions. As the process becomes more selective and inequality makes a college degree more valuable, many parents feel they have no choice but to double down on anything that might make their kids' application shine.

Of course, the road to a golden application does not come cheap. Parents whose children do extracurricular activities spend an average of $731 per child annually. For families with kids in travel sports teams and music lessons the bill is significantly higher. But it's a cost parents are unwilling to cut. In fact, 79 percent of parents surveyed in a 2021 study said they have gone into debt to pay for their kids' extracurriculars.

That doesn't take into account the time parents devote to these activities. We've spoken about the second shift—time women spend doing housework and childcare after they come home from work. But now, many parents take on a third shift, shuttling their kids to activities between meetings, editing their teenager's essays on the weekends, and finishing science projects long after their kids go to bed.

Then there's the mental toll on children. While intensive parenting may benefit children economically in the long run, it hurts them psychologically. Studies show intensive parenting makes children feel less competent, more anxious, and more depressed.

But once you start helicopter parenting, it can be tough to quit. Take one study by the University of Michigan of over seven hundred employers hiring *college* graduates. One-third said parents had submitted their kid's resume, some without their consent. A quarter of employers reported being contacted by parents urging them to hire their kids. Four percent said parents actually showed up at job interviews.

Many parents want to give their kids more independence but don't know where to start. A poll of parents conducted by Mott Children's Hospital in Michigan found that even though 97 percent said they wanted to help their teens become independent, a quarter of them struggled because when crunched for time, they found it easier to do tasks themselves.

Yet just because both the stakes and dangers in America are higher than in other parts of the world doesn't mean that families can't sprinkle some Dutch parenting into their lives. They just need help learning how to safely step away. Luckily, they can find inspiration closer to home.

## Tips from the Worst Mom in America

Lenore Skenazy has dedicated her career to freeing America's bubble-wrapped children. In 2008, after she wrote an article about letting her nine-year-old son navigate the New York City subway on his own, the Internet dubbed her America's worst mom.

Skenazy embraced the moniker. The slew of hate she received from readers claiming she was endangering her child by letting him find his way home was proof for her that parental anxiety had gone off the rails. Skenazy became an early advocate of what became Free Range Parenting, a movement that calls for parents to foster more independence in their kids. Speaking with psychologists, she found that there had been a shift in American parenting since her own childhood. Parents were engaging in what she calls "worst-first" thinking. They might appreciate the benefits of a child walking to school, but they are quick to follow that thought with a catastrophizing one. If the worst were to happen, they think, I could never forgive myself. Nobody wants to be the parent on television explaining how their child went missing, she said.

It's a train of thought that I've traveled many times with my own kids, and inevitably it makes me hold them closer. "But fear is a terrible prison to live in, for you and your children," Skenazy told me.

Part of the problem, she said, is that we know too much. Parents today can have constant information about their children from infancy through adolescence. We track our babies' breathing, our kid's locations, and our teenagers' Google searches. Many daycares ping parents throughout the day to let them know about their child's every bowel movement, snack eaten, or playground disagreement. "It's somewhere between an ICU and maximum security prison," said Skenazy.

The data gives us an illusion of control over our children that previous generations never had. Once you've experienced that kind of 24/7 access, letting go of it, even to let your kids walk to the park on their own, can feel terrifying. Skenazy realized that childhood independence was something this generation of parents had to be taught.

In 2017, she partnered with psychologists, professors, and other parents to launch Let Grow. The nonprofit, whose slogan is "When adults step back, kids step up," has a curriculum for parents and teachers designed to foster independence in children safely. Parents can download an "independence kit" for their kids with checklists of activities to stretch their children's sense of autonomy, like cooking their own breakfast or taking the bus. The kit also comes with a kid's license for children to carry around to assuage anxious strangers that they are not neglected, just practicing independence.

The program gives parents social permission to let their kids experiment. "It takes somebody else, a third party, a trusted authority—whether that's the school or your kid's teacher to tell you that you can do this, that you're not the only parent, you are not the crazy person." She encourages parents to start small. "We aren't going to get forest droppings soon, but maybe we will get walking to the 7-Eleven or going to the park during the day."

When parents give their kids more freedom, they are often surprised at how capable their children are. Success in each baby step of independence reinforces a child's competence and confidence. But even failures can turn into important life lessons.

American mom Erin Stubbs Braun moved from Alabama to Germany with her three sons. The independence afforded to children in her German town shocked her. Her elementary school–aged son was allowed to walk to stores to purchase snacks during the school break. Her middle schooler could take public transit into town for lunch before attending his afternoon classes. At first, she was nervous about letting her children take the bus on their own. "Now I'm a huge advocate of letting children ride on public transit," she told me. The experience came with a learning curve both for Erin and her boys. But she urges parents looking to give their kids more liberty that it is all part of the process. "They are going to make a few mistakes, but you should let them," she said.

One day, her middle school son fell asleep and missed his stop. He had to walk nearly two miles to make his way home. But he learned an important lesson in responsibility. "Let's just say that never happened again."

Now back in America, she is shocked at how little independence her children's friends have. "It's wild to see. There is a huge difference between them and their American peers. My kids seem so much more mature."

Ying Li grew up with a similar amount of freedom in Canada. By second grade, he was walking home from school alone, his house key tied to a string around his neck. Now living in the United States with his American wife and two children, he's tried to implement a similar culture. His ten-year-old son, Cameron, is allowed to roam his Brooklyn neighborhood freely after school as long as he's home before dark. He doesn't have a phone or an air tag and is responsible for getting himself to piano and soccer on his own.

But Ying stresses that Cameron was not handed these responsibilities overnight. They were gradually introduced, allowing him to adapt and grow in his independence.

"We would observe him and see, is he ready?" Ying made sure that Cameron knew not only his parents' telephone numbers and addresses, but that he was comfortable asking neighbors or security staff at the park for help if he needed it. When walking home with the children, Ying made up a game he called "GPS," where the kids had to guide him home on their own to improve their sense of direction. "You can't throw a kid in the deep end overnight. You have to give them some training wheels." In time, his children learned their way home, and Ying was reassured they were ready for a little more independence.

But, as they began walking home alone, Ying realized they weren't the only ones adjusting to this newfound freedom. "When we started, we would get frantic texts from neighbors saying, 'I just saw Cameron walking around, or I stopped Cameron because he was hanging out in the neighborhood.' And I would tell them no, don't worry about him. He's fine."

Ying realized that like in the Netherlands, Cameron's neighbors in Brooklyn were keeping an eye out for him. Eventually, they got used to Cameron wandering. Some even allowed their kids to join him.

## BRING IT HOME

There's plenty we can learn from the Dutch about fostering independence in our children, without dropping them in the woods. Here's how you can safely and slowly step away from your kids.

1. **Scout Your Location:** Be mindful of where you test your children's independence. Start in low-stress situations that make sense for your child's age. You don't even have to leave them alone to let them taste freedom. Have them order at restaurants and schedule their own doctor appointments. Unstructured play and bike riding can be done with minimal supervision in appropriate places like parks and playgrounds. Learn from my mistake and look for neighborhood streets with little traffic and few hazards. Scale up to busier or more dangerous areas as children grow, pointing out risks they may not be able to see for themselves ahead of time.

2. **Hide Behind Trees:** Allow kids to test their independence by giving an illusion of freedom while ensuring you are nearby in an emergency—but remember to step in only when absolutely necessary. For example, when Oliver turned six, I let him ride the elevator on his own to his after school activities. He was equal parts thrilled and terrified the first day the elevator doors closed and I stayed behind. For the first few weeks I would take the very

next lift up, checking in with the teachers to make sure he made it. One afternoon, I saw he exited the elevator and was headed toward the wrong door, but I stopped myself from swooping in. Instead, I waited for him to make his mistake and watched as the teachers redirected him to the right location. Even when I'm right next to them, I like to practice taking a breath when my kids spill or break something and asking them what they think we should do next. They get to practice problem-solving skills and often come up with creative solutions. Cuts and bruises, both physical and emotional, can be a small price to pay for the knowledge and social skills gained.

3. **Leave Them in the Woods:** Make unstructured outdoor time a priority for your kids. Lessons American parents are desperate to teach their kids—grit, independence, and resilience—may be easier taught in the forest than in front of the piano. Remember, time outdoors is not meant for science experiments, educational lectures on bugs, or organized games. If your kids (like mine) are used to you facilitating play at all times, make sure you bring a book or activity for yourself so they know you are unavailable. Let them be bored and, in time, they will learn to entertain themselves. When I first tried this, it took two weeks for my kids to detach from me at the playground. When they realized I wasn't going to drum up activities for them, they started to venture to the jungle gym on their own. I stayed back and watched as their creativity soared. They thought up games and created make-believe worlds richer than anything I could have come up with. Even when they got into arguments with other kids about whose turn it was to go down the slide or who a toy belonged to, I bit my tongue and let them talk it through. It was uncomfortable, but it taught them valuable conflict-resolution skills.

4. **Drop Some Breadcrumbs:** Like the Dutch, identify the greatest risks to your children, then focus on giving them the tools needed to protect themselves. Knowing how to swim or cross the road are breadcrumbs you can leave to help ensure they are safe even as they grow in independence. Carve out time to teach them the skills that can help them in emergencies. Make them memorize your phone number and address. Teach them to ask others for help if they get lost and identify community leaders, like teachers, police officers, or security guards who may be able to step in, in case of an emergency. Expand their independence only once they have mastered these critical skills. Focus on one skill every six months to keep everyone from getting overwhelmed.

5. **Discern Risk from Fear:** Try to tap into the Dutch discernment and separate your phobias from substantive risks. How likely are your kids to actually encounter the situation you fear? Does it justify keeping them close? Remember that while driving your child to school may prevent the improbable kidnapping, it will also keep them from picking up invaluable skills like learning how to deal with boredom at the bus stop, make conversations with friends walking to school, or navigate home. Be mindful of these tradeoffs.

6. **Tap Their Talents:** Remember that you are not your child. Their achievements are not a reflection of your success and their interests should not be defined by yours. Spend time kindling your child's innate passions. If they are interested in film, make a list of top movies of the decade to dissect together. Get them a camera and let them explore the art on their own. Look out for opportunities to apply these talents in the community, volunteering to help organizations that could use an extra hand. Help them identify mentors in these fields to speak to. Think of these activities as

experiments to suss out a potential profession or passion, not as resume builders for a college application. The time will strengthen your bond and infuse them with a clarity of purpose their college classmates may never know. Even if your child's interests don't blossom into a career, finding a hobby or passion they love is worthwhile and the independence they'll gain in the process is golden.

7. **Find Your Troop:** Link up with other parents who share a desire to give their children more freedom. Banding together eases the transition into independence for both children and their parents. Kids can learn from their more independent friends. Other parents can provide you with the moral support to ease your anxieties as your children scale the independence ladder. Plus, a group walking to school together is safer than a child walking alone.

# Give Your Toddler
# Blue Cheese

## A Daycare to Remember

Once upon a time, there was a daycare system created with working parents in mind—a network of government-subsidized community centers where parents, regardless of their income, could access childcare for as little as seven dollars a day. It was a program that provided six hundred thousand children with free lunch, snacks, and a first-rate education. The quality of these daycares was so exceptional that kids who attended would go on to make more money for the rest of their lives than their peers who did not. As foreign as the picture I'm painting may sound, I'm describing the childcare infrastructure of the United States—at least, the United States of the 1940s.

At the height of World War II, the United States passed the first, and so far only, national childcare program. The 1940 Lanham Act created federal grants for community groups to provide

201

childcare services for as little as fifty cents a day (seven dollars adjusted for inflation). Congressional approval of the network was explicitly tied to the wartime need for female labor. The country desperately needed women to take up jobs once filled by men in factories around the country, and it was willing to invest $52 million in childcare (more than $1 billion in today's currency) to make it happen.

At its peak in 1944, the program subsidized over three thousand centers responsible for caring for 130,000 children. Though that was a small fraction of America's forty million children, it was the largest national childcare program the country would ever see. Following the Allied victory in Europe, the childcare party was over. The Federal Works Agency responsible for the distribution of funds announced it would end the program as soldiers came back from Europe and their wives went back home. There was an avalanche of protests from families who had come to rely on the aid. They sent no less than 1,155 letters, 318 wires, and 794 postcards and petitions urging the program to continue. The government agreed to extend the program, but only through February 1946. Thus ended America's only experiment in federally subsidized childcare. What if it had been allowed to continue?

Across the Atlantic, a similar exercise was budding in a newly liberated France. Daycares had been around for a century as a way to reduce the number of neglected and abandoned children in industrialized cities. These small-scale centers were primarily supported by religious institutions and aimed at poor, working mothers. But in 1945, the country passed the Mother and Infant Protection Act, which tasked the government, not the church, with the responsibility of caring for the country's children. The act paved the way for what would become a crown jewel in France's welfare state: an affordable and extensive daycare system catering to families of all incomes and backgrounds. Childcare was no longer a private problem for families and religious institutions to solve but a public matter. It was a leap their American counterparts would never quite be able to make—at least not permanently.

France's subsidized daycare was cheap. But for decades, the quality was poor, and conditions were sometimes even abusive. Reports of children being strapped to their cribs haunted parents, who were not allowed inside the daycares and had little say over policies. That would change a few decades after the war when a cultural revolution brought the country to a standstill.

## When Toddlers Go Wild

Paris was burning. It was May of 1968, and France was in the throes of a cultural revolution that would forever redefine gender and labor roles. At the Sorbonne, the oldest university in France, student protesters were clashing with the police. Their demands included everything from greater autonomy on campus to the end of the Vietnam War. Workers calling for higher pay soon joined the marches. The protests swelled. Nearly eleven million workers joined the students in a general strike that stopped the country for seven weeks. Nurseries and schools shuttered. In downtown Paris, barricades fenced in the growing crowd. On the streets, children squeezed next to their parents as they marched.

Across town, Françoise Lenoble-Prédine, a teacher living in the suburbs, drove toward the action in search of children. "Parents have to liberate themselves, but the children must be cared for," Prédine recounted in an article looking back on the time. She hopped off the bus at Saint-Michel, the student neighborhood in Paris's Left Bank, and followed the crowd to the Sorbonne, the heart of the protests. Ducking behind the library, she took over an empty storage space at the university, determined to make it a place where children could be cared for amid the chaos. She would need paper for crafts and milk for sustenance, she told the protesters. These materials, along with beds, toys, and books, arrived at her doorstep, and so did the children. Prédine and other colleagues cared for 250 toddlers as their parents marched. Hers was the first of several "wild daycares" set up to care for the children of striking parents. Because she did not have to answer to anyone but the parents, Prédine decided to experiment. She invited not just teachers but also parents into the daycares, a rotating system of volunteers who actively participated in their children's education. Kids were not separated by age but by developmental stage. Similar daycares soon sprouted across protest sites around the city.

One by one, these daycares would be dismantled by police, but they showed that a different kind of care was possible. Demands for wild daycares cropped up around the country, culminating in protests known as the "Daycare Spring." Once relegated to the pickup lines outside their children's daycares, parents now wanted to actively participate in their children's schools. They demanded affordable, quality care—starting at birth.

France answered their calls. The number of daycare spots almost doubled between 1961 and 1971, thanks to a family allowance fund that tried to make daycare available nationwide. Today, more than 1 million children—almost a third of kids under five—are cared for by a government-subsidized daycare or nanny.

The daycares, known as crèches, have become a permanent feature of the family services provided by France's social security program. Even as different administrations have tried to slim down France's welfare state, its crèche system has only expanded. This has contributed to a view of childcare not as a need-based welfare program or a market-regulated commodity but as a right of every French child and their parents.

Today, the French government covers up to 85 percent of the cost of attending daycare. But that doesn't mean parents don't have a say in what happens inside. The local mayor's office operates most daycares, but thanks in part to the wild schools started by Prédine, parents can also choose to send their child to a state-subsidized co-op with other families of their choosing or to hire a state-approved and subsidized nanny. These options allow parents much greater control over what their children learn and how.

May 1968 made childcare political. Who cares for France's children, how, and at what cost would forever be a part of the country's political discourse. Today, the number of students enrolled, teacher salaries, and even what's on the menu is a source of debate for the country's dozens of political parties. "It was the beginning of another way of thinking," Janis Santos, a kindergarten teacher and childhood education activist for La France Insoumise, a left-wing political party, told me. "The way you raise a child is the way you raise a nation."

## The Right to Art, Organic Blueberries, and of Course, Cheese

Lunch is served at Anne Sylvestre Daycare. Today, the chef prepared an appetizer of cucumber sprinkled with mint. The entree offers a choice of pork or fish with blue cheese sauce and a side of creole rice. The children cap off the meal with a cheese course, apple sauce, and blueberries for dessert. It makes cafeteria hot dogs and frozen pizza look downright barbaric.

Menus at French daycares have gone viral on social media in recent years as examples of the level of care provided at government facilities. But the food is just the tip of the iceberg when it comes to services. Some crèches even have resident artists sent to "democratize and integrate" art into the daily lives of the toddlers. The government sees daycare as a great equalizer, where children can be provided the same starting point—exposure to art and organic meals for all—no matter their socioeconomic background.

The daycare system has been cemented not only as a solution for working parents but as an integral part of the country's social policy. "It is important for the child to be introduced to equality of opportunity early on, for their social origin not to be a handicap from the start," said Patrick Bloche, deputy mayor of Paris responsible for education, childcare, and families.

The government views an investment in daycare as an investment in its future citizens. For every Euro the city of Paris invests in a child, it estimates it receives seven Euros in return in tax contribution and productivity. "There is a virtuous cycle. You invest in public funds and get a return in a strong contribution of the population," said Bloche.

Not only do the crèches help provide a strong foundation for all children, but they offer an access point for early intervention services. A psychologist drops by monthly to serve children and parents, and a doctor visits weekly. Many also provide services for the whole family. Tara Maudet, an urban sociologist, worried about women dropping out of the labor force in France because of the lack of childcare. She set up a foundation to build daycares around the city, including the Anne Sylvestre Daycare in the Saint-Denis suburb that offers twelve-hour daycare for kids and includes job coaching sessions to help parents build resumes and apply for work. "A healthy child has healthy parents," explains daycare director Sandra Launet. "A crèche is a place where parents are cared for too."

The government subsidizes the daycare, covering up to two-thirds of its costs. Tuition covers the rest, with parents paying a sliding scale based on their income. Rates start at 30 cents an hour.

"If my daughter weren't in crèche, I would have to stay at home," said Saloua Bakhelal. The twenty-eight-year-old pays seventy dollars a month for her three-year-old daughter to attend the crèche four days a week. The daycare allowed her to hold on to her job as a medical secretary and attend training courses in accounting. The affordable rate means that she and her husband, a food delivery driver, have enough money at the end of the month to save and even go on vacation to her parent's native Morocco every now and then. She beams as she tells me about the trips. "I'm proud to be able to bring my family on vacation. Because I'm working, I can afford it."

The affordable rates also help tip the balance for parents weighing the opportunity costs of working outside the home. "If not for crèche, I would have divorced," said Virgile Quenum, a thirty-eight-year-old digital marketer. At-home childcare for their twin three-year-olds consumed most of his wife's paycheck. But she loved her job and was reluctant to give it up. The tension weighed on the marriage, and they decided to try crèche. Now, they pay $1,200 a month for full-time care for both girls, 30 percent less than they paid for a nanny.

The parents I spoke to understood how essential crèche was to their quality of life and credited their children's care with allowing them to affordably juggle work and family. "When your basic needs are cared for, you can take care of everything else," said Mathilde Duval, thirty-nine, who works as a director of human resources at a government agency while her eight-month-old twins attend the daycare. "With the crèche, we found the best balance."

## Daycare Distrust in America

While France saw daycare as a tool for social change, in America, it remained a private problem addressed with private solutions. Large-scale childcare aid programs in the United States were limited in scope. The Civil War, the Great Depression, and of course, World War II, saw the most significant experiments in childcare subsidies. Still, these programs never expanded to form a permanent, nationwide framework as they did in France.

When the country wasn't at war, daycare was not a matter of national interest. In fact, it was seen as detrimental, sociologist Kaspar Burger wrote in his study comparing the evolution of childcare in America and France.

Throughout the twentieth century, politicians in America portrayed daycare as a threat to the family and in particular, to mothers' authority over their children. The argument was that any government-provided daycare was akin to a takeover of the family. Parents who sent their kids to daycare would be stepping aside and ceding command over their children to the state. It was the stuff of communist nations and, in Cold War America, not something patriotic politicians were eager to endorse. In 1971, an act proposing universal childcare for three- and four-year-olds passed the House and Senate, only to be vetoed by President Richard Nixon for its "family-weakening implications."

In a statement, Nixon explained his reasoning: "For the federal government to plunge headlong financially into supporting child development would commit the vast moral authority of the national government to the side of communal approaches to child-rearing over against the family-centered approach." In other words, daycare just wasn't the American way.

His veto sent a message once again that childcare was a private issue for families, i.e., mothers, to tackle themselves. Institutionalized care was, in the mind of many politicians, an inferior option to the alternative—staying home with mom.

These family policies designed for working fathers and stay-at-home mothers no longer serve us, but they still define our political framework regarding childcare. And though millions of women joined the workforce in the decades that followed Nixon's veto, legislation never caught up. Today, politicians still talk about daycare as a private decision, though 73 percent of mothers work outside the home, according to the US Bureau of Statistics.

Absent a public option, America turned to the private sector for answers. But what happens when you let the market dictate the price of a service so central to social welfare? In twenty-eight US states, full-time infant childcare is now more expensive than in-state university tuition. Childcare in America for a baby comes with an average price tag of $13,000 a year per child.

In most developed countries, the government helps foot this bill. But the United States is an outlier in investment in childcare. It spends only 0.3 percent of its GDP on children two and under, or $200 per child, compared to an investment of over 1 percent of GDP in France. In the United States only the poorest families with kids under three qualify for childcare subsidies. Even so, most families eligible for government aid do not receive it. Of the 12.5 million children eligible for childcare subsidies in 2019, only 16 percent actually got them. That's in part because states have the right to set further restrictions on the subsidies, including aid caps, fees, and income requirements.

And while the price of daycare is prohibitive for most families, tuition barely covers the cost of running a center. Quality infant care requires a small student-teacher ratio, extended opening hours, and college-educated professionals. When prices are not subsidized, too often parents can't afford to pay, and daycares can't afford to stay open.

That has led to a shortage of daycares across the country. More than half of America's children live in what is known as a "childcare desert," where there are as many as nine children and toddlers for every daycare slot. Eighty-three percent of parents with children under six reported serious problems finding quality, affordable childcare in their area, according to a 2018 survey.

Treasury Secretary Janet Yellen summarized the problem in a 2021 speech. "Childcare is a textbook example of a broken market, and one reason is that when you pay for it, the price does not account for all the positive things it confers on our society," she said. "The free market works well in many different sectors, but childcare is not one of them. It does not work for the caregivers. It does not work for the parents. It does not work for the kids. And because it does not work for them, it does not work for the country."

Our threadbare childcare system backs many two-income families into a corner. Working can quickly become unaffordable when you have to fork over all your income to pay the daycare bill. That was the case for Brittney Robey, a teacher who quit her job when she couldn't find affordable daycare for her three children. "I decided it was best to stay home because my salary was not enough to cover childcare for all three of them, so it didn't make sense for me to be working and losing money at the end of the day," she said. Her husband now works three jobs to try and make up for her salary loss.

Kaytie Etheredge Ellis found herself in a similar situation. She spent five years in college getting a bachelor's degree in nursing and then landed her dream job at a prestigious pediatric hospital. Over the next three and a half years, she worked her way up to a position that paid thirty dollars an hour. But after she had her son, she was surprised to find no daycares around her had open slots. She quit her job and lived on her husband's income while they waited for a place to open up at her local daycare. Six months later, when a spot finally opened up, she took a pay cut for a job at a different hospital. But the twenty-four-dollars-an-hour salary was barely enough to cover her son's $1,000 monthly daycare. Now pregnant with her second, she feels she has no choice but to leave the job market altogether. "It's definitely a double-edged sword. We need my income, but at the price of everything else, it saves us more money for me to stay home," she said. "I just worry that my skills and career that I spent so much money and so much school and hard work to obtain will suffer. I wish there were a better balance for sure."

Brittney and Kaytie's dilemma is heart-wrenching but predictable. Millions of families face similar decisions every year. And because men still make more than women in most heterosexual marriages, it often makes more economic sense for women to tap out of the labor force to stay home. In fact, one 2023 study found that a 10 percent increase in median childcare prices would lower maternal employment rates by one percentage point.

The 2020 coronavirus pandemic laid bare that childcare is the linchpin of the economy. With children unable to attend daycare thanks to the virus, parents, especially mothers, left the workforce in droves. As much as we may talk about daycare as a private problem, the consequences of our crippled care infrastructure ripple throughout society, and the bill inevitably washes up at the taxpayer's door. As many as one hundred thousand Americans have been forced to stay home from work because of childcare problems, according to the US Bureau of Labor Statistics. In 2018, those absences cost the country an estimated $122 billion each year in lost earnings, productivity, and revenue.

While daycare in France is seen as a tool to fight inequality, in America, it contributes to it. High childcare prices pull women out of the labor market, depleting family earnings and preventing low-income children from accessing the quality early childhood education of their peers. Children who cannot afford daycare are disadvantaged before they even set foot in a public school. It's not just about memorizing the ABCs. Kids cared for in nurturing environments with low student-teacher ratios and engaged teachers learn everything from emotional intelligence to impulse control.

If the American childcare system was cracked before the pandemic, it is shattered now. Federal aid that kept some two hundred thousand centers alive during the pandemic has now dried up, jeopardizing care for thousands of children. Childcare, one of the sectors worst hit by pandemic lockdowns, has also been one of the slowest to recover. The industry lost some eighty thousand workers to office and retail jobs during the pandemic, a casualty that still has not recouped.

In an attempt to deal with the crisis, President Joe Biden included a provision in his 2021 Build Back Better infrastructure bill to provide universal pre-K in all states. The bill would limit childcare spending to 7 percent of most families' income. But the childcare provision was cut from the bill after it received opposition from Senator Joe Manchin, a centrist Democrat who received campaign funding from several of the country's largest private daycare chains. One of those chains, Bright Horizons, concluded in a 2021 report that any kind of broad-based childcare benefit could "place downward pressure on the tuition and fees we charge, which could adversely affect our revenues." In the end, the infrastructure final bill included zero dollars for family policy programs, childcare, and pre-K or parental leave. And so, a pattern that began over a century ago continued. Childcare in America remains a private problem.

Some parents decided to take matters into their own hands.

Homeschooling became America's fastest growing type of education during the pandemic, and that growth continued even as schools opened their doors and lifted masking restrictions. Many parents traded the rising costs of childcare expenses for home-based learning options where they felt they had more control over what and how their children were learning. Like the mothers of the Daycare Spring in Paris, these parents are demanding more say over their children's care.

Interest in co-op and microschools also ballooned. These alternative schools run the gamut of styles and philosophies. Some microschools are made up of half a dozen neighborhood children, take place in living rooms and do not employ any professional teachers. Others offer a mix of parent and teacher-led learning. Co-ops tend to be more affordable than traditional daycares and demand higher levels of parental involvement.

Sarah Keiger sends her two sons to the Family Preschool in North Carolina, a co-op daycare where parents are required to volunteer one to two days a month. She pays $125 a week for twelve hours of care. Sarah works from home as a social worker and finds that spending time with the children every month at the co-op provides her with precious insight into their day.

"I get to know their friends, and when we are sitting around the dinner table, and they are talking about their day, I can say, 'I know exactly what you are talking about. I played with your friend today, too!"

At Family Preschool, teachers and parents are constantly learning from each other. Sarah takes mental notes of how teachers deal with behavioral and developmental challenges and applies them to her own parenting. She also asks the teachers to incorporate lessons or behaviors that she feels would be valuable to the children, like teaching them to clean up after their meals.

The exchange levels the playing field between parents and teachers. Just like with the wild daycares of 1968, the walls between home and school become more porous when everyone is invited into the classroom.

## BRING IT HOME

France's remarkable network of daycares shows us what is possible when we rely not just on our extended families, neighbors, or communities but on our governments for help in parenthood. Here are some tips on how you too can fight for better, more affordable care for your family.

1. **Reframe the Problem:** The first step in fighting for better child-care is to wrap your mind around the fact that this is not a personal problem—it is a systemic one. Families cannot and should not have to figure out a solution to childcare on their own. Your child deserves quality, affordable daycare. Be their advocate in fighting for it.

2. **Take What's Yours:** Millions of kids who are eligible for daycare support do not receive it. Tap into the funding that is rightfully yours. Childcare.gov is a great resource to find out what programs and benefits your state offers and how to apply.

3. **Fight for Change:** You can influence the type and quality of care your children receive. Don't stand on the sidelines. Like the parents during France's Daycare Spring, find your voice when it comes to your children's care. Meet with your daycare administration regularly. Think through suggestions to alleviate pain points (and fundraise if you have to!). But don't be afraid to speak up for the kind of care you'd like to see.

4. **Call Your Representatives:** Parents from across the political spectrum favor more funding for childcare, but that support has not translated into bipartisan action. Calling your representatives to let them know you would like to see them support expanded funding for childcare is one way to bring this "private" problem into the public sphere. Put your weight behind politicians voting to increase daycare subsidies. Canvas parents at your school and in your neighborhood to do the same.

5. **Go Wild:** Eager to experiment with different kinds of daycare? Take a page from François Lenoble-Prédine and shake things up. Start small—find out how your children respond to different teaching styles by testing them out at home. Consider your kids' personalities and the skills you'd like them to pick up. Many

parents who have been priced out of private daycares are creating local cooperatives with their neighbors. These co-ops are more flexible than formal daycare and allow parents to tailor childcare to their schedules, wallets and preferred curriculum. Neighborhood groups on social media are great places to inquire about informal daycare options. As with anything that is not regulated, investigate health, safety, and quality standards before choosing an option that works for you.

6. **No Parent Left Behind:** The struggle to find dependable, affordable daycare affects families around the country. Look for ways to help your fellow parents whenever possible. Step in to fill childcare gaps for those close to you and help other parents find financial resources that may benefit them. Look beyond chains that may be actively lobbying against federal childcare programs, and if you can, opt for ones that support families from a wide variety of backgrounds. As we learned from the French, childcare is not a problem that anyone should tackle alone.

# Cross the Finnish Line

## Baby in a Box

When she was five months pregnant, Johanna Isopuro received a cardboard box in the mail, the kind you pack when you are unexpectedly fired from your office job. But this one was painted a festive, turquoise blue and adorned with stenciled yellow leaves. Johanna opened it to find it packed to the brim with merino wool onesies, a knit reindeer blanket, a hooded towel with little ears, a fluffy snowsuit, and snow boots puffy enough to keep the smallest toes warm. There was a baby book of nursery rhymes, a stuffed toy, and a sleeping bag. There were also items for her: pads, nipple cream, and even condoms. The box itself transformed into a bassinet, providing an infant with a safe place to sleep.

Johanna was receiving her baby box—a government-issued kit with everything she would need to care for her baby boy. It was a moment Johanna had been looking forward to for months—a right of passage that anointed Finnish mothers for generations.

In Finland, parents look to the government for the time, money, and even the onesies required to grow and care for a baby. Today, Finnish moms who attend at least one maternity care appointment before eighteen weeks are given a choice of receiving a baby box with all the supplies they need to care for their little one or a cash equivalent. Ninety-five percent take the box.

"My mom got the box, and I wanted to have it too because it feels so special. It means I'm becoming a mother," said Johanna. Plus, she added, "Us Finns are quite proud of the box."

There's good reason to be proud. When the Finnish government first started giving out baby boxes to low-income mothers in 1938, infant mortality in Finland was one of the highest in Europe, with 65 out of 1,000 babies dying. Many parents slept with their babies in their beds, raising their risk of sudden infant death syndrome. The box bassinet provided babies with a safe place to sleep and served as a way to lure women to the doctor early. It was also meant to provide women with compensation for the loss of income during their pregnancy and was the only government benefit offered to support pregnant women at the time.

By the 1940s the box became a universal benefit given to all expectant mothers who attended a doctor's appointment for prenatal care. In the years that followed, infant mortality plummeted. Today Finland has one of the lowest rates in the world. More than sixty countries have copied the baby box model with similar programs of their own. These boxes have already been shown to increase breastfeeding uptake rates and decrease babies' exposure to tobacco smoke. Experts stress that the box is not magical. While it provides babies a safe place to sleep, it also crucially connects women to Finland's robust healthcare system, one that will continue to care for them throughout their pregnancy.

## Finns' Favorite Word

It's striking that accepting help is the first public step you take as a parent in Finland. It is a sign not of defeat, but of transition into a new social role—one, it is understood, that will require the support of an entire society, not just a nuclear family.

It's a remarkable norm in a country that prides itself on independence. Tossed among the Swedish, Russian, and German possessions for centuries, Finland has developed a culture of self-sufficiency and resilience. Grandparents drilled into their grandkids tales of how they survived invasion, war, and displacement.

It's a trait so central to the Finnish way of life that there's a word for it: *sisu* (pronounced see-soo) or stoic determination in the face of hardship. The word has no precise translation in any other language. But it is a trait is so central to Finnish identity that the *New York Times* deemed it in a 1940 profile of the country as "A word that explains Finland."

You can sense this spartan self-reliance walking around Helsinki. While riding the subway my translator asked me if silence was alright or if I would like to engage her in small talk. It's not something Finns normally do, she explained, but she could make an exception for me. No need, I assured her. Save for the clanging of vessels on the wooden sailboats lining the harbor, downtown was quiet. It's a place where people mind their own business and solve their own problems.

Even within relationships, Finns maintain a level of independence foreign to most couples in America. All the people I spoke with split their rent fifty-fifty with their partners, even if married. They kept separate bank accounts and planned on dividing childcare expenses evenly.

Still, when it comes to paying for the cost of raising kids, there's no qualms about accepting outside help. Parents are given a total of 360 days of "parental allowance" or paid days off, starting 40 days before the baby's due date for the birthing parent. It doesn't stop there. Families also receive "child benefit" payments until their children turn seventeen. These tax-free payments start at $100 a month but increase depending on the number of children in a family. On average, the government pays $15,000 in parental benefits to birthing parents and $3,100 to their partners.

"It's a lot of work to raise a baby. This aid shows respect to the parents and to the mother who does the work," said Johanna. A yoga teacher with no fixed income, she was still reeling from the fallout of the pandemic. She had to dig into savings and work part time as a substitute teacher to make ends meet. Still, thirty-five weeks into her pregnancy, Johanna stepped away from the mat. The $1000 a month she receives while she's on leave helps to cover Johanna's half of the rent and food for the months she will be home with the baby.

The aid also ensures that women with difficult pregnancies are not pushed out of the workforce. Pamela Jokisalo, a thirty-two-year-old nursing professor, spent the first months of her pregnancy rushing out of class to throw up. She was diagnosed with hyperemesis gravidarum, a severe type of morning sickness that lasted throughout her pregnancy. Pamela was on her feet all day, balancing her full course load with constant trips to the bathroom. "I was just trying to survive," she said.

Fiercely independent, at eighteen she left home and started her studies, working on the side as a supermarket cashier to pay the bills. She loved her job teaching future nurses and was even pursuing a PhD on the side. But by her last trimester, she could no longer endure the strain. "I was exhausted."

Pamela used the Finnish government's forty-day leave policy to step away from work early without losing her job. The Finnish government pays her 90 percent of her average monthly salary, roughly $2,500 before taxes.

Now, just days before her baby is due, Pamela spends her days getting the house ready, while her husband works from home. The anticipation of the last weeks of pregnancy hangs in the air. An empty stroller waits by the front door. A tower of rolled-up diapers—gifts from her friends at her baby shower, sits on the table by the window. A plastic banner reading "Hello baby" is pinned to the wall.

Not only does the money give Pamela the time and resources to prepare for her baby, but it also secures her ability to provide for him in the future. By paying for the cost of Pamela's leave, the government separates her health needs from her employer's bottom line, ensuring she has a job to return to when her maternity leave is up.

"The policy says that parenthood is valued and that it is financially supported. Because the aid is based on earnings, it also says that employment is important," said Anneli Miettinen, a researcher at KELA, Finland's government agency that manages Finland's maternity benefits. When I asked her why she thought parents in Finland go through parenthood surrounded by financial support, while parents in America are left to go it alone, Miettinen paused at the question. Her eyes lowered, and when she spoke her voice was softer, heavier. "It is very difficult to imagine this situation," she said. "I think women would feel so insecure without this support."

## When Parents Go on Strike

While in Finland parenthood is seen as a social good that must be compensated, in America, it is still viewed as a private choice that comes with personal costs and benefits. For a while, this was the case. In agrarian societies, parenthood was an economic investment that benefitted family more than government. Farms with more children were more productive, and parents recouped the time and money they invested in their kids.

However, the Industrial Revolution erased many of these economic benefits. As parents flocked away from the farm and to the factories, children turned from economic asset to liability. A big family meant more mouths to feed, as children spent more time in school and less time growing the family bank account.

Even as their economic contributions fell, children's emotional real estate in the family grew. The amount of time parents, especially mothers, spent caring for, nurturing, and playing with their children only increased with the passing of generations. Parents continued to birth, house, and sustain the next generation free of cost. They were now also tasked with maximizing their children's academic performance, athletic ability, emotional intelligence, and SAT scores.

Society reaped the benefits of better-educated, emotionally regulated, high-achieving young adults. Yet the economic support for parents has stagnated.

Of course, parenting, when it is a choice, is not a solely economic one. There is something off-putting about placing any kind of a dollar sum on love. Critics say that the economic argument for children misunderstands a fundamental aspect of parenthood. Parents care for their children not as investments, but because they love them. The return happens not in dollars and cents, but in hugs and kisses, a moral sense of duty, and the fulfillment of watching your firstborn walk across the stage at graduation.

However, pretending money plays no role in the decision to have kids is an illusion many parents can no longer afford. Raising a child now costs parents a quarter of a million dollars, not including college tuition. That doesn't take into account income lost for parents who drop out of the workforce to care for their kids.

Increasingly, it's a cost parents are not willing or able to shoulder on their own. And thanks to contraception, now they don't have to. For a generation squeezed by student loan debt, rising inflation, and lack of affordable housing, there is just no room in the budget left for kids.

Many Americans would decry the cost of programs like the ones in Finland. But the alternative may be even more expensive. America's fertility rates, already at a record low before the pandemic, are now below the necessary replacement level for a post-industrial economy. A woman in America now has only 1.6 children, below the 2.1 needed to replace her and her partner.

This trend is likely to accelerate. Almost half of childless adults ages eighteen to forty-nine in the United States now say they don't expect to have children, according to a 2021 Pew Research Survey. That's an increase of 7 percentage points from 2018. While there are a myriad of reasons people choose not to have children, the top nonmedical one today is money.

As a society, we fail to see the social and economic contributions of parents at our own peril. When people stop having kids, what was once a personal choice becomes a public problem. The consequences ripple through generations. A shrinking population saps our workforce and eats into our tax base, not to mention our social security system, which after all, is built on borrowed income from future generations. Social security benefits to retired, disabled workers and their families are paid for by taxes drawn from the income of current employees. That system worked well for decades. But falling fertility rates compounded by rising life expectancy means there are fewer current workers paying for a larger number of retirees than ever. In 1940, there were 159 workers contributing taxes to fund each retiree receiving social security benefits. Today, there are only 2.8 workers for every retiree. Officials estimate that at this rate, the program's ability to pay for benefits will run out by 2035.

Fertility norms, once in place, are incredibly difficult—and expensive—to reverse, even with family-friendly policies. It's what demographers call the "low fertility trap." First, there is the mathematical reality that fewer births today mean fewer potential mothers in the future. But demographers have also seen that reductions in fertility can affect norms for generations. People look at the size of the families around them to determine how many children they want to have. Parents who grow up in smaller families tend to want few children of their own. Fertility norms affect not only parents' desired family size but also the material and economic sacrifices adults are expected and willing to make in order to support that family. If their families of origin were used to a certain level of affluence and comfort, it is unlikely that they will be willing to sacrifice that in the name of having a larger family.

It turns out that once people stop having kids, it's very hard to change their minds.

The trap begins, for many demographers, when fertility falls below a rate of 1.5 children per woman. In other words, just below the United States' current level. "Possible action to counteract this trend will have a far greater chance of succeeding if it is implemented soon," one study from the Vienna Institute of Demography warns. In other words, if we want to reverse the trend, we have to act now.

Policy can only do so much, but it's better than nothing. France, with its expansive crèche infrastructure, and the Nordic countries that have generous welfare states and family leave policies, have been able to slow the fertility decline that has plagued many of their European neighbors. However, government support isn't a silver bullet for fixing fertility issues. Even Finland, with all its social support, finds itself battling a fertility rate that hovers at 1.5. But fertility issues can present such a pressing problem that experts agree countries must take some action to prevent even more drastic declines.

We have seen the alternative, and it isn't pretty. South Korea is one example that haunts other developed countries. The country's fertility rate began to drop below two children per woman in the 1980s. By 2018, the average South Korean woman had 0.7 children. It's a population decline faster than that caused by the Black Plague.

As the demographic pyramid inverts, countries look to automation or immigration to fill the void of young workers. But those solutions are incomplete. What to do about shrinking armies, a dearth of innovation, and economic stagnation? Who will pay those costs?

Rather than fix the problem after the fact, economist Nancy Folbre has argued that it is high time society pays parents for the social services they provide. "Because children are social goods that benefit the economy as a whole, familial commitments to children deserve consistent and equitable public support," she writes in her book *Valuing Children: Rethinking the Economics of the Family*. "Current policies have not done enough to help parents meet the growing costs of child-rearing. Indeed, they have, in a sense, exploited parents by taxing the younger generation to help finance the spending of the older generation with little regard for who devoted time and money to raising those taxpayers."

Part of the problem, experts say, is that parents have struggled to fight for change. It's not their fault. "Generally I think parents are the worst at advocating for themselves because they are just too damn tired. It's one more thing in the lives of people who already have too much expected of them," Jennifer Glass, professor in the Department of Sociology and Population Research Center at the University of Texas, told me. By the time they come up for air, it's a problem for the next generation. "It's going to hit everybody, but it doesn't hit everybody all at once," she said. "Until there is a crisis."

That crisis came in 2020. Battered by the pandemic, when the full weight of supporting the next generation was dumped on their shoulders, many parents began to rethink the kind of support they are demanding from their government.

When families simultaneously cried out for help, leaders were forced to respond. In 2021 lawmakers passed a bill to expand the existing child tax credit. American families below a certain income were eligible to receive tax refunds of up to $300 a month for each child under the age of six.

The impact was seismic, affecting education, nutrition, and childcare access. The aid cut the country's child poverty rate in half, to 5 percent, a historic low. Some 3 million children were lifted out of poverty, according to the US Census Bureau.

But attempts to extend the tax credit did not gain bipartisan support and the measures expired at the end of 2021. As the money dried up, the poverty rate for children more than doubled the following year to 12.4 percent.

Still, the effects of the Child Tax Credit lingered. Americans have historically been opposed to European-style welfare programs—and the high taxes that come with them. But the pandemic gave them a taste of what that kind of support feels like. Now that those programs have ended and the aid is receding, the gaps in support are more glaring than ever. Parents from all backgrounds are demanding more.

More than four in five parents say Congress should reinstate the Child Tax Credit expansion, according to a 2022 survey. That support is bipartisan, with 77 percent of parents who voted for a Republican and 94 percent of parents who voted for a Democrat listing it as a priority.

## The Flint Experiment

Leaders in Flint, Michigan, are paying attention. The city, where almost 70 percent of children live in poverty, is implementing the country's first city-wide project to give parents a monthly allowance throughout the first year of their child's life.

Beginning in 2024, any pregnant Flint resident is eligible for a one-time payment of $1,500, delivered halfway through their pregnancy, followed by $500 a month for the first year of their child's life. The program, called Rx Kids, was inspired by similar family cash transfer programs around the world and comes with no income requirements or prerequisites.

But while parental support is widely accepted in Finland, the picture is a bit more complicated in America, where many see government aid as an admission of failure. To combat that narrative, Rx Kids talks not about handouts but about empowerment. The website promotes the cash as "no-strings-attached love." Raising children, the website reminds families, "takes a village of love and support."

Dr. Mona Hanna-Attisha, founder of the program, said that phrasing is purposeful. "We are trying to send a message that this is how it's supposed to be. Having a baby and raising a child is hard for everybody, and it is in society's best interest to care for the future of its nation," she said. "This is how it is in many other countries. When we fail to invest in moms and babies during this critical window, we pay the consequences."

Beyond questions of fertility, or morality, helping children get out of poverty has proven health benefits. Low-income status in childhood has been associated with everything from shorter life expectancy to depression, substance abuse, and infant mortality. But when societies support parents financially, their children benefit via better academic performance, higher earnings in adulthood, and even increases in brain activity.

Flint resident Alana Turner was twenty weeks pregnant with her second baby when she found out about the Rx program. At first, she thought it was too good to be true. But a few weeks after signing up she checked her bank account and saw it had grown by $1,500. The relief was immediate. "I will never forget it. It was completely life-changing," she said.

Alana, who works two jobs to make ends meet, used the cash to buy a stroller, car seat, and start a savings account for emergencies. The aid also means she won't have to rush back to work immediately after giving birth, an experience that left her traumatized after she had her first baby four years ago.

At the time she was working at a hotel that gave her no paid maternity leave. She asked for six weeks of unpaid leave to recover, but a month in, her boss demanded she return to work early or find another job.

Forced to return weeks after giving birth, she said the separation from her newborn was brutal. She was still breastfeeding, having to pump several times a day, and constantly worried about whether he had enough milk at home, where her mom was caring for him. This time around, Alana is determined to have a more peaceful transition out of postpartum for her and her baby. The Rx money has given her peace of mind that she will be able to pay her bills while working one part-time job from home until both she and her baby are ready for her to return. "It feels like a weight has been lifted off my shoulders. I am going back into the workforce knowing I will have a lifeline."

## BRING IT HOME

How can we adapt Finnish financial support for parents in our own lives?

1. **Move to Finland?:** This, dear reader, is where the self-help portion of our book ends. The solutions to these issues, unfortunately, cannot be found within ourselves. Societies invest in what they value. We cannot build an economy dependent on

future generations' productivity and not support parents—the people investing the most in their care. Policies and programs like Rx Kids that recognize both the challenges and the collective contribution inherent in parenthood make a statement. They protect and exalt parents' role as a cherished, cared-for member of society. Fighting for those policies is the only way to ensure that parents get the financial support they need. Absent that, we will have to move to Finland.

# Home Again

THE CHRISTMAS DECORATIONS WERE STILL UP, BUT THE WEATHER was a balmy 70 degrees. We were enjoying our last day of vacation in Florida with my parents before heading back to Singapore. Outside, my dad was barbequing with his best friend, Ozzie, who was visiting for the week. Despite our upcoming departure, it was a joyous day, the kind you want to burn into your memory as it is happening. The kids were splashing in the pool while my mom threw toys for them to catch. Laughter floated from all sides.

I went inside to grab snacks for the kids when Ozzie followed me in. "Can I talk to you for a minute?" I was suddenly worried. Ozzie was like a second dad to me. He had been in our lives since his daughter Ashley and I met and became fast friends in the fifth grade. To our surprise, our parents had become close too. He was there for every birthday and graduation; he took me to my first concert and ski trip.

Standing in the kitchen, he shifted his weight and chewed on his thoughts. "So, what's the plan?" he finally asked. "When are you guys moving home for good?" It was a question that had come up several times during the trip. I repeated what I had told my parents days before. "Honestly, we aren't sure we are ever coming back. We love Singapore." Our lives felt balanced, I explained. The kids were thriving. We lived next to friends who had become family. It would be hard to give all that up. And for what? The difficulties of parenting in America had become clearer to me than ever.

He hesitated and looked at me for a long time before continuing. "I'm going to tell you what I wish I had known at your age. This..." he said, pointing at the scene outside, the kids in the pool, splashing my parents, "It doesn't last forever. You have something really great going here. Don't miss out on it."

His words twisted inside me for the rest of the afternoon. My parents were in good health, but I knew that with each passing year things could go south fast. They had already missed so many of the kids' milestones. Dahlia's first steps and Oliver's lost tooth were not the same when viewed through grainy FaceTime videos. How many more holidays with them did we have left?

A few weeks later, Rudy got a call from his mom. Earlier that evening, while walking to the kitchen to make dinner, she tripped and hit her head against the floor. She was just lucid enough to crawl to her phone and call 911 before passing out. Rudy flew up to see her. At the hospital, while rifling through her medical records, he was shocked to learn she had been diagnosed with dementia months earlier. She had never mentioned it. They discussed her options. She could move into a nursing home, hire help, or come live with us in Singapore. She rejected them all. She didn't want to leave the home she had known for four decades, especially not to move halfway around the world. She insisted she was fine. But a few months later, a handyman replacing the air-conditioning filters at her house heard her speaking to Rudy on the phone and asked if he could have a word. "I might be stepping out of line here," he said, "but if I were her son, I would want to know that this is not someone who should be living alone. She left the gas on two times this month."

Rudy was heartbroken. It was the start of a different kind of caretaking journey, one that would define the next few decades of our lives. We could no longer put off our decision about whether to stay in Singapore. We pondered our options over a bottle of wine, a heavy stillness settling between us.

"I want to be there," Rudy said, breaking the silence. "I want to do it right." I saw that, when the time came, I would want to be there for my parents too.

We sat Jeremy and Melissa down and shared the news. Our Kampung was breaking up. "I guess we have to get a dog now or something," Melissa said, teary-eyed.

So we gathered our things for one final move from Singapore. I packed the lessons I learned from Stockholm to Shanghai with me. But would I be able to use them in America to create the sense of community I had come to admire around the world?

## Frozen at the Popsicle Party

"I'm not sure I can do this," I whispered to Rudy. The air was thick with late-summer humidity. On the playground, dozens of parents new to the neighborhood formed a ring around the swings, arms clinging nervously to their spouses.

It was the back-to-school Popsicle party for new families, sponsored by the Wood Acres Elementary School PTA, and the stakes felt high.

After months of job hunting, Rudy found an opportunity that would take us back to Washington, DC. But this time, we weren't recent grads looking for the neighborhood with the hottest restaurants. Instead, we dove into research on the American school system, trying to find a neighborhood where our kids could experience a Dutch level of freedom and a Mozambican sense of community, but with good schools to boot.

At first, we were spooked by the suburbs, with their empty, manicured lawns and lack of sidewalks. But before long, the school systems lured us in like so many parents before us, and we moved into the most family-friendly neighborhood we could afford, just outside the city. Broad roads, tall trees, stability all around—just what the children needed after years of moving, I thought. Taking a page from the Mozambicans, I put up a swing in our front yard, hoping it would serve as an open invitation to the neighborhood kids.

But to our disappointment, the swing sat empty, except when Ollie or Dahlia wandered over there alone. I walked the length of our block, hand outstretched to meet our neighbors, only to find that most were much older than us. They spoke fondly of raising children on our street, of the good schools and safe roads, but the fog of parenting had long evaporated for them.

For two months, our lives had been a whirlwind of appointments, purchases, packing, unpacking, and endless trips to Target when the Popsicle party invite popped up in my email. We hadn't seen anyone but family in weeks. Our social skills were rusty, and it dawned on me that it had been years since I had been forced to make a new friend.

While the kids happily played with their new peers at the party, I froze. My insecurities bubbled to the surface, and my heart pounded. I felt like I was ten years old again, the last kid to be picked for the kickball team. Gathering my courage, I introduced myself to some families, but I did not know how to navigate past the small talk, and we went home discouraged. I video-called Jeremy and Melissa that night, craving the easy intimacy of old friends.

Over the next few weeks, Rudy and I started to wonder whether we had made a mistake. In Singapore, life was communal by definition. The city, one of the densest in the world, required daily interaction. You couldn't ride the elevator or check your mail without running into a neighbor curious about where you were headed. But in America, isolation was standard. Apps seamlessly allowed us to hire plumbers, order groceries, and even check on neighborhood gossip from our phones. After spending a week locked up in the house, the only sign of life was the daily shove of mail through the slot in the door.

Lying in bed on yet another friendless Saturday, I realized I was waiting for a phone call that would never come. If I wanted plans, it was up to me to make them. I channeled my inner Suki and got to work.

At a back-to-school night event that week, I beelined to a set of parents who had also just moved. That's when I met Jen, a real estate agent fresh from Columbus, Georgia, with a son of Oliver's age. I knew Suki would have invited her over immediately for a playdate. Half our house was under renovation and the place was a mess, but that was no excuse. So I swallowed my pride, baked some cookies, and sent the text.

It was hard to tell who hit it off faster—the boys or us moms. We commiserated over the difficulty of moving, finding new friends, and understanding the school dropoff system. "Where have you been all my summer?" Jen asked at the end of the playdate.

With our friendship established, I decided to take it a step further and put some commune-like events on the calendar. We kept running into each other at school pickup, where the boys would beg for playdates. So Jen and I set up a pickup schedule to take the boys home on alternate days, with a mini-playdate before we dropped them off. It was our version of Mozambique's street moms. One day, I was dropping her son off after school, and she swung by the car and handed me a Greek feta pie. "So you don't have to worry about dinner." A few weeks later, when she caught a cold, I paid back the favor, sending her soup as I remembered the Iban who carried their sick.

Inspired by the Danish moms' groups, I created one of my own. I gathered the parents' emails in Dahlia's school directory and added them to a common WhatsApp group. Dozens joined within the hour. I tried to keep messages short and events optional. The group not only made it easier to coordinate class events, but it also meant that I had all the parents' contact information at my fingertips. I approached friendship methodically and made my way through the list, inviting parents and their kids for brunch and playdates. Like Suki, I tried to be a superconnector and invited moms I thought would hit it off to meet each other. I found a wine bar I loved and decided that would be my regular spot. For two weeks, I cast my net wide and invited rotating groups of moms to happy hours and wine-and-cheese nights. All of them said yes.

With fall came a deluge of flyers advertising more children's activities than we knew what to do with. I tried to keep it balanced and resisted my temptations to sign up for the extracurricular arms race, rejecting robotics and chess lessons in favor of unstructured outdoor time. But I knew soccer would be a great way to plug Oliver into a group of boys in his grade, so I took the plunge.

Though his team met at the school field, parents were forced to escort the kids over, lest they get kidnapped on the way. The paranoia annoyed me at first. Why couldn't a group of seven-year-olds walk themselves to their school field for soccer? But the rule had an unexpected benefit: it forced a group of moms together with nothing to do but watch their first graders stumble over their soccer balls for an hour a week.

On the first day of practice, we all stood around the field, glued to our phones. At the second practice, we talked about the weather. On the third week someone brought a picnic blanket for us to sit on. By October, we were picnicking under the auburn trees, planning girls' night out and brunches. It quickly became my favorite day of the week, and I recognized yet again how regular meetings lubricate social relationships.

These meetings and playdates served dual purposes. They filled my extroverted cup but also meant that the kids did not start school alone. When Oliver looked out into the sea of students at his public school cafeteria, he had a handful of kids he had already played with to sit next to.

We still didn't have the depth of relationships we had in Singapore. But we were on our way.

## Labor Divided

It is usually a bad sign when your husband goes to bed saying another woman's name, but for the first month after we moved, Rudy and I would take turns sighing, "I miss Frelyn." After four years of working for us, her absence was palpable. Breakfast was harried and stressful for the first time in years as we figured out how to handle the morning rush of filling lunch boxes, brushing teeth, and putting on shoes minus one pair of hands. The children, who for years had been impeccably dressed in matching outfits, rolled out the door with whatever clothes they could put on themselves. But most of all we missed the love she poured into the kids, the laughter that echoed through the house in Singapore. She kept in close touch after we moved, calling every Sunday to hear how the kids' week went.

As our housework piled up, we took a tip from the Swedes and decided to divide and conquer. I took over meals and cleaning; Rudy was responsible for bath time, dishes, and decoding Maryland's Byzantine recycling schedule. At first, the gap between our knowledge was palpable. After our first week in the US, I was absent-mindedly running my fingers through Dahlia's hair when they got stuck. Her curls were tangled in knots the size of my fist. "Haven't you been combing her hair after you wash it?" I snapped at Rudy, sitting Dahlia down for a one-hour detangling session. "Wait, you have to put conditioner on *and* comb it?" he asked incredulously.

Like the Japanese men at cooking school, it was time for Rudy to level up. I explained to him the right order of hair washing, how to detangle and dry Dahlia's hair after the shower, and the power of a shower cap on days when her hair was already clean. We went through the minimum standard of a full shower (clean hair, bodies, and trimmed nails). Once those standards were met, I stepped back and bit my tongue to avoid commenting on the mismatched pajamas or the flooded bathroom floor after they were done.

The kids also had to step up and contribute in ways they never dreamed of in Singapore. I drew up a list of tasks Frelyn would have done for them, and, keeping in mind the children I met in Mozambique who were eager to contribute to their households, I doled out assignments.

Rather than forcing the chores on them, I attempted to instill a sense of ownership in the children like the moms I saw in Mozambique did. "You're hungry. I am too! Oh no! It looks like the table isn't set. How will we eat our food?" I'd ask. They would often take the bait, smiling big as they finished a task they wouldn't have been allowed to do in Singapore.

The big prize was the laundry, a low-stakes, high-impact chore the kids loved and I dreaded. I discovered that, with a step stool and some instruction, they could help me load, start, and unload the machines. If I presorted our laundry, there wasn't too much that could go wrong. They loved the beeps of the buttons, the slam of the door, and the independence of pouring the detergent on their own.

Next, I tackled the most chaotic parts of our days—the mornings and evenings. We spent the summer practicing a morning routine that would allow them to get themselves ready for school and an evening routine that got them in bed, teeth brushed and pajamas on independently. I drew a visual chart of what needed to be done each morning and night and made it into a competition between us. Whoever finished their morning routine first chose our breakfast for the day. The first under the covers at bedtime picked that night's story. By August, the children had their morning ritual down, and even if the beds weren't perfectly made, I checked the items off my to-do list and moved on. The routine kept the kids moving without constant shouting or reminders.

If I'm honest, moving to the US also meant lowering my standards for a clean home. Sparkling counters, organized toys, and ironed clothes came at a cost that was too steep for us to bear as a family, a realization I only came to after a few too many sessions of angry tidying. So I set time limits on how long I would allow myself to spend cleaning. If my time was up, I was off the clock, and whatever mess was left would have to wait.

Still, after a month of trying to navigate meal prep, cooking, and cleaning, Rudy and I could sense a burnout building again. But when we looked at our budget, hiring help felt like an impossible luxury. It turns out many other parents were feeling overwhelmed but cash-strapped. On a local Facebook group, I found a post from a neighboring mother looking for someone to split the costs of a "household manager," who could watch the children and do the occasional cooking, cleaning, and maintenance required to keep things moving smoothly. A third family was soon interested, and by splitting the cost three ways, we could all afford a few hours of support.

## Grandparents to the Rescue

Other aspects of our move were easier than expected. Leaving Singapore after four years felt like diving off a cliff into the unknown. Luckily, we had family waiting to catch us. To say my parents were excited about our return to the US is an understatement. When Rudy snagged the job that allowed us to move back, my mom burst into tears. In so many ways our move was prompted by a desire to be closer to them. Now that we were back, we would need their help.

My parents jumped into action. My mom measured the entire house and was my go-to consultant as we filled it with furniture and organized the cupboards. Dad, still a few years away from retirement, took a week off work to help us move in. There were so many aspects to adulting in America that confounded me. He helped me negotiate buying our car, figure out insurance, and discover the wonders of a Costco membership. "I really don't know how to thank you guys for this," I told my dad at the checkout line. "One day, you'll be in a checkout line with your kids while they move in, and I want you to remember this moment," he told me. "Do the same for them." I thought of Albertina in Mozambique, who was raised by her neighbor only to care for her in her old age, their social debt swapping and revolving through the generations. I vowed to do the same not only for my kids but for my parents too.

As we settled in for our first night in our new home, I weighed our to-do list and sudden lack of childcare. I knew I'd have to ask my parents for one more favor. It was time for granny to nanny. "I need you to take them," I told my mom. The kids were playing in the backyard, climbing trees for a better view of their new domain. My mom didn't blink, taking both kids to her house for ten precious days of quality grandparent time while I raced around the city in a whirlwind of errands that would have bored even the most patient toddler to death.

Our move meant even bigger changes for Rudy's mom, who put her house up for sale as soon as Rudy accepted his new job. Rudy helped her look for an apartment nearby. A week before we closed on a house, she unpacked her bags three blocks down the road.

Being closer to his mom meant the world to Rudy, who was finally able to accompany her to doctors' appointments and talk her down from increasingly frequent bouts of anxiety. The children were good for her; whenever they visited, she seemed lighter and happier. Seeing this, Rudy began taking the kids with him for weekly visits that sometimes stretched into sleepovers the children loved. His mom was also available for the occasional emergency childcare, allowing us to dash out for a parent-teacher meeting or quick dinner. We now understood on a whole new level the logic of Singapore's tax breaks for families that live close to grandparents.

It wasn't just Rudy's mom. A cast of old friends and family rotated through our home during our first months back. My childhood best friend visited for a weekend, and my brother stayed for a week. Rudy's aunt came from New York with a suitcase and no return ticket. She lived with us for nearly a month, filling our fridge with homemade tofu, scallion pancakes, and dumplings. Rudy was in heaven with the home-cooked food, and we welcomed the cooking and childcare help. The need for company was now reciprocal.

But accommodating a new family member with her own routines, preferences, and organization doctrine was tricky. I have been told that my obsession with tidiness borders on disease. This is especially true in the kitchen. I spent weeks arranging our spices in matching jars, finding beautiful storage containers for our pantry staples and concealed shelving for our appliances. Few sights soothe my soul more than a clear surface. But for Rudy's practical aunt, the space was unusable. "Everything in this house is hiding! The trash, the fridge, the food, all of it, hiding," she would complain, piling sauces, pans, and cutlery on the counter where she could see them. One day, she hauled a human-sized sack of yeast onto the kitchen island. "You always buy such little portions! This way, you don't have to shop so soon."

On the days when I felt my frustration build, I tried to remind myself that I was simply stretching my community-living muscles. A little pain was just part of the process. The disruptions were difficult for me but barely noticeable to the children, who delighted in the attention of their newfound extended family. Just as we had wanted, they were becoming fluent in the flexibility and tolerance required of multigenerational relationships.

In a culture where self-reliance is celebrated, shifting the responsibility of childrearing beyond the immediate family to include friends, extended family, and neighbors requires more than just good intentions—it demands communication, constant flexibility, and, sometimes, living with a year's supply of yeast on your kitchen counter.

The trade-offs are real, especially in a country with limited resources to support families striving to live more communally. It requires vulnerability—going out to yet another playdate with a potential friend, knowing it may be a flop, or opening up your home and your heart to neighbors, even when you are at your worst. Taking time to nurture these relationships often means putting personal preferences on the back burner and optimizing for the greater good. Moving closer to relatives can curtail career paths. Traveling to see friends can consume budgets. In a place where success and fulfillment are frequently measured by personal achievements, committing to a communal way of life requires reevaluating what it means to thrive, not just as individuals but as part of a greater whole.

But it is possible, even in America. As we settled into our new life, I realized that, despite the lack of infrastructure, rampant individualism, and gaps in policy and community, the United States had something no other country could give us: family. Love is, after all, the scarcest resource. Surrounding your kids with love, whether by blood or bond, and building everything else around those relationships—that's something all cultures can agree on.

# Conclusion

No MATTER WHERE YOU DO IT, RAISING A HUMAN BEING FROM BIRTH to adulthood is challenging. All parents I spoke to, from Sweden to Mozambique, talked about the frustrations and exhaustion inherent in parenting. But none were as desperate for support and understanding as American parents. There was an indignation about their grievances that I did not find in other places, even those where families struggle to get their basic needs met.

In writing this book, I traveled to ten countries and spoke to hundreds of parents of all races and economic backgrounds, trying to uncover an alternative to the American approach. While I don't think any single country has it all figured out, my research crystallized at least one understanding: what American families are trying to do is extraordinary both in time and place. We were not made to parent alone. Both parenthood and childhood were never supposed to be this isolating.

Political, economic, and social trends in America over the past decade have only made it worse. We are more polarized and fragmented than ever before. While we are more connected online, our virtual lives have exacerbated our loneliness and decreased our tolerance, to the detriment of our extended families. Though more women have joined the workforce, they spend more time caring for their kids than previous generations. Meanwhile, growing inequality has raised the stakes. In an increasingly unequal society, a child's academic performance, musical talent, and athletic abilities weigh even heavier on their financial future. Parents are scrambling to do it all themselves, with thinning family, social, and political support. The result is not sustainable.

American parents are not just tired. They are angry, and justifiably so. Unlike in developing countries where families and communities band together to help fill in gaps in care, parenting in America has been atomized to the nuclear family. And while in Europe government policies have sustained families and helped redistribute the burden of care, in America, parents struggle for basic concessions like parental leave and daycare subsidies.

Compounding their frustration is the unrelenting pressure of self-reliance in the United States, which dictates that parents must find solutions to these problems within themselves. Those who need help are reluctant to ask for it because, for generations, family problems were private problems.

It makes sense that parents feel like they are floundering. But they aren't the only ones hurt by the vacuum of support. When we fail parents, society feels the consequences for generations in the capacity of our workforce, the quality of our voters, and the size of our taxpayers' funds. It is high time that parents demand more support than they are receiving. But while we wait for policy to shift, change can start at home.

Reporting on birth parties in Brazil and my own not-so-festive labor showed me the importance of inviting others into our lives, even when things don't go according to plan. My birth party prompted me to turn outwards and ask for help in my bleakest hour. Even for those who don't want guests watching their C-section, the tradition encourages parents to lean on their community through good times and bad as their family expands.

Confinement nurses in China underscored this idea, calling on us to bring our village into our homes, even when they are messy. The forty-day confinement period calls for an essential pause for the postpartum parent to adjust to their new responsibilities from the comfort of their home. The tradition understands that the recovery of the postpartum mom is important for the health of the whole family. You, too, can plan for a period of postpartum confinement, even if you want to leave your house. Delegating chores and creating a nutritious meal plan (that you are not responsible for!) is one way to ensure you receive the rest and recovery that is essential after giving birth.

In Denmark, we learned that letting babies sleep outside is just one way that Danes make space for the ambivalence of parenthood, the push and pull desires to be close to but far from our babies. With the help of support groups and encouragement from postpartum nurses, parents learn to hold on to their identity even as they transition into a new phase. It offers a lesson in self-preservation for Americans who feel lost after the birth of their baby. We should not leave our identities at the door when we become parents. That means investing in our hobbies and passions and introducing them to our children. It requires bringing your whole self to parenthood and not trading your identity for the all-consuming title of mom or dad.

Sweden presented an example of how to strive for gender equality in parenthood from the start by giving spouses room to find their own parenting style and take on equal responsibilities. But even as American parental leave policies struggle to catch up, the Swedish case study illustrates the importance of allowing your partner the time and space to parent. American parents can apply these lessons to their own lives and remember that the duties and expectations assigned in the early days of parenthood have a way of sticking around. Letting your partner learn from their mistakes and create their own systems will encourage an equitable division of childcare long after you return to work.

In Mozambique, we examined what happens when neighbors are invited to parent alongside families. In a country where many struggle to get their basic needs met, community matters. It was a lesson that came naturally for my friend Suki. After we moved in next door to each other in Brazil, I saw that a good neighbor can be a game-changer in the early days of parenthood. Through Suki and the parents I spoke to in Mozambique, I learned the value of stitching together a support network in your neighborhood by having an open-door policy and initiating cycles of help.

Trekking through Malaysia with the Iban tribe, I learned the importance of showing up for hangouts and how communal living can ease the load for everyone. I put these methods to the test in my own little commune in Singapore. Living with Jeremy and Melissa taught me that being close to the people you love is worth sacrificing individual freedoms. Creating a commune does not have to be daunting. You can start small, sharing chores like carpooling or making dinner, and gradually fold in other elements of your life, like housing and budgets if it makes sense for your family.

In Singapore, I watched grandparents actively participate in caregiving and grasped the value of multigenerational parenting.

I also learned the importance of honing communication and conflict-resolution skills in keeping the peace and maximizing the time spent with grandparents. Giving grandparents a concrete task, like asking them to pick kids up from activities or teach them a new skill, is a great way to expand their role in your children's lives. Best of all, caring for grandkids improves grandparents' cognitive function and mental health and boosts kids' levels of empathy.

Parenting in Singapore also showed me the importance of hiring help and expanding my support team. Hiring a helper made me confront the ambivalence I had about domestic help. It allowed me to prioritize my time and attention to show up for my family as a whole person and ditch the martyrdom I had come to associate with parenthood. As I learned from Singaporean moms, there is nothing selfish about hiring someone to care for your kids while you care for yourself. Making a list of your priorities as a parent can help you define what roles you'd like to take on and budget for what you'd like to outsource.

The Dutch tradition of forest dropping—leaving your kids in the woods to find their way home—provided an insight into the benefits of giving children more responsibility and independence. While parenting in America is objectively more risky, parents can learn how and when to back off their kids. Dutch parents taught us to keep safety in mind, phobias at bay, and kids outside.

In France, an extensive daycare network contrasted with a persistent vacuum of care in America. While subsidized daycare systems arose in America, they were snuffed by an obsession with independence and limited government. But the rise of the crèche system in France showed what is possible when parents band together to demand better support. French parents revealed how to take existing aid available for childcare and then fight for more, while maintaining an active say in the care your children receive. American parents don't have to settle for the status quo. They, too, can fight for funding, calling their representatives and supporting bills that expand childcare aid.

Finally, in Finland, we saw a financial support system so robust that it begs Americans to reframe parenting from a private to a public act. Finland shows us that even a country that prides itself on individualism can support parenthood and that accepting help is not an admission of defeat but an integral part of the journey.

The families I spoke to differed in their approaches to child-rearing. Some favored co-sleeping, while others sleep trained. Some parents stayed home. Others worked at the office. Some yelled at their kids, many didn't. Yet similar threads emerged in their advice to American parents.

They agree that parents should take what is theirs and not leave allowances or benefits on the table. That means maxing our day-care subsidies and parental leave, even as you fight for more. Don't be ashamed to rely on the public support already there. Accepting help doesn't mean you are a failure. It means you are a member of a collective society.

These parents had social skills that are rusting in the United States, where we are quick to draw boundaries against those who may disagree with us. The parents I interviewed had daily practice, either due to choice or necessity, in the flexibility required to live in community. When you have to deal with your crazy cousin at family dinners every weekend, you naturally become better at conflict resolution. They showed me that when you increase your tolerance for activities, philosophies, and prac-tices that are not perfectly aligned with yours, you leave room for others to step in and help—whether that's your partner, a grandparent, or even your child themselves.

Parents abroad understand that perfection is the enemy of intimacy when creating community. Allowing others in means letting them see all of you—the beauty and the mess. Don't wait for the perfect moment, mood, or house to invite others in.

Finally, these parents understand that communal life doesn't just happen. It must be curated. Prioritize living close to those you love and investing in the relationships around you. After raising children in three countries and interviewing parents worldwide, I can confirm parenting is much more joyful, rewarding, and fun when we do it together.

# Acknowledgments

I'D LIKE TO EXPRESS MY HEARTFELT GRATITUDE TO THE FOLLOWING people who made this book possible:

To the families across the world who opened up their homes and their lives to me, I am honored by your trust and generosity and hope I have done justice to your experiences.

My agent, Jenna Land Free, championed this book into existence and molded it into a practical, optimistic guide. Her insight never led me astray. Gwen Hawkes at Hachette Go took a chance on a first-time author and immediately understood my vision for the book. Nana Twumasi and the Balance team carried that mission forward with seamless dedication.

Annabella Stieren, Mateus Fotine, Elina Kinos, Miranda Wang, Chris Ningkan, Mehdi Ouldsaad, and Charlene de Wang helped me color the chapters of this book with the most vibrant characters.

Flannery Salkeind showed me that a blank page is nothing to fear and was the best accountability partner I could have asked for. Mary Beth Sheridan and Matt Brown at the *Washington Post* believed in my wildest story ideas—like Brazilian birth parties—and gave me the confidence to carry this project forward.

# Acknowledgments

The Singapore National Library, where many pages of this book were written, became my haven, with views that inspired words. Thank you for the quiet.

Frelyn, Edith, Fatima, Cynthia, Odette, Angela, and Marlene, my "other mothers," helped raise my children and me with unfailing love within unfair systems.

Ozzie, Patty, and Ashley Marchante, my first chosen family, reminded me of the importance of coming home.

Suki Chung, my partner in crime during the early days of parenthood, taught me the art of stitching a community together with generosity and creativity. The commune continues to provide, thanks to you.

CATPT was my first audience, my most honest critics, and the perfect guinea pigs for my tales. Jeremy and Melissa, thank you for choosing us. For yelling at my kids, celebrating the wins, wiping away the tears, making the dinner reservations, arguing until midnight, and committing to the Kampung, even when everyone thought it was weird. You are the embodiment of family.

My wise little brother, Eduardo Lopes, continually surprised me with his insights on parenthood and family. He shaped entire chapters of this book with his thoughtful feedback.

My mom, Valeria, ensured that no matter where we were, our language, culture, and connection to family remained strong. She cheered me on through every journey, even when what she most wanted was for me to come home. My dad, Ernesto, the original storyteller, sparked my love for narrative with every tale. He taught me to always have an exit strategy, how to drive stick, and to never stop dreaming. Being your daughter is a gift I hope to live up to daily.

# Acknowledgments

Ruddy, you promised me adventure and made it our home. I love the story we continue to write.

To Oliver and Dahlia, my constant inspiration. This book is an account of our early years together, full of love, discovery, and the joy of learning who we are as a family. My love for you knows no borders.

# Resources

*Babysitter: An American History Paperback*, by Miriam Forman-Brunell, 2011.

*The Danish Way of Parenting: What the Happiest People in the World Know About Raising Confident, Capable Kids*, by Jessica Joelle Alexander and Iben Sandahl, 2016.

*Everyday Utopia: What 2,000 Years of Wild Experiments Can Teach Us About the Good Life*, by Kristen R. Ghodsee, 2023.

*Fair Play: A Game-Changing Solution for When You Have Too Much to Do (and More Life to Live)*, by Eve Rodsky, 2019.

*The First Forty Days: The Essential Art of Nourishing the New Mother*, by Heng Ou and Amely Greeven, 2022.

*Hanging Out: The Radical Power of Killing Time*, by Sheila Liming, 2023.

*The Happiest Kids in the World: How Dutch Parents Help Their Kids (and Themselves) by Doing Less*, by Rina Mae Acosta and Michele Hutchison, 2017.

*A Life's Work: On Becoming a Mother*, by Rachel Cusk, 2021.

*Screaming on the Inside: The Unsustainability of American Motherhood*, by Jessica Grose, 2022.

*Why We're Polarized*, by Ezra Klein, 2020.

# Notes

## Rule 1: Invite Guests to Your C-Section (Brazil)

14 **Up to 45 percent of women:** Jenny Patterson, Caroline Hollins Martin, and Thanos Karatzias, "PTSD Post-Childbirth: A Systematic Review of Women's and Midwives' Subjective Experiences of Care Provider Interaction," *Journal of Reproductive and Infant Psychology* 37, no. 1 (2019): 56–83, https://doi.org/10.1080/02646838.2018.1504285.

14 **In the United States, one in three women:** R. Reed, R. Sharman, and C. Inglis, "Women's Descriptions of Childbirth Trauma Relating to Care Provider Actions and Interactions," *BMC Pregnancy Childbirth* 17, no. 1 (January 2017): 21, doi: 10.1186/s12884-016-1197-0, PMID: 28068932; PMCID: PMC5223347.

17 **One 2012 study:** M. R. de Oliveira and M. A. Dessen, "Alterações na rede social de apoio durante a gestação e o nascimento de filhos" [Changes in mothers' social support network during pregnancy and childbirth], *Estudos de Psicologia* 29, no. 1 (2012): 81–88. doi:10.1590/S0103-166X2012000100009.

18 **By 1950, 88 percent:** Judith Walzer Leavitt, *Brought to Bed: Childbearing in America 1750–1950* (New York: Oxford University Press, 1986).

21 **The maternal mortality rate:** Donna L. Hoyert, "Maternal Mortality Rates in the United States, 2021," NCHS Health E-Stats, 2023, doi: https://dx.doi.org/10.15620/cdc:124678.

21 **That's ten times the rate:** "Maternal and Infant Mortality," OECD Data Explorer, 15 January 2024, www.oecd.org/health/health-data.htm.

21 **One study found that 13 percent:** Chen Liu et al, "Disparities in Mistreatment During Childbirth," *JAMA Network Open* 7, no. 4 (2024), e244873, doi:10.1001/jamanetworkopen.2024.4873.

21 **They are three to four times:** Centers for Disease Control and Prevention, "Trends in Pregnancy-Related Mortality Ratios in the United States: 1987–2019," n.d., CDC.gov.

21 **Studies attribute the disparity:** United Nations Population Fund, "Maternal Health Analysis of Women and Girls of African Descent in the Americas," July 2023, UNFPA, www.unfpa.org/resources/maternal-health-analysis-women-and-girls-african-descent-americas.

## Rule 2: Don't Wash Your Hair for Forty Days (China)

46 **"Following birth, many cultures prescribe":** American College of Obstetrics and Gynecology, "Optimizing Postpartum Care," Committee Opinion no. 736 (May 2018), https://www.acog.org/clinical/clinical-guidance/committee-opinion/articles/2018/05/optimizing-postpartum-care.

## Rule 3: Let Your Baby Sleep Outside (Denmark)

58 **And unlike the Danes:** Lee Rainie, Scott Keeter, and Andrew Perrin, "Trust and Distrust in America," Pew Research Center, July 2019, https://www.pewresearch.org/politics/2019/07/22/trust-and-distrust-in-america/.

59 **There are an estimated:** Alyson Krueger, "When Mom Slams a Brand on Instagram," *New York Times*, 26 November 2019, https://www.nytimes.com/2019/11/26/business/mommy-influencers.html.

60 **These artificial depictions:** Ciera E. Kirkpatrick and Sungkyoung Lee, "Comparisons to Picture-Perfect Motherhood: How Instagram's Idealized Portrayals of Motherhood Affect New Mothers' Well-Being," *Computers in Human Behavior* 137 (2021): 107417, https://doi.org/10.1016/j.chb.2022.107417.

63 **While controversial:** Gina Ford, *The New Contented Little Baby Book: The Secret to Calm and Confident Parenting* (London: Vermilion, 2013), 56.

## Rule 4: Develop the Paternal Instinct (Sweden)

70 **Every child she has dents:** Jeremy Staff and Jelyan T. Mortimer, "Explaining the Motherhood Wage Penalty During the Early Occupational Career," *Demography*, no. 49 (2000): 1–21, https://www.ncbi.nlm.nih.gov/pmc/articles/PMC3272159/.

70 **That's just 2 cents:** Rakesh Kochhar, "The Enduring Grip of the Gender Pay Gap," Pew Research Center, 2023, www.pewresearch.org/social-trends/2023/03/01/the-enduring-grip-of-the-gender-pay-gap/, accessed 1 March 2023.

74 **When fathers took time off:** M. Lidbeck and S. Bernhardsson, "What Happens to the Couple Relationship When Sharing Parental Leave? A Prospective, Longitudinal Study," Scandinavian Journal of Psychology 62, no. 1 (2021): 95–103, https://doi.org/10.1111/sjop.12682.

74 **A 2012 change in the policy:** P. Persson and M. Rossin-Slater, "When Dad Can Stay Home: Fathers' Workplace Flexibility and Maternal Health," National Bureau of Economic Research, 25902 (2019), https://www.nber.org/papers/w25902.

77 **The percentage of men:** "Findings from the May 2021 American Perspectives Survey," Wikipedia, Wikimedia Foundation, 8 June 2021, www.americansurveycenter.org/research/the-state-of-american-friendship-change-challenges-and-loss/.

83 **While most fathers take:** Department of Labor, "Why Parental Leave for Fathers Is So Important for Working Families," *Policy Brief* (2012), https://www.dol.gov/sites/dolgov/files/OASP/Paternity-Leave.pdf.

83 **Research from 2019 shows:** R. J. Petts, C. Knoester, and J. Waldfogel, "Fathers' Paternity Leave-Taking and Children's Perceptions of Father-Child Relationships in the United States," *Sex Roles* 82 (2020): 173–188, https://doi.org/10.1007/s11199-019-01050-y.

83 **But men who do take leave:** Laurie A. Rudman and Kris Mescher, "Penalizing Men Who Request a Family Leave: Is Flexibility Stigma a Femininity Stigma?" *Journal of Social Issues* 69, no. 2 (2012): 322–340, https://spssi.onlinelibrary.wiley.com/doi/abs/10.1111/josi.12017.

## Rule 5: Love Thy Nosey Neighbor (Mozambique)

97 **Over the last three decades:** Centers for Disease Control and Prevention, "Mozambique: CDC Division of Global HIV and TB Country Profile," CDC.gov, September 2023, www.cdc.gov/globalhivtb/where-we-work/mozambique/mozambique.html.

102 **For the first time:** "Church Membership Falls Below Majority for First Time," Gallup, 30 March 2021, news.gallup.com/poll/341963/church-membership-falls-below-majority-first-time.aspx.

102 **The resulting echo chambers:** "The Polarization in Today's Congress Has Roots That Go Back Decades," Pew Research Center, 10 March 2022, www.pewresearch.org/short-reads/2022/03/10/the-polarization-in-todays-congress-has-roots-that-go-back-decades/.

103 **Seventy percent of millennials:** "Cigna 2020 Loneliness Factsheet," Cigna, 2020, legacy.cigna.com/static/www-cigna-com/docs/about-us/newsroom/studies-and-reports/combatting-loneliness/cigna-2020-loneliness-factsheet.pdf.

103 **Only 14 percent of Americans:** "Facts About Neighbors in U.S.," Pew Research Center, 15 August 2019, www.pewresearch.org/short-reads/2019/08/15/facts-about-neighbors-in-u-s/.

103 **By August 2020:** Ed Choice: Morning Consult Intelligence Poll, 12–17 August 2020, chrome-extension://efaidnbmnnnibpcajpcglclefindmkaj/https://edchoice.morningconsultintelligence.com/assets/52605.pdf.

## Rule 6: Propose to a Friend (Malaysia)

119 **There are over ninety million:** "Number of Homes in the United States in 2021, by Type," *Statista*, 14 February 2023, www.statista.com/statistics/1042111/single-family-vs-multifamily-homes-usa/.

119 **Only half of Americans have:** "New Cigna Study Reveals Loneliness at Epidemic Levels in America," Cigna, 1 May 2018, www.multivu.com/players/English/8294451-cigna-us-loneliness-survey/.

119 **According to a 2021 study:** "The Loneliness Epidemic Persists: A Post-Pandemic Look at the State of Loneliness Among U.S. Adults," The Cigna Group, 12 December 2021, newsroom.thecignagroup.com/loneliness-epidemic -persists-post-pandemic-look.

120 **"We often measure":** Kristen R. Ghodsee, *Everyday Utopia* (New York: Simon & Schuster, 2023).

120 **Some three thousand of these:** Gary Wills, *A Necessary Evil: A History of American Distrust of Government* (New York: Simon & Schuster, 1999).

121 **Faith in institutions:** "Historically Low Faith in U.S. Institutions Continues," Gallup, 6 July 2023, news.gallup.com/poll/508169/historically-low-faith -institutions-continues.aspx.

## Rule 7: Make Granny Nanny (Singapore, Part 1)

138 **Grandparents are the primary:** Chan Qing Rong et al., "The Infancy Study: The Impact of Caregiving Arrangements on Early Childhood Development," Singapore Children's Society, 2019, https://www.childrensociety.org .sg/wp-content/uploads/2022/11/The-Infancy-Study-Research-Monograph -2019.pdf.

138 **In the United States, by comparison:** Pew Research Center Analysis of American Community Survey, "Children Living with or Being Cared for by a Grandparent," 2011, https://www.pewresearch.org/social-trends/wp-content /uploads/sites/3/2013/09/grandparents_report_final_2013.pdf.

141 **Singaporean mothers who:** Inland Revenue Authority, Singapore Government Agency, www.iras.gov.sg/taxes/individual-income-tax/employees /deductions-for-individuals/personal-reliefs-and-tax-rebates/grandparent -caregiver-relief.

142 **Or as a 2019 study:** S. Narayanankutty, "Grandparenting and Intergenerational Solidarity in Multi-Ethnic Singapore," Master's thesis, Nanyang Technological University, Singapore, 2019.

143 **"Because intergenerational transfers":** Michael Gurven and Raziel Davison, "The Importance of Elders: Extending Hamilton's Force of Selection to Include Intergenerational Transfers," *Proceedings of the National Academy of Sciences* 19, no. 28 (2022), https://www.pnas.org/doi/full/10.1073/pnas.2200073119.

143 **Even today, most older peoples:** United Nations Department of Economic and Social Affairs, Population Division, "Living Arrangements of Older Persons Around the World," Population Facts no. 2019/2 (April 2019), https:// www.un.org/en/development/desa/population/publications/pdf/popfacts /PopFacts_2019-2.pdf.

144 **The United States is one:** Neli Esipova et al., "381 Million Adults Worldwide Migrate Within Countries," Gallup, 15 May 2013, news.gallup .com/poll/162488/381-million-adults-worldwide-migrate-within-countries .aspx?utm_source=alert&utm_medium=email&utm_campaign=syndication &utm_content=morelink&utm_term=All%20Gallup%20Headlines.

145 **Nearly one-third of Americans:** Merril Silverstein et al., "Older Parent-Child Relationships in Six Developed Nations: Comparisons at the Intersection of Affection and Conflict," *Journal of Marriage and Family* 72, no. 4 (August 2010), Wiley Online Library, doi:10.1111/j.1741-3737.2010.00745.x.

146 **"I learn[ed] it's the best way":** S. Narayanankutty, "Grandparenting and Intergenerational Solidarity in Multi-Ethnic Singapore," Master's thesis, Nanyang Technological University, Singapore, 2019.

149 **This is especially true:** Sara M. Moorman, PhD and Jeffrey E. Stokes, MA, "Solidarity in the Grandparent–Adult Grandchild Relationship and Trajectories of Depressive Symptoms," *Gerontologist* 56, no. 3 (June 2016): 408–420, https://doi.org/10.1093/geront/gnu056.

149 **Children who are regularly:** Generations United and the Eisner Foundation, "All in Together: Creating Places Where Young and Old Thrive," GrandFam Report, 2018, https://www.gu.org/app/uploads/2018/06/SignatureReport -Eisner-All-In-Together.pdf.

150 **According to some studies:** Sonja Hilbrand et al., "Caregiving Within and Beyond the Family Is Associated with Lower Mortality for the Caregiver: A Prospective Study," *Journal of Evolution and Human Behavior* 38, no. 3 (May 2017): 397–403.

150 **In fact, grandparents who only received:** Moorman and Stokes, "Solidarity in the Grandparent–Adult Grandchild Relationship," 408–420.

151 **By 2021, a quarter of adults:** "Young Adults in U.S. Are Much More Likely Than 50 Years Ago to Be Living in a Multigenerational Household," Pew Research Center, 20 July 2022, www.pewresearch.org/short-reads/2022/07/20 /young-adults-in-u-s-are-much-more-likely-than-50-years-ago-to-be-living -in-a-multigenerational-household/#:~:text=The%20share%20of%20young%20 adults,in%20the%20home%20in%202021.

154 **More than four in five Americans:** Generations United and the Eisner Foundation, "All in Together: Creating Places Where Young and Old Thrive," GrandFam Report, 2018, https://www.gu.org/app/uploads/2018/06 /SignatureReport-Eisner-All-In-Together.pdf.

## Rule 8: Shout for Help (Singapore, Part 2)

171 **And while gender dynamics at home:** Richard Fry et al., "In a Growing Share of U.S. Marriages, Husbands and Wives Earn About the Same," Pew Research Center, 13 April 2023, https://www.pewresearch.org/social-trends/2023/04/13/in -a-growing-share-of-u-s-marriages-husbands-and-wives-earn-about-the-same.

171 **According to an ongoing online:** Katrina Alcorn, "Do You Have a 'Hospital Fantasy'?" Workingmomsbreak.Com, 6 December 2010, www.workingmoms break.com/2010/12/06/do-you-have-a-hospital-fantasy/.

171 **"[F]or them to take a vacation":** Gabi Garrett, "I Interviewed the Newest Mom Coach, and She Told Me About the "Hospital Fantasy": It's a Thing," Today.Com, 12 January 2021, community.today.com/parentingteam

/post/i-interviewed-the-newest-mom-coach-and-she-told-me-about-the
-hospital-fantasy-its-a-thing_1610549959.

## Rule 9: Abandon Your Kids in the Woods (Netherlands)

184 **"When the police officer looked"**: Genine Babakian, "A Sinister Tradition for the Happiest Kids in the World," Wordsworth, Purveyor of Fine Phrases, 26 September 2018, https://www.finephrases.com/post/2018/09/25/A-Sinister -Tradition-for-the-Happiest-Kids-in-the-World.

184 **A United Nations study:** Anna Gromada, Gwyther Rees, and Yekaterina Chzhen, "Worlds of Influence: Understanding What Shapes Child Well-Being in Rich Countries," United Nations Children's Fund, Innocienti Report Card 16, 2020, https://www.unicef.org/innocenti/reports/worlds-of-influence.

184 **They are also easier to:** Eric Desmarais et al., "Cross-Cultural Differences in Temperament: Comparing Paternal Ratings of US and Dutch Infants," *European Journal of Developmental Psychology* 16, no. 2 (2019): 137–151, doi:10.1080/17 405629.2017.1356713.

184 **Childhood over here consists:** Rina Mae Acosta and Michele Hutchison, *The Happiest Kids in the World: How Dutch Parents Help Their Kids (and Themselves) by Doing Less,* (New York: The Experiment, 2016).

186 **Almost 75 percent of kids:** Eleftheria Kontou et al., "U.S. Active School Travel in 2017: Prevalence and Correlates," *Preventive Medicine Reports* 17 (March 2020): 101024, https://doi.org/10.1016/j.pmedr.2019.101024.

186 **Deaths involving vehicles:** "Early Estimates of Motor Vehicle Traffic Fatalities and Fatality Rate by Sub-Categories in 2021," National Center for Statistics and Analysis, vol. DOT HS 813 298, National Highway Safety Administration, May 2022.

186 **In 2020 alone, road deaths:** Emily Badger and Alicia Parlapiano, "The Exceptionally American Problem of Rising Roadway Deaths," *New York Times,* 27 November 2022, www.nytimes.com/2022/11/27/upshot/road-deaths -pedestrians-cyclists.html.

186 **Compared to twenty of the:** Ashish P. Thakrar et al., "Child Mortality in the US and 19 OECD Comparator Nations: A 50-Year Time-Trend Analysis," *Health Affairs (Project Hope)* 37, no. 1 (2018): 140–149, doi:10.1377/hlthaff.2017 .0767.

187 **America has fifty-seven times the:** Chip Grabow and Lisa Rose, "The US Has Had 57 Times as Many School Shootings as the Other Major Industrialized Nations Combined," CNN.com, 21 May 2018, edition.cnn.com/2018/05/21/us /school-shooting-us-versus-world-trnd/index.html.

187 **In a 2004 study, 82 percent of moms:** Rhonda Clements, "An Investigation of the Status of Outdoor Play," *Contemporary Issues in Early Childhood* 5, no. 1, 2004, https://doi.org/10.2304/ciec.2004.5.1.10.

187 **That adds up to an:** Anthony P. Carnevale et al., "The College Payoff: Education, Occupations, Lifetime Earnings," Georgetown University Center on

Education and the Workforce, 2011, https://cew.georgetown.edu/cew-reports /the-college-payoff/.

188 **In other words:** Matthias Doepke and Fabrizio Zilibotti, *Love, Money, and Parenting: How Economics Explains the Way We Raise Our Kids* (Princeton, NJ: Princeton University Press, 2019).

190 **"You don't have to tell him"**: Richard Winton, "Former TPG Exec Bill McGlashan Says He Never Paid a Bribe to Get His Son into College," *Los Angeles Times*, 27 March 2019, www.latimes.com/local/lanow/la-me-college-admissions -bribe-defense-20190327-story.html.

191 **In fact, 79 percent of parents:** Dawn Papandrea and Julie Sherrier, "Kids' Competitive Activities Lead to Debt for 79% of Parents," LendingTree, 11 May 2021, www.lendingtree.com/credit-cards/study/kids-competitive-activities -may-lead-to-debt/.

191 **Studies show intensive:** Mara A. Yerkes, Marit Hopman, F. Marijn Stok, and John De Wit, "In the Best Interests of Children? The Paradox of Intensive Parenting and Children's Health," *Critical Public Health* 31, no. 3 (2021): 349–360, doi: 10.1080/09581596.2019.1690632.

192 **A quarter of them struggled:** C. S. Mott Children's Hospital, "Parent Efforts Insufficient to Promote Teen Independence," *National Poll on Children's Health* 34, no. 4 (July 22, 2019), https:////mottpoll.org/reports/parent-efforts-insufficient -promote-teen-independence#:~:text=Parents%20recognize%20the%20 benefit%20of,give%20their%20teen%20more%20responsibility.

## Rule 10: Give Your Toddler Blue Cheese (France)

202 **The country desperately needed:** Thalia Ertman, "The Lanham Act and Universal Childcare During World War II," Friends of the National WWII Memorial, 27 June 2019, www.wwiimemorialfriends.org/blog/the-lanham-act-and -universal-childcare-during-world-war-ii.

203 **Reports of children being:** "Le printemps des crèches," France Culture, Radio France, n.d., www.radiofrance.fr/franceculture/podcasts/lsd-la-serie -documentaire/le-printemps-des-creches-1869231.

204 **Today, more than 1 million:** Noémie Lair, "200.000 Nouvelles Places En Crèche D'ici 2030: Les Détails Du Plan D'Élisabeth Borne Pour La Petite Enfance," Radio France, 1 June 2023, www.radiofrance.fr/franceinter/200 -000-nouvelles-places-en-creche-d-ici-2030-les-details-du-plan-d-elisabeth -borne-pour-la-petite-enfance-6203494.

208 **When the country wasn't at war:** Kaspar Burger, "A Social History of Ideas Pertaining to Childcare in France and in the United States," *Journal of Social History* 45, no. 4 (2012): 1005–1025, JSTOR, http://www.jstor.org/stable /41678948, accessed 14 December 2023.

208–209 **In 1971, an act proposing:** Richard Nixon, "Veto of the Economic Opportunity Amendments of 1971," Speech, 37th President of the United States, 1969–1974, 6 September 1971, The American Presidency Project, University

of California, Santa Barbara, www.presidency.ucsb.edu/documents/veto
-the-economic-opportunity-amendments-1971.

209 **Today, politicians still talk:** US Bureau of Labor Statistics, US Department of
Labor, "Employment Characteristics of Families, 2022."

209 **In twenty-eight US states:** Baylee Patel, "The U.S. States Where Childcare
Costs More Than College Tuition," NetCredit, 31 August 2023, www.netcredit
.com/blog/cost-of-child-care-by-state/.

209 **It spends only 0.3 percent:** "Public Spending on Childcare and Early Education." OECD Family Database, 1 February 2023, www.oecd.org/els/soc/PF3_1
_Public_spending_on_childcare_and_early_education.pdf.

210 **Of the 12.5 million children:** Nina Chien, "Factsheet: Estimates of Child Care
Eligibility & Receipt for Fiscal Year 2019," Office of the Assistant Secretary for
Planning and Evaluation, US Department of Health and Human Services, 1 September 2022, aspe.hhs.gov/sites/default/files/documents/c348c484e48774718
ffee84aab34a91b/cy2019-child-care-subsidy-eligibility.pdf.

210 **More than half of America's:** Steven Jessen-Howard et al., "Understanding
Infant and Toddler Child Care Deserts," Center for American Progress, October 2018, https://www.americanprogress.org/wp-content/uploads/sites/2/2018
/10/IT-ChildCare-Deserts-13.pdf.

210 **"And because it does not:"** Janet L. Yellen, "Remarks by Secretary of the Treasury Janet L. Yellen on Shortages in the Child Care System," US Department
of the Treasury, 15 September 2021, home.treasury.gov/news/press-releases
/jy0355.

212 **In fact, one 2023:** "New BLS Report Finds Price of Child Care Untenable for
All Families," First Five Years Fund, 2023, www.ffyf.org/resources/2023/01
/new-bls-report-finds-price-of-child-care-untenable-for-all-families/.

212 **As many as one hundred thousand Americans:** "Labor Force Statistics from
the Current Population Survey," US Bureau of Labor Statistics, data.bls.gov
/timeserie, accessed 14 December 2023.

212 **In 2018, those absences:** Nancy Fishman et al., "$122 Billion: The Grow-
ing, Annual Cost of the Infant-Toddler Child Care Crisis." Ready Nation:
Council for a Strong America, February 2023, https://www.strongnation
.org/articles/2038-122-billion-the-growing-annual-cost-of-the-infant-toddler
-child-care-crisis.

212–213 **The industry lost some eighty thousand:** Dana Goldstein, "Why You Can't
Find Child Care: 100,000 Workers Are Missing," *New York Times*, 13 October
2022, https://www.nytimes.com/2022/10/13/us/child-care-worker-shortage
.html.

213 **One of those chains, Bright Horizons:** Dana Goldstein, "Can Child Care Be a
Big Business? Private Equity Thinks So," *New York Times*, 16 December 2022,
https://www.nytimes.com/2022/12/16/us/child-care-centers-private-equity
.html.

213 **Homeschooling became America's:** Peter Jamison et al., "Interactive Map: Homeschooling Growth Data by District," *Washington Post*, 31 October 2023, www.washingtonpost.com/education/interactive/2023/homeschooling -growth-data-by-district/.

## Rule 11: Cross the Finnish Line (Finland)

218 **When the Finnish government:** Ella Näsi and Karoliina Koskenvuo, "The Finnish Baby Box: From a Volunteer Initiative to a Renowned Social Security Benefit," *Successful Public Policy in the Nordic Countries: Cases, Lessons, Challenges*, edited by Caroline de la Porte et al. Oxford Academic online, 2022, https://doi.org/10.1093/oso/9780192856296.003.0020.

223 **That's an increase of 7 percentage points:** "Growing Share of Childless Adults in U.S. Don't Expect to Ever Have Children," Pew Research Center, 19 November 2021, www.pewresearch.org/short-reads/2021/11/19/growing-share -of-childless-adults-in-u-s-dont-expect-to-ever-have-children/.

224 **Today, there are only:** "Historical Social Security Benefit Ratios," Social Security Administration, https://www.ssa.gov/history/ratios.html.

224 **Officials estimate that:** Barry F. Huston, "Social Security: Demographic Trends and the Funding Shortfall," Congressional Research Service, November 4, 2019, https://crsreports.congress.gov/product/pdf/R/R45990.

225 **"Possible action to counteract":** Wolfgang Lutz, Vegard Skirbekk, and Maria Rita Testa, "The Low-Fertility Trap Hypothesis: Forces That May Lead to Further Postponement and Fewer Births in Europe," *Vienna Yearbook of Population Research* (2006): 167–192, https://pure.iiasa.ac.at/id/eprint/8465/1/RP-07 -001.pdf.

225 **It's a population:** Ross Douthat, "South Korea's Birth Dearth," *New York Times*, 2 December 2023, https://www.nytimes.com/2023/12/02/opinion /south-korea-birth-dearth.html.

227 **That support is bipartisan:** "Parents Support for Expanding the Child Tax Credit November 2022 Survey Analysis," Morning Consult, https://www .zerotothree.org/wp-content/uploads/2022/11/ZTT-MC-Survey-Analysis -November-2022.pdf?_ga=2.135259569.1422472677.1669658007-1774533288 .1662584846. 2021.

228 **But when societies support:** Sonya V. Troller-Renfree, Molly A. Costanzo, and Greg J. Duncan, "The Impact of a Poverty Reduction Intervention on Infant Brain Activity," *Proceedings of the National Academy of Sciences* (24 January 2022), https://doi.org/10.1073/pnas.2115649119.

# About the Author

Marina Lopes is a Brazilian-American journalist who has written about feminism, caregiving, and motherhood across five continents. From 2016 through 2020, Marina covered Brazil for the *Washington Post*.

Her reporting took her from the remote corners of Brazil's Amazon rainforest, where she interviewed female shamans challenging gender norms in their tribes, to Rio's gang-controlled favelas, where she spoke to mothers who lost their children to gun violence. In Brazil's Zika-infected northeast, she chronicled the devastation of the epidemic on families living in poverty.

Her 2019 article on the spread of the Venezuelan diaspora in South America was nominated by the *Washington Post* for a Pulitzer Prize. She was also a 2019 recipient of an International Women's Media Foundation Grant for her coverage of sex trafficking rings in the Amazon. Her 2018 series on how gay Brazilians confronted the rise of homophobia in Bolsonaro's Brazil was nominated for a GLAAD award for outstanding newspaper article. Before joining the *Post*, she was a correspondent for Reuters in Mozambique. Her work has been published by the *New York Times*, the *Boston Globe*, the BBC, PBS, *Vice*, and others. She lives in Washington, DC, with her husband and two children.